Ski Faster

Lisa Feinberg Densmore's Guide to High-Performance Skiing and Racing

Lisa Feinberg Densmore

Ragged Mountain Press / McGraw-Hill

Camden, Maine • New York • San Francisco • Washington, D.C. • Auckland • Bogotá • Caracas • Lisbon • London • Madrid
Mexico City • Milan • Montreal • New Delhi • San Juan • Singapore • Sydney • Tokyo • Toronto

Ragged Mountain Press

A Division of The McGraw-Hill Companies

10 9 8 7 6 5 4 3 2

Library of Congress Cataloging-in-Publication Data

Densmore, Lisa Feinberg.
    Ski Faster : Lisa Feinberg Densmore's guide to high-performance skiing and racing / Lisa Feinberg Densmore.
        p.   cm.
    Includes index.
    ISBN 0-07-134381-4
    1. Downhill ski racing. 2. Downhill skiing—Training. I. Title.
II. Title: Lisa Feinberg Densmore's guide to high-performance skiing and racing.
GV854.9.R3D46   1999
796.93'5—dc21
99-30599
CIP

Questions regarding the content of this book should be addressed to
Ragged Mountain Press
P.O. Box 220
Camden, ME 04843
www.raggedmountainpress.com

Questions regarding the ordering of this book should be addressed to
The McGraw-Hill Companies
Customer Service Department
P.O. Box 547
Blacklick, OH 43004
Retail customers: 1-800-262-4729
Bookstores: 1-800-722-4726

This book is printed on 70-lb. Citation
Printed by Quebecor Printing, Fairfield, PA
Design by Paul Uhl, Design Associates
Production by Faith Hague and Dan Kirchoff
Edited by Tom McCarthy and Larry Floersch
Illustrations by John Hinderliter

Gummi, P-Tex, Scotch-Brite, Teflon, and Velcro
   are registered trademarks.

Photo courtesy of Head USA: p. 9.
Photo courtesy of Lisa Feinberg Densmore: p. 62 (top).
Photos courtesy of Swix: 156, 157, 158, 159, 160 (top), 166, 167.
Photos by Barrie Fisher/Sports File: pp. 87, 114, 116 (middle).
Photos by Tim Hancock/Sports File: pp. 11, 12 (top), 110, 111, 112, 115, 116 (top); inset photos on chapter-opening pages.
Photo by Scott Smith/Sports File: p. 116 (bottom).
All other photographs by Dennis Curran/Sports File.

For my husband, Jason, whose unwavering support, counsel, and love have gotten me through every challenge, including writing this book.

And for my parents, Philip and Phyllis Feinberg, who gave me the opportunity to pursue my ski racing dreams.

Contents

Foreword

Lisa Feinberg Densmore has found a niche in her latest book, *Ski Faster: Lisa Feinberg Densmore's Guide to High-Performance Skiing and Racing*. Any clever aspiring ski racer with a good grasp of research technique can find a multitude of ski racing information—eventually. A bit here, a bit there, but nothing short of an all-out web power-search in four languages will yield the information contained in this single book.

Having known Lisa since her collegiate ski racing days, I knew that at some point in her career she would write a book on alpine ski racing. Probably sooner than later. This is the kind of book that "happens" when a world-class athlete has a passion for the sport, a world-class brain, and an interest in sports journalism. How fortunate for those of us who share that passion!

Lisa is a doer extraordinaire. Her ski racing prowess goes without saying. But what about being able to nail a passing shot down the line off the backhand or carry on a nonstop dialogue while hiking the steepest inclines of the White Mountains or going from zero to sixty in under ten seconds on in-line skates or (this really gets me) water skiing so that she carves trenches that cast sheets of water onto both shores of the Connecticut River.

Lisa's skills have developed from her willingness to undertake challenges and then to meet them head-on. Many top athletes have difficulty teaching others the steps leading to athletic accomplishment, but Lisa is able to pass along her knowledge succinctly and clearly to those at all levels of learning.

Lisa's athletic background is only one of the reasons behind the success of her book. The other key ingredients are her insistence on perfection and her love of the sport, both of which are apparent on every page. Lisa is certainly a credible source on any ski racing topic. But she goes to extra lengths to ensure the veracity of her information by seeking out the sharpest, cutting-edge experts on every aspect of the sport. Whether offering tips on packing a wax kit, prepping new skis, or how to make your new shaped skis lay rails in the snow, the information is complete and accurate.

Although the book is oriented toward newcomers to alpine ski racing, the depth and quality of information contained in the book is invaluable to all who have ever stepped into the starting gate. As a former ski academy headmaster, the current managing editor of *Ski Racing* Magazine, and a life-long ski racing enthusiast, I have the opportunity to read, write, and edit articles on all aspects of the sport. In addition to enjoying the personal anecdotes that Lisa relates of her own experiences, I am better informed after having read *Ski Faster*. The book has updated my technical understanding, eased my aversion to the tuning process, and provided a blueprint to whip me into top shape next fall.

Taking the challenge posed by *Ski Faster* will indeed help you ski faster, and Lisa takes us on an exhilarating ride.

Bill McCollom
Managing Editor, *Ski Racing International*

Acknowledgments

Writing a book of this nature is far from a solo effort, and it would not have been possible without the guidance, assistance, and input of the following people: Charles Everitt, who had the idea for this book in the first place and who guided it toward my publisher and through the writing process; Tom McCarthy, my patient, encouraging editor; the Stratton Mountain School, where I perfected my ski racing, and that also provided the courses for the original ski racing photography used in this book; the Stratton Mountain ski resort, which provided the perfect location for all of the original pictures in this book; Dennis Curran, whose original and stock photographs gave this book a visual life; Swix Sports USA, which provided photographs of various ski tuning tools; and Head USA, which provided either photographs or the ski for many of the ski diagrams.

A special thank you goes to the following people, who contributed their expert knowledge: Ron Kipp, Director of Athlete Preparation, U.S. Ski Team; Edgar Pollman, General Manager, Tyrolia Worldwide; Thor Verdonk, Race Director, Rossignol Ski Company (USA); Horst Weber, Program Director, New York Ski Education Foundation; Pavel Stastny, Head Coach, Stratton Mountain School; Peter Dodge, Men's Alpine Skiing Coach, Dartmouth College; Mike DeSantis, Product Development Manager, Volkl USA; Hilary Lindh, 1997 World Downhill Champion, 1992 Olympic Silver Medalist (downhill); Felix McGrath, Men's Alpine Skiing Coach, University of Vermont; Geoff Hamilton, Alpine Service Technician, Swix Sports USA; and the members of the 1999 U.S. Alpine Masters Ski Team.

Introduction

Remember the book *Everything You Always Wanted to Know about Sex: But Were Afraid to Ask?* This book is ski racing's version. If you are a junior racer or the parent of a junior racer, this book covers the sport of alpine ski racing from A to Z, including the nuances of slalom, giant slalom, Super G, and downhill; equipment; off-snow training; travel tips; the elements of course inspection; and ways to mentally prepare yourself to help put you in the winner's circle. If you started ski racing as an adult, you will find this book a shortcut to the secrets of faster skiing that you may have missed in your youth, such as waxing tricks, faster starts, course tactics, and on-snow drills. If you participate in NASTAR (National Standard Race) or any of the hundreds of fund-raiser competitions that take place at ski resorts each winter, this book will help you take the mystery out of ski racing, so that you can enter the starting gate like a prowling tiger rather than a quivering butterfly. If you have no interest in ski racing but wish to improve your skiing ability, this book will help you, too. You will gain a better understanding of shaped skis and other options in new equipment and learn more effective technique, allowing you to ski faster and on more difficult terrain with more confidence.

Confidence in skiing, as in any other pursuit, comes with knowledge and experience. This book will give you the knowledge, and although it cannot put snow under your skis, it is filled with personal anecdotes from myself and a number of other top racers, equipment manufacturers, coaches, and technicians. You will gain a deeper understanding of the sport and perhaps be entertained by the various adventures that have gone into a lifetime of skiing and competition. At the very least, you will be able to watch a replay of Hermann Maier's spectacular crash in the 1998 Olympic downhill race and see what he did wrong. You may even figure out where Picabo Street, in the 1998 Olympic Super G race, gained $\frac{1}{100}$th of a second over the competition to take the gold.

Why Ski Faster?

Every four years, ski racing takes center stage during the Olympic Winter Games. The gold medalists in the women's and men's downhill races are heroes of the Olympics for their bravery and athleticism in the face of excessive speed and outrageous "air" time off the bumps, typically on a course glazed with unforgiving ice. Although those spectacular crashes and hair-raising finishes capture the public eye, there is much more to ski racing than the Olympics. Unfortunately, it is these Olympic images that come to mind 99 percent of the time when the words *ski race* are uttered. Most recreational skiers would never consider entering such a race for fear of going too fast, getting out of control, and falling. They think racing means you must go 85 mph, not a prudent activity for anyone who gets anxious gliding down the intermediate slopes at 15 mph. Although going fast is inherent to ski racing—that is, after all, why it is called "racing"—in reality, only a few hundred people in the entire world are truly capable of skiing faster than they drive a car. The rest of us race for fun.

What makes skiing fun? The majesty of the mountains, the cold, refreshing air, the people, and the après ski parties are certainly part of the landscape that draws people to the slopes. However, it is the glide, the sense of freedom, the challenge presented by a slope, the arcing turns, and the thrill of accomplishment at the bottom of each run that make skiing addictive. Skiing evokes physical and mental sensations that are matched by only a few other activities. It is the desire to continually heighten those sensations that draws us back to the slopes time and time again, and the only way to feel better on skis is to ski better.

What Does It Mean to Ski Better?

Your initial reaction to the question of what it means to ski better is probably to make more technically correct turns. This is only partially correct. To perform at a higher level, you must also be comfortable at faster speeds. By its nature, a carved turn is faster than a skidded turn. The more the arcs your skis leave in the snow look like railroad tracks, the more speed your skis carry; you even accelerate. Talk about an awesome feeling! A fast, carved turn beckons to your sense of athleticism. It delivers an addictive dose of explosive power that starts at your feet and zooms up your body to the top of your head. To ski better, you have to control this increase in your speed and power. Also, you must be able to summon that control, regardless of the snow conditions or the steepness of the slope. Once you do, you will have the confidence to continue improving. That is how this book will help you.

Ski Faster will give you the tools to raise your performance level, whether or not you ever ski through a slalom gate. However, if you are intrigued by ski racing, by the last page of this book you will not only know how to handle faster speeds competently, but you will also be able to step into the starting gate of any race course with confidence.

Why Should You Ski Race?

Ski racing is not just a challenge, it's a *fun* challenge! It challenges like a round of golf. After you play 18 holes, you are sure you can lower your score, so you come back another day for another round. Every time you cross the finish line of a ski race, you are sure you can lower your time. It's addicting. For many, even those without Olympic aspirations, it is a passion. The adrenaline is addictive, too. Although you may never go as fast as Alberto Tomba, you can get the same rush. Of course, many skiers race for reasons other than speed.

Can You Ski Race without Going Fast?

Speed is not always essential. Instead of going for maximum speed, many skiers try a course for entertainment. If you are limited to only one ski area or a few smaller resorts, skiing the same trails a hundred times can become boring. Whether you go fast or not, skiing in a course makes the sport stimulating again. On the open slopes, you can turn anywhere. In a course, you have to turn where the gates dictate. It is harder than it sounds. Skiing around gates proficiently requires precise technique and anticipation. If your technique is flawed, those flaws will be magnified in a course.

At the most basic level, in order to make it to the finish line, you have to ski correctly. The technical demands of ski racing help you improve on the open slopes. You will carve better turns. You will be more agile in the bumps and in the trees. You will be more confident on the ice and the steep terrain. This is the minimum guarantee that ski racing offers.

The Best Skiers Are Ski Racers

Ever notice how the best skiers in the world, particularly those who have influenced ski technique the most, were top racers? Jean Claude Killy, Stein Eriksen, and Ingemar Stenmark can still out-ski most people 20 years their junior. Need more proof? The elite in every discipline of skiing have all raced at some point in their past. Donna Weinbrecht, the first Olympic Gold Medalist in freestyle skiing (1992, Moguls) cofounded her high school ski team. The members of the Professional Ski Instructors of America (PSIA) Demonstration Team, considered the top instructors in the country, are required to have proficiency in skiing gates in order to qualify for the team. Before making their marks as National and World Extreme Skiing Champions, Kim Reichhelm and Noel Lyons spent time on the U.S. Ski Team and the pro tour.

Besides becoming a better skier, there are other reasons to race on skis. With high-speed quad chairlifts putting multitudes of people on the slopes at once, one of the only ways to solo a trail is in a ski race. What a luxury! No need to worry about other people getting in the way. When asked why she continues to race after more than a decade of involvement, Wendy Hill, an instructor at Killington, Vermont, and a three-time member of the U.S. Alpine Masters Ski Team, said, "I love the exhilaration of having a whole trail to myself."

Hill, and many others like her, also race because it attracts a fun group of people. Friendships abound. It has a huge leg up on the personal ads. Even after skiing the mildest course, everyone who has competed has something in common: an exciting moment about which to reminisce, a gate that was almost missed, an amazing recovery, or a big crash. . . . What better way to meet people for more than a chairlift ride than to get involved in a ski-racing program! Every course is an adventure to be shared. If you already have a lot of pals, how about challenging them to a "dual"? Ski racing is a terrific competitive outlet. By pushing yourself to go faster than a buddy, you will push yourself to a higher level of skiing.

Ski racing is also an activity that the entire family can do together. Dad can race Mom. Sammy can race his sister Susan. Dad can race Sammy. And everyone can laugh about it for the rest of the day. At a more structured level, club or school ski teams provide kids with an excellent outdoor physical activity at a time of the year when their sports options are limited. Also, they can participate in ski racing whatever their size or shape! Unlike gymnastics or football, skiing is a sport that can be pursued for life. With a racing background, you have the ability to explore and enjoy any part of any mountain, rather than being relegated to the open, groomed slopes. Ski racing can be enjoyed for life. Some Alpine Masters program racers compete into their 80s, and these octogenarians look for speed just as avidly as people half their age.

For most skiers, there is no denying that the underlying purpose of ski racing is to go fast. Once you have been down a course or two, you will agree that the faster you go, the more fun you have. Many skiers already feel the need for speed and resent that resorts post "slow zones." The race course is the only place at a ski area where the ski patrol will not yank your ticket for going too fast. The faster you go, the freer you feel.

The cheer, "Let 'em run!" is often shouted from the side of a course as racers pass. The phrase implies throwing caution to the wind and pushing your accelerator to the floor. If you have never quite trusted yourself to relax at faster speeds, you have picked up the right book. There are many reasons for a fear threshold, some physical and some mental. This book explores each one of them, then reveals how to go down a course with confidence.

If you are already confident but slow, this book will help you go faster. Inexperienced racers will learn how to trim seconds off their times by choosing the correct equipment and using proper technique. Did you know that you can waste a second or more just getting out of the starting gate? A second is an hour in ski racing, given that many races are won by mere tenths or hundredths of a second. If you are a veteran racer who finds yourself out of the medals by a few eye-blinks, this book offers the insights for training, waxing, travel arrangements, and race day preparations that will help put you ahead of those racers you are currently trailing.

This book is meant to be a reference for anyone interested in ski racing at any age or ability level. Also, it could save you some embarrassment. For example, every weekend, ski resorts host fund-raising events for charities. Many involve corporate teams. As a skier, you could be recruited by your office-mates for a weekend at a ski area, all expenses paid. All you have to do is socialize and, at some point, ski down a course. Sounds great, until you are standing in the starting gate, trembling with anxiety, praying you make it to the finish line. This book will turn those 30 seconds of hell into 30 seconds of excitement because you will know what to do. Do not underestimate the value of this confidence, both personally and professionally. At the very least, you will enjoy these types of events while you raise money for charity, and in many cases, win free trips, equipment, and other prizes.

Yes, faster skiing has many benefits: some are material, such as a trophy; others are intangible, such as self-esteem. And even if you never leave your living room, with this book, you will at least be able to watch the Olympics and know what is going on.

The New Carved Turn

A carved turn is a perfect turn. It is efficient and elegant.

It is the signature move of an expert skier.

The Basics

A carved turn is a turn that involves no skidding. The evidence of a carved turn is two clean lines, one from each ski, in the snow behind the skier. As recently as the early 1990s, the evidence of a carved turn was only one line in the snow because 100 percent of the skier's weight was on the downhill ski. Today, although most of your weight should still be on the downhill ski, the uphill ski gets about 30 percent of the pressure—more on a flatter slope, less on a steep, icy slope. The reason for this change in technique is found in just two words: shaped skis.

Shaped skis were first seen at ski areas as a teaching aid around 1995. They promised a quicker learning process because they required less steering than traditional, straighter-edged skis. Most first-time skiers could make carved turns after only a morning lesson. After a day or two, a newcomer could handle a groomed intermediate slope with some technical prowess. Before the advent of shaped skis, it often took a week of ski school just to negotiate an easy slope with some confidence. For many, carving a turn was a lifetime pursuit.

Why the dramatic improvement? Because of the pronounced sidecut (wide tip, skinny middle, and wide tail) and soft longitudinal flex of shaped skis, turning on them takes only two key skills, maintaining a balanced stance over the center of the skis

SKI CAMBER

Take any ski and place it with its base down on a hard floor or table. Notice how only the tip and tail areas of the base touch the floor. The amount of space under the middle of the ski is the ski's "camber." Camber varies from model to model, even from ski to ski. You can also see the camber of skis if you hold a pair of skis base to base.

While holding the tip of a ski with your left hand, wedge the tail of the ski on the floor under the instep of your right foot. Now press down on the middle of the ski with your right hand. This causes the ski to reverse camber. If you now were to put the ski on the floor base down, the middle would touch the floor and the tip and tail would be in the air. The same thing happens when you stand on the ski on the snow. The more you bend the ski,

the tighter it will turn. In general, more camber indicates a stiffer ski, but this is not always the case. A ski can have a small amount of camber, yet be relatively stiff, and vice versa.

The more camber and the more stiffness a ski has, the more pressure it takes to bend it and thus the more energy it takes to make a turn. However, shaped skis are relatively soft flexing compared with their predecessors, which is one of the reasons they are easier to turn and less fatiguing to use over the course of a day on the slopes.

Shaped skis are relatively soft flexing. As a result, they bow under your feet, into reverse camber, just from your body weight. If you roll them on edge, the combination of their reversed camber and pronounced sidecut leaves parallel tracks in the snow.

Ski camber. (A) The shaded area shows the camber of the skis. (B) **Regular ski camber** is visible when no pressure or weight is on the ski (top); **reverse camber** is apparent when the ski is under pressure, as when a person is standing on it during a turn (bottom). (C) Skis in reverse camber during a turn leave parallel tracks in the snow.

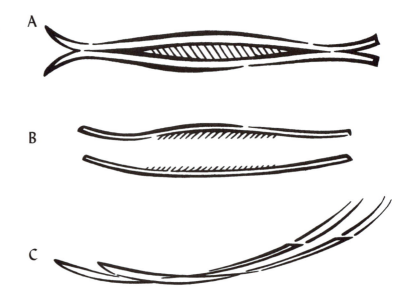

A

B

C

and rolling the skis on edge. By just standing on shaped skis, your body weight provides enough pressure to bend them into reverse camber. Once in reverse camber, if you roll them on edge, they automatically make a turn with a radius between 18 and 25 meters, similar to the radius of an average giant slalom turn.

Shaped versus "Straight" Skis

Any ski designed over the last hundred years has some sidecut. Even though older skis look straight by today's standards, they do differ in width between the ends and the middle. Otherwise, they would not turn. The sidecuts of shaped skis are just more pronounced. On average, they are 10 millimeters wider in the tip and the tail, a few millimeters thinner in the middle and 10 centimeters shorter than their predecessors. (Actual measurements vary depending on the manufacturer.)

The extra wide tip and tail and technological advances in vibration dampening have made shorter length possible. Even though a shaped ski is not as long as a "straight" one, it typically has more surface area on the snow and more edge, because of its added width fore and aft. For example, if you use a 200-centimeter "straight" ski, then switch to a 200-centimeter shaped ski, the shaped ski will feel like a 210-centimeter straight ski. A 190-centimeter shaped ski may look short at first, but it feels surprisingly fast, stable, and responsive.

High-Performance Carving

The introduction of shaped skis is one of the few times in the history of skiing that ski design produced a dramatic change first at the recreational level. In fact, many expert free skiers and elite racers were rather underwhelmed the first time they tried shaped skis, usually because they tried to steer them too much. As manufacturers figured out ways to make shaped skis torsionally stiffer for better edge grip and to make them better at dampening vibration for more control at faster speeds, top racers began to ski faster on them and switched.

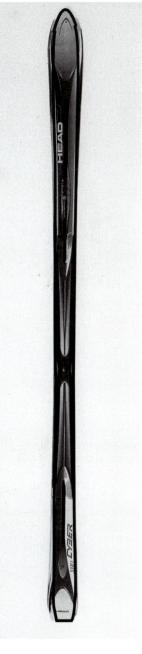

Shaped GS ski about 1999 (190 cm), compared with outline of unshaped GS ski circa 1989 (200 cm).

SKI NOMENCLATURE

Shaped skis went by several names when first introduced: *parabolic skis, super-sidecut skis*, and *hourglass skis*. Today, the accepted term is *shaped ski*.

In the early days of shaped skis only one ski manufactured by Elan was truly parabolic in shape, meaning its tip and tail were the same width, with its thinner midpoint halfway between them. The performance of these parabolic skis proved to be too limited, however, because you could only make carved turns of one size or arc comfortably.

At a glance, a shaped ski looks like a stretched-out hourglass because of its wide tip and tail and narrow middle, but the term hourglass skis didn't stick, perhaps because it implied inaccurately that symmetry existed between the tip and tail. In fact, most shaped skis have a tip that is wider than the tail. The difference in width between the tip and the tail creates the ski's taper angle. The taper angle of a ski helps determine how easily the ski enters and exits a turn. Draw straight lines down both sides of the ski from the widest part of the tip to the widest part of the tail. The angle formed where these two lines intersect is the taper angle. Some manufacturers have experimented with reverse taper angles, where the tail is wider than the tip.

Also synonymous with the term *shaped* is the term *super-sidecut*, because the sidecut of a shaped ski is very exaggerated compared with the sidecut of an older, straighter ski. The term super-sidecut is not widely used because it is more of a mouthful and because deep sidecuts have now become so normal among ski designs—much like wide-body tennis racquets or oversized golf club heads—that they no longer seem "super."

taper angle

The taper angle of a ski is the difference between the width of the tip and the width of the tail. The wider the tip relative to the tail, the greater the taper angle. The skis shown are *shaped skis*, which have a greater taper angle than traditional skis.

The first real success for the new design came in 1997, when Deborah Compagnoni, an Olympic gold medalist from Italy, won the World Cup giant slalom title and the World Championship giant slalom race on shaped skis. High-level skiers took notice. Before long, racers marveled that their new giant slalom skis had shrunk 5 to 10 centimeters and were about the same length as their slalom skis. Today, slaloms are the only races where you can find straight skis, and even slalom skis are beginning to have more shape.

Compagnoni, however, did not single-handedly raise the performance bar by competing on shaped skis. Earlier, the success of her compatriot, Olympic hero Alberto Tomba, and Norwegian World Cup star Ole Christian Furuseth, had produced a tremendous influence on technique—and thus on the ski designs that best accommodated that technique. This influence eventually filtered down to the black diamond masses.

In the late 1980s, Furuseth gained recognition among World Cup watchers with his first of seven World Cup wins. During his career, he also garnered two World Cup discipline titles and one World Championship gold medal. As coaches analyzed his technique, they made a startling discovery. Furuseth put pressure on both skis rather than only on the downhill ski when he turned. Other Norwegians were doing the same, but Furuseth was winning. He seemed turbocharged. By putting pressure on both skis, he got more acceleration out of every turn because two skis have more rebound than one ski. Furuseth figured out how to channel that power into smooth, flowing turns. The classic "step to the new ski, roll it on edge" style made popular by Swedish champion Ingemar Stenmark was out; two skis on the snow was in.

In 1992, the flamboyant Alberto Tomba won the Olympic slalom and giant slalom races in Albertville, France. He went on

THE FOUR DISCIPLINES OF ALPINE SKI RACING

Although alpine skiing is often called *downhill skiing*, downhill is really just one of four alpine ski racing disciplines, and the least likely pursuit for most people on the slopes. The four disciplines of alpine ski racing are slalom, giant slalom, downhill, and Super G. **Slalom** is a short sprint through a forest of ski poles. **Giant slalom** most closely resembles free-skiing on the open slopes, with its smooth arcing turns, back and forth across the hill. In **downhill**, racers seem to go straight down the mountain at speeds upward of 80 mph. The only turns in downhill typically follow the terrain. **Super G** is a hybrid between giant slalom and downhill: racers ski fast, around 60 mph, but also make high-speed turns, particularly if the trail is wide and steep. (See chapter 4 for more on giant slalom, chapter 5 for slalom, and chapter 6 for Super G and downhill.)

Alberto Tomba (Italy) performs his trademark tight, aggressive GS turn.

Above
Ole Christian Furuseth (Norway) in mid-GS turn, his weight on both skis.
Below
Deborah Compagnoni (Italy) on the victory stand after winning the GS at the 1998 Winter Olympics.

to dominate the World Cup in those two events through the middle of the 1990s. Tomba backed up his bravado with the strength and confidence to take a straighter line at each gate, then carve a turn with a tighter radius without losing speed. In addition, he maintained a lower body position throughout his run, regardless of where he was in the turn. To enhance his performance, his ski supplier, Rossignol, began experimenting with the shape and length of his skis, shortening them and increasing their sidecut a little bit at a time. When other racers started emulating Tomba, other ski manufacturers started experimenting with shorter skis and deeper sidecuts.

The 10 Secrets of Faster Skiing

Although the carved turn is the essence of expert skiing, your skiing will not truly be high performance until you also can handle speed, regardless of how steep the terrain might be. Forget about skiing through gates until you hone your technique and speed on the open slopes. Whatever your speed limit is while free skiing, it will be less when skiing through gates, perhaps much less depending on your mental toughness.

Assuming you can carve a turn, here are the ten secrets of faster skiing. Practice them one at a time while free skiing until each one becomes automatic:

1. FINISH YOUR TURNS, BUT DO NOT OVER-TURN

A fast turn has just enough arc in the snow to finish it (place the size and shape of the turn where you want it) while allowing you to maintain your speed. The shape of a fast turn in the snow is never more than a half-circle (180 degrees). If your skis turn past this 180-degree half-circle, even by one degree, you will decelerate. Also be careful to avoid incomplete turns. If you feel yourself going faster and faster but in an uncontrolled way as a result of gravity and not the power you have generated in the turn, you are not finishing your turns. Link your turns in a rhythmic way; try to feel the pressure build and release under your boots over and over again. It is this combination of fluidity and directed pressure that will allow you to ski faster with confidence.

FIRST PERSON: A SPEED BREAKTHROUGH

Skiing faster takes good technique, physical strength, and a mental leap in confidence. Throughout my ski-racing career, I had a reputation for excellent technique. I could always run faster, jump higher, and do more sit-ups per minute than most of my competitors, but my speed threshold, although higher than most, held me back. During my second year on the Women's Pro Tour, I lost three races in a row by less than 1/100th of a second. It was maddening, yet I couldn't find that fraction of an eyeblink no matter how hard I trained.

About halfway through the winter, the tour stopped at Winter Park, Colorado, where an old college friend of mine, Mack Lyons, lived and trained. (He was racing on the Men's Pro Tour at the time.) One afternoon, Mack and I went free skiing. I had never been to Winter Park before and was curious about the mountain. I followed him everywhere, not because he was playing tour guide, but because the pace at which he skied was faster than mine.

I never did see much of the mountain. I was too busy trying to keep up with Mack. I constantly felt on the edge of or just beyond my comfort zone, yet my sense of pride prodded me to make respectable turns. I had to keep up. I wasn't scared, just nervous.

The next weekend, instead of losing the race by almost nothing, I won a number of runs by significant margins. (Pro races are dual format, set up like a tennis tournament. Two competitors race side by side. The fastest racer in each round moves on to progressively tougher rounds. The top finishers take up to 10 runs per day.) By following my faster friend for a day, I became faster, too. Since then, whenever I have the chance to ski with someone faster than me, I don't hesitate to go. I can inevitably ski faster as a result.

fall line

Linked turns along the fall line will appear as connected half circles.

2. KEEP YOUR EYES AND TORSO ORIENTED DOWN THE HILL

Unless you have exceptionally fast feet, your maximum speed in a short-radius turn is around 20 mph. Faster skiing not only is more comfortable when the turns have a wider radius, but also more graceful and practical. One of the most common mistakes in a wide-radius turn is letting your body face in the same direction that your skis are traveling, or worse, letting your body rotate into the hill. The result is too much weight on the uphill ski, which leads to skidding, and, if the slope is steep, falling. If you feel your tails slip to the side midway through the turn instead of following in the same path as the tips of your skis, your body is not oriented properly down the hill.

You should always keep your upper body oriented down the trail, if only slightly, to help facilitate the angulation of your hips to the side and to keep most of your weight on the downhill ski. It helps to look down the fall line continually—the direct line a snowball would travel down the slope. If your body position feels awkward when you look down the fall line, your torso is oriented incorrectly.

The author making a wide radius turn. Notice the orientation of her body as she moves downhill.

3. ALLOW PRESSURE TO BUILD UNDER YOUR SKIS AS LONG AS POSSIBLE IN EACH TURN.

Moving faster requires more energy. You are not an internal combustion engine, so you cannot speed up by simply giving your legs more gas. You have to create energy through your turns.

You have two sources available, the centrifugal force created by the turns themselves, and the gravitational force pulling you down the hill. To get the most energy out of a turn, you have to allow as much pressure as possible to build up under your feet. It is a matter of strength and timing. Assuming you have the strength to handle the pressure, hold each turn until the last moment before starting a new turn. If you release the turn too early, you lose potential energy. Even if you take a more direct line, you still have to pressure your skis until you reach the transition between each turn. In other words, allow pressure to build on your skis through the whole apex of the turn.

4. RELEASE WEIGHT FORWARD, NOT UPWARD

Ten years ago, ski technique emphasized up-and-down motion. You came up to release the turn, then sank down as you progressed into the next turn. Forget up! Think forward! Skiing faster means moving down the hill faster. Focus your movements in that direction. Rising up dissipates energy into the air. Keep low, by angulating to the side and slightly curving your back. When it is time to release the pressure that has built up in a turn, use it to propel yourself forward into the next turn.

5. KEEP YOUR SKIS ON THE SNOW

Air is slow. That is why downhill racers fight to keep their skis on the snow. They try to time jumps so that they spend the least possible amount of time in the air. A ski in the air can only glide. It cannot generate speed. It is also difficult for a skier to maintain a compact body position in the air.

Part of the air control game in skiing has nothing to do with a jump. Sometimes the pressure created in a turn pops you into the air when you release it. This may feel energetic, but it is misdirected. The fastest skiers are the ones who keep their skis on the snow the most.

6. ANGULATE TO THE SIDE, DON'T BEND AT THE WAIST

In an attempt to apply more pressure to their skis, many people collapse at the waist. To increase the pressure on your skis aggressively, flex forward at the ankles and knees, not at the waist, and let your body angulate to the side at the hips. This angulation should increase through the turn, then decrease as the turn ends. It should be a movement in which your feet and legs move out to the side, then back under your body, then out to the other side, while the upper body stays relatively quiet. However, do not think of the upper body as inactive. The muscles in your back,

Move laterally. **1–2.** At the most angulated part of the turn, the author's legs extend to the side. **3–4.** As the finishes the turn, she draws her legs under her body. **5–8.** Then she extends them out to the other side as the next turn progresses.

side, and stomach must constantly make adjustments to keep the rest of the upper body under relaxed control. At the most angulated part of the turn, a skier resembles a large, moving comma.

7. TRANSFER WEIGHT LATERALLY BETWEEN TURNS

The transition between turns is just as important as the turn itself and not a time for a quick rest. In the old days, the legs straightened during the transition between turns as part of the motion to "unweight" the skis. Today, because of shaped skis, the opposite is true. The legs are at their most extended during the turn, out to the side. Between turns, your knees come up under your body (this is done by contracting your stomach muscles), while the upper body stays relatively level in relation to the ground. As the next turn begins, the legs drift quickly to the other side.

8. FEEL THE CARVE

Even the tiniest amount of skidding reduces speed. Skiing requires acute sensory perception in the feet. Feel the snow, the terrain, and, most of all, what your skis are doing. Are they carving or skidding? Expert skiers strive to make every turn perfect. Sometimes it is subconscious, but the feeling for the snow, for the edge, is always there.

9. ONLY EDGE THE SKIS INTO THE SNOW ENOUGH TO MAKE THE TURN, NO MORE

This may sound like a contradiction to building as much pressure on your skis as possible, but it is not. There is a fine line between too much and too little edging. With so much concentration on building pressure on the skis to generate speed, you may be edging too much, particularly if the snow is soft. Each type of snow condition and each type of terrain has its speed limitations based on the skier's ability, fitness level, and equipment. Once you reach that limit, doing more is beyond a matter of no added gains. It is a matter of reduced results. Allowing your edges to dig too deep into the snow will slow you down. Part of the acute awareness of body and skis that comes with high-performance skiing is a "touch" for the snow. The next time you are cruising on packed powder, experiment to see just how little edging you have to use, compared with that on an icy slope, to make turns.

10. KEEP YOUR HANDS FORWARD FOR STABILITY

The faster you go, the more important it is to keep your hands forward for balance. For many downhill racers, that is their lone thought; the same is true for many gate skiers, too. For example, Billy Kidd, 1964 Olympic Silver Medalist in slalom (Innsbruck, Austria) and 1970 World Champion in the combined (slalom and downhill) is a hand man. As a racer, he believed that if his hands were doing the right thing, the rest of his technique would fall into place. If he was having trouble, he could usually trace it to his hands. Today, as director of his own performance center in Steamboat Springs, Colorado, he still practices and preaches the benefits of keeping your hands forward.

One common mistake is to drop your hands by your sides, which will cause you to sit back. If you sit back while going slow, it is more difficult to initiate your turns. If you sit back at speed, you will crash. Dropping one hand is not as risky, but it is not conducive to high-performance skiing. Usually the uphill hand is the culprit, especially toward the end of a wide-radius turn. Dropping

Correct hand position. The faster you ski, the more you have to press forward with your hands, ahead of your knees, to stay in control.

the uphill hand causes your upper body to tip into the hill; this pulls your weight off the downhill ski and ends the carve. Beware of a lazy hand after your pole plant, too. Plant your pole quickly with just a flick of the wrist, not a big arm movement. As you pass the spot in the snow, do not let the hand drop. Both hands should be in the bottom edge of your peripheral vision at all times.

Keeping your hands forward helps drive your body forward, too. To be effective, your hands must be forward and parallel to the slope. In other words, unless the trail is flat, the downhill hand is lower than the uphill hand. This concentrates more of your weight on the downhill ski, which is essential for edge grip. The steeper the slope, the more the downhill hand has to press down the hill, as if it has a weight in it.

If you find yourself about to crash, your best hope for recovery is to drive your hands forward. Imagine a fall in slow motion. Picture your hands as you start to lose your balance. At least one jets over your head, out to the side, or behind your body. Get your hands under control, and your skis will be in control, too.

Going Too Fast

It is not enough to push off the chairlift thinking, "I am going to ski faster." Safe speed comes with many miles of competent, relaxed skiing. You ski faster as a result of your technique, strength, and mental attitude. It should never be a reckless endeavor. If you do get nervous about your speed, slow down immediately, either by intentionally skidding or by making rounder turns. Avoid inadvertently sitting back!

The first step in the "flight" instinct is to recoil from danger, or back off. The second is to get closer to the ground to lessen a potential fall. This is why many people sit back too much on their skis and/or lean into the hill. They are simply recoiling from a perceived danger. When you go beyond your comfort zone in skiing, the safest move is contrary to your natural instinct: you should drive your hands forward and lean down the hill more in the middle of each turn. And remember, always ski within your limits to lessen your chance of injury.

Dryland or Off-Snow Training

Preparation plus preparation plus preparation equals confidence.

The Focus

Practice is the key to unlocking the gate to faster skiing. Only after you have trained your body and your mind to the fullest extent in practice can your skiing reach higher levels of performance and eventually allow your skiing ambitions to come true. You can ski better. You can race. You can race faster.

Although accumulating mileage on snow is certainly critical to better skiing, training for skiing should begin well before the first snowflake drops from the sky. This is not a revelation. Any skier who has felt unrelenting leg burn after only a run or two knows the importance of getting in shape before heading to the slopes. Skiing exerts unique forces on the body. The only way to get your muscles fine-tuned for this sport is by skiing—a lot. If this is not an option, take heart. You can get very close off the snow, so close that the transition from off-snow training to skiing is virtually seamless, but you must focus. It is not enough to simply get in generally good physical condition.

Being in overall good condition won't prevent leg burn, let alone improve your technique, but it is much better than going from the couch to the chairlift. To ski faster (and longer), your conditioning must be skiing-specific. Top ski racers mix precise doses of weight training, speed and agility drills, and other sports

U.S. SKI TEAM FITNESS STANDARDS

Did you ever wonder just how fit a World Cup racer really is? The U.S. Ski Team Alpine Medals Test is a series of eight exercises that assess the physical condition of a skier. How do you stack up compared with America's best?

U.S. Ski Team Fitness Standards

Activity	USST Men	USST Women
40-yard dash	4.8 seconds	5.3 seconds
Push-ups	75 without pause	55 without pause
440-yard run	56 seconds	69 seconds
Hexagonal jump (total time, both directions)	27 seconds	29 seconds
Vertical jump (without a step)	28 inches	25 inches
High box jump progression	105 jumps per 90 seconds	95 jumps per 90 seconds
Sit-ups (bent knees)	70 per minute	65 per minute
1-mile run	5 minutes 30 seconds	6 minutes 30 seconds

SOURCE: U.S. Ski Team Sports Science Department, 1998

into a specific preseason regimen. The recipe changes depending on the time of the year.

If you think you will never be able to run a sub-7-minute mile, don't worry, your skiing career is not over. What's more, off-snow training does not have to feel like boot camp. It can be part of an active lifestyle. It should be fun and relieve stress as well as get you in shape for the slopes. Any form of physical activity will help your skiing, but some forms help more than others. To make the workouts you already do more skiing-specific takes an understanding of cross-training and the addition of a few basic exercises, if you don't already do them.

Conditioning for skiing can be separated into five areas of fitness: strength, quickness and agility, balance and coordination, flexibility, and endurance. Professional athletes have the luxury of making physical training the priority each day. The rest of us have work, family, and social obligations constantly cutting into workout time. Some days we might have 2 hours to exercise, other days we might have only 20 minutes. Given the time restriction, it is important to choose your daily activity wisely, understanding how it will help your skiing and spending the right amount of time on each area of fitness. If you run every day, you may be in excellent aerobic shape, but you will be in worse shape for skiing than someone who runs now and again, but also hikes, lifts weights, plays tennis, and stretches.

Let's look at the five areas of fitness and how they relate to skiing.

Strength Training

Strength is the most important area of fitness when it comes to skiing. Strength allows you to control your body and thus your skis against the forces and vibrations created in a turn. The stronger you are, the faster you can ski, because you can withstand higher amounts of pressure generated by your turns and absorb the rattles and shocks that your skis receive, particularly on hard-packed conditions. Once your skiing is technically correct, the only way to increase your performance level is to make yourself stronger.

Strength is also a confidence builder. If you know you are stronger, you will be more self-assured and believe in your ability to handle higher-speed turns because of your off-snow preparation. Sometimes you may even find yourself skiing faster without realizing it because of your improved strength.

Strength is also your safety net. When you lose your balance, it is your strength that helps you recover. For example, if you ever sit back while skiing, or worse, get thrown back off a bump, it will be your strength, particularly in your abdomen, that will spare you from a dramatic crash and possible injury.

What can you do to make your strength more skiing-specific? Building your strength for skiing involves a combination of weight training (with free weights, weight machines, or both), calisthenics, and a form of exercise called *plyometrics*.

It is critical to your strength-training program that you always work out opposing muscle groups equally to help prevent injury. In skiing, the hamstrings and the quadriceps, and the back and the stomach are the most obvious and critical opposing muscle groups. The hamstrings and quadriceps support the knee joint. If the quadriceps are significantly stronger than the hamstrings, you will be more susceptible to knee injury. In the case of the back

WEIGHT-TRAINING BASICS

Proper weight training is critical to faster skiing, but improper weight training and a resulting injury can prevent you from skiing at all. Here are some simple rules of thumb to ensure that your weight-training program has the desired effect.

1. Before beginning any fitness program, including a weight-training program, consult your physician to make sure you are physically capable of the anticipated exertion.

2. Never begin your weight-training session until you have properly warmed up. Try running on a treadmill, riding a stationary bike, using a step machine, or jumping rope for at least 5 to 10 minutes. You should begin to sweat.

3. Don't worry if the "big boys" are pumping heavy iron. Begin with lighter amounts of weight, for example, 60 percent of your maximum. It is always better to err on the side of lighter weight and add some than to lift too much weight and strain your muscles.

4. If you are using free weights, never lift without a spotter.

(continued on page 23)

and stomach, the stomach helps support the back and vice versa. If your abdominal muscles are weak, your back will get sore. If a bump throws you back, your stomach muscles pull you forward again. If you start to fall forward, your back muscles tense more to help you recover. A strong torso, or core, allows you to maintain a "quiet" upper body. It also allows you to angulate to the side in a turn, letting your upper body "separate" from your legs as your legs travel to the side. If you are a racer, your midsection is the turbo-booster that gets you out of the starting gate.

Also, keep in mind that whether you opt for free weights, weight machines, or a combination of the two in your strength training, you should first determine how much weight you should lift. Opinions vary, but given the fact that skiing places more emphasis on power and control than on endurance, if you lift 80 percent of your maximum ten to fifteen times per set and you do three sets, you will be a stronger skier. For many areas of your body (e.g., legs, torso), that is the equivalent of making 45 turns, which is about the number of turns in a giant slalom race.

After you have performed a weight routine to the point that the last repetitions of the last set are as easy as the first repetitions of the first set, increase the weight a little. When you are comfortable with your weight routine, add some explosive power to your lift (without jerking or throwing the weight), but remember, the recovery phase of the lift—the phase when you return the weight to its original position—should always be slow and controlled.

Although skiing engages all of the major muscle groups in the body, the legs and torso bear the brunt of the work. For this reason, front squats are the bread and butter of strength training for skiing.

Given a choice, select free weights over a weight machine. Free weights require you not only to lift the weight, but also to balance it. You might not be able to lift as much using free weights, but the quality of each lift is more important than the amount of weight or the number of repetitions.

The back is made up of long, stringy muscles that are more susceptible to tiny tears than a big chunky muscle, such as the quadriceps, and many skiers, even those at the world-class level,

(continued from page 22)

Have the spotter help you position the weight for the lift and then return it to the rack when you are done.

5. Exhale as you press the weight. Inhale as you return to the starting position.

6. Be sure to exercise through your full range of motion in order to fully strengthen a muscle group.

7. Constantly check your alignment as you lift to prevent injury. Is your back straight? Are your knees bending over your toes?

8. Control the weight in both directions and at all times.

9. Be sure to strengthen opposing muscle groups, such as the hamstrings and quadriceps, equally to prevent injury.

10. Be courteous. Always return weight machines to zero and a neutral position and return barbells and dumbbells to their racks when finished. Also, don't forget to wipe your sweat from the area.

11. If you are unfamiliar with weight training or have any questions whatsoever, consult a certified strength and conditioning specialist (CSCS).

Above Left
Front squats. If you're just starting a weight program, begin with front squats, which are easier to do correctly. Hold the weight bar closely in front of your neck, on your collarbone, just under your Adam's Apple. With a straight, supportive back (your back muscles should feel tight), bend your knees—but not past 90 degrees—then return to a standing position.

Above Right
Back squats. For back squats, the weight bar rests on your shoulders, behind your neck.

suffer from back soreness. Because of the *eccentric* nature of ski racing, the highest forces are on the back, not the legs. In physiological terms, during eccentric activities, the muscles must lengthen under tension, which produces a pulling sensation. Most trainers advise starting a weight-training program with *concentric* exercises (the opposite of eccentric), in which your muscles feel the most stress as they contract against gravity. For example, the "up" half of a biceps curl is concentric and harder than the "down" portion, which is eccentric. Gravity tries to pull the weight toward the ground as your biceps flex to raise it to your chest. The biceps lengthen as you lower the weight.

A common exercise that strengthens the back for skiing is called *Good Mornings*. It is an off-snow training standard because, like skiing, the eccentric portion of the exercise is more strenuous than the concentric portion. Bear in mind, however, that because some eccentric exercises, such as Good Mornings, exert more stress on the muscle, if you use too much weight, you may end up too sore to train.

Good Mornings. With your hands behind your head, a straight back, and your knees bent slightly, bend forward at the waist, then straighten up again (left). As you get stronger, add weight in small increments, starting with just the weight bar or a dumbbell resting on your shoulders (right). Traditional Olympic bars weigh 20 kg (45 lbs.); however, many weight rooms now have bars that weigh 35 lbs. or less. Before using a bar, find out its weight to monitor your workout properly.

Another helpful back strengthening exercise for skiing is called "back extensions."

Although free weights are more desirable, weight machines are not bad. For novice weight lifters, weight machines ensure proper form and usually do not require a spotter.

If you use weight machines, try different ones for a particular muscle group, particularly if the exercise influences the hip area.

Back extensions. This exercise is easiest to perform on a back-extension apparatus. With your feet held securely, bend forward at the waist into the resting position (left). Holding your hands behind your head, lift your torso until your back is straight, but no further—never arch your back (right). Don't add weight (e.g., a weight plate held to your chest) until you can easily do 30 repetitions.

For example, some machines for hamstring curls make you lift sitting up, whereas on others you must lie down. By alternating between both types of machines, in addition to having stronger muscles, the muscle groups will be better balanced.

Weight machines are also a common way to strengthen your abductor and adductor muscles (outer and inner thighs). These opposing muscle groups help stabilize the hip, leg, and knee while you are angulating to the side in a turn.

Most people have a weaker side. If you work out on weight machines, try to work each leg separately, even if the machine is set up to allow you to exercise both legs at once. For example, if you are doing quadriceps extensions, alternate between a set for the left leg and a set for the right leg. One leg recovers while the other one lifts. If you are on a leg press machine, push the weight up with two legs, but lower it slowly with one. Warning! Never use only one leg or arm during any phase of a lift if doing so changes your position on the machine, causes you to do the exercise with poor form, or results in less than complete control of the weight through the whole range of motion. It can result in injury.

Any of the usual abdominal exercises, such as crunches, sit-ups, and bicycles, will strengthen your abdominal muscles. As with the hip area, the key is to vary your routine. "With your abdominals, if you can do 40 reps, it is time to change to another exercise," advises Ron Kipp, Director of Athlete Preparation for the U.S. Ski Team. Kipp particularly favors stomach exercises that

Abdominal lift using a large rubber ball. Lie on the ball with your pelvis slightly lower than the highest point (left). With your feet parallel, your hands behind your head, and your elbows out to each side, lift your upper torso about 6 in., then lower yourself (right). Look at the ceiling to keep your chin up. Concentrate on using just your abdominal muscles. Your hands act only as a support for your head and neck.

incorporate a large rubber ball, a half meter to one meter in diameter, depending on your size, because the ball forces you to stabilize your torso in space, as skiing does.

As your level of skiing gets better and you develop a "go for it" attitude, you not only need strength, but also power. Power on skis is an explosive yet controlled movement. It is focused high energy. To teach your muscles how to handle consecutive blasts of power requires a type of exercise called *plyometrics*. Plyometrics involve a leap or a jump, either forward or straight up into the air, such as frog jumps, one-leg hops, and lateral jumps. Your body serves as the weight. Plyometrics have a reputation of making even a top athlete sore after the first session. Start modestly, doing only ten of each exercise. Build up to twenty repetitions, then up to three sets, interspersing a lot of rest—3 to 5 minutes—between each set.

Another common skiing-specific exercise is the forward lunge. Forward lunges can be done with or without weights. In either

Lateral jumps. Lateral jumps look a lot like skiing. With your hands forward as if you're holding ski poles, stand on your right foot, knees bent. Leap laterally to your left foot, then back to your right foot. Try to develop a rhythm as if you're going from turn to turn on skis.

Forward lunges with light dumbbells. With a straight back and eyes looking forward, take a big step forward, allowing both knees to bend to 90 degrees. Your hands should hang by your sides, and your front knee should point in the same direction as your toes. Start with no weight, then add light dumbbells—no more than 3–5 lbs. per hand at first.

case, like plyometrics, they are advisable only after you have achieved a high fitness level. Lunges are highly eccentric as you step forward and lower your body; this is terrific training for skiing but also a potential cause for the use of ibuprofen a day or two later. Start modestly, ten repetitions on each leg, alternating legs with each lunge.

What about the wall-sit? It's exactly as its name implies. Your back rests against the wall while your knees form a 90 degree angle, as if you are sitting in a chair. The wall-sit has the oldest, most widespread reputation as an exercise for ski conditioning, but its use has become controversial. Some skiers, especially mogul skiers, swear by it, but others have recognized its pitfalls. Although it does strengthen the quadriceps, the knees bear most of the load, especially if you hold them at 90 degrees. If you already have a knee injury, forget about wall-sits. In addition, the wall-sit positions your hips and torso well behind your feet. In skiing, your hips should be over your feet. Finally, it is a static (isometric) exercise. "Isometrics strengthen the muscle at only the joint angle, plus and minus three degrees," says Kipp. "Therefore, if wall-sits are performed at 90 degrees of knee flexion, the athlete is really only getting stronger at 87 to 93 degrees of knee flexion, not exactly the range of motion that is used in skiing." Isometric exercises are fine as part of a larger strength-training program, particularly if you are teaching your body to deal with accumulations of lactic acid. In simple terms, lactic acid is a waste product that forms in your muscles as you exercise. If you exercise harder (faster) than your blood can remove it, it accumulates in the muscle. Skiers feel it most as leg burn.

If you have limited time, you are better off choosing an exercise that's a closer simulation to skiing, such as one-leg knee bends. One-leg knee bends are beneficial for several reasons. They strengthen your hamstrings and your quadriceps. You are not static; you move up and down, as if you are absorbing bumpy ter-

rain on skis. They also exercise one leg at a time, which helps equalize your right and left legs and improves your balance.

Even though skiing places the greatest demand on the body below the chest, don't forget to strengthen your arms and shoulders, too. The upper body is involved in several basic functions for all skiers, such as poling along a flat area, getting up after a fall, carrying gear, and just keeping your hands in the proper position for a pole plant. For anyone aspiring to faster skiing, particularly in a race, strong arms and shoulders are critical for starts. They can mean the difference between winning a race or being a couple seconds out of the trophies.

The most skiing-specific upper-body exercises on weight machines are triceps extensions and latissimus pull-downs. Both target the triceps, which are the dominant poling muscles. As with other muscle groups, it is important to strengthen opposing muscles to stabilize your joints and to help prevent injury. At the

Wall-sit versus one-leg knee bends. In the wall-sit (left), the torso and hips are well behind the feet. In the one-leg knee bend (right), the hips are over the feet and the body is balanced. In both exercises, the knee or knees are bent 90 degrees, but the one-leg bend more closely simulates skiing.

very least, do some push-ups or arm dips for your triceps and some biceps curls for balance. If you have access to weights, add a full upper-body circuit, including chest flies, bench presses, upright rows, biceps curls, triceps extensions, overhead presses, overhead pull-downs, shrugs, and lateral raises. "A good rule of thumb for muscle balance is that if one exercise pushes, it should be balanced with one that pulls," says Kipp. "For example, the bench press is a push. This could be balanced with a bent-over row, which is a pull."

If you cannot or will not go to the weight room, many weight-training exercises can be simulated with a rubber cord. Rubber cords are also a great substitute if your travel plans take you away from the gym. As with your weight training, be sure to select a cord that offers the correct tension. You may need two cords, a stronger one for your legs and a lighter one for your arms.

U.S. ALPINE MASTERS SKI TEAM (1996–98) MOST POPULAR OFF-SNOW ACTIVITIES

Rank	Activity	Percentage of Participants (%)
1	Weights/exercise	52
2	Biking (road)	46
3	Hiking	42
4	Running	40
5	Tennis	33
6	Mountain biking	29
7	Golf	21
8	In-line skating	19
9	Sailing	13
10 (T)	Stretching	12
10 (T)	Swimming	12
10 (T)	Aerobic equipment*	12
13 (T)	Soccer	10
13 (T)	Water-skiing	10
13 (T)	Fishing	10
13 (T)	Gardening	10
13 (T)	Hunting	10
18 (T)	Windsurfing	8
18 (T)	Walking	8
18 (T)	Aerobics class	8
18 (T)	Canoe/Kayak	8
18 (T)	Equestrian	8

(T) signifies a tie.
*Treadmill, stationary bike, stepmachine, rowing machine, etc.
Information gathered from author's annual questionnaire to team members

Cross Training for Skiing

Simply defined, cross training is playing one sport to get in shape for another, in this case, skiing. Although there are myriad drills that have been invented to improve your quickness, agility, and balance, you can get as much or more benefit, have a lot more fun, and stay motivated by doing activities you enjoy. Almost any other sport you participate in will help your skiing in some way.

The U.S. Alpine Masters Ski Team is a group of elite adult racers in the United States who are considered the fastest in their respective age groups. Except for class 1 (ages 21 to 29 years), groups are divided by age in 5-year increments, up to 80-plus years. One man and one woman from each age group—up to 24 total racers—are named to the team each year based on their results at the annual U.S. Alpine Masters Championships. Not only are the members of the team fast skiers, they are also busy people, with jobs, families, and other obligations off the slopes, much like any skier. Their opportunities for off-snow training are based primarily on what is available where they live and, to a lesser extent, on age. A survey (see table at left) of the 52 individuals who qualified for the team for the years 1996, 1997, and 1998 revealed their favorite ways to get in shape for the slopes.

In the table, the percentage of participants adds up to more than 100 percent because most team members do more than one activity. Other off-snow activities that team members mentioned were yoga, volleyball, softball, surfing, cutting and stacking firewood, rowing, flag football, bowling, scuba diving, and squash. The message from this group is, the more active your lifestyle, the higher your performance on the slopes. There is no one perfect way to cross-train for skiing. In fact, varying your workouts is more beneficial than concentrating on one off-snow activity. "Just doing one activity for training will not enhance your skiing. In fact, it could be a detriment," says Ron Kipp. "For example, if an

FIRST PERSON: THE PRO RACER FROM NEW YORK CITY

During the summer of 1986, between my first and second winters on the Women's Pro Ski Tour, I received the job offer of my dreams. There was only one problem: I would have liked it better had it come about three years later. Grey Advertising in New York asked me to become an Assistant Account Executive, a one-in-a-million chance, particularly since I did not have a Masters in Business Administration. I knew that the advertising and marketing field was my ultimate calling and that this opportunity would not come again, yet I had some unfinished business on the pro tour. After all, I had just gotten my skis under me again after a year-long hiatus, during which I had worked in New York in a bank training program. I wasn't really ready to move back to the corporate rat race.

Because an acceptable apartment became available and the agency agreed to let me use my meager vacation time here and there, instead of in the usual two one-week blocks, I made the decision to take the job and to continue ski racing. My only dilemma was the lack of snow-covered vertical terrain in the concrete jungle. My competitors would undoubtedly ski every day. My solution was to get in the best physical condition of my life on the theory that it would make up for lost time in the gates.

I convinced myself that two workouts a day were possible despite spending 12-hour days at Grey Advertising. In my mind, my workday did not end until I had finished my evening exercise program. Yes, I was nuts. I ran or biked every morning at 5:30 in Central Park, lifted weights, took aerobics classes, and escaped the city on weekends to hike, water ski, play tennis, and, of course, run gates once the snow fell. The only window in my life for socializing was dinner around 10:00 in the evening, if I could keep my eyes open.

It worked! I had my best year on the tour, finishing tenth overall, while helping introduce Americans to Sucrets Spray and convincing them to let Calgon bath products "take them away." Shortly after the end of ski season, I was promoted to a full-fledged account executive.

athlete only runs, her aerobic system will be greatly enhanced. The downside is that her leg production will decrease dramatically. Most marathoners cannot high jump over 10 inches. Skiers need to do a mix of strength/power, anaerobic endurance, and aerobic activities."

Quickness and Agility

Most other sports require a modicum of agility. That is what makes them a sport. However, not all sports involve quick reactions, which are vital to high-performance skiing. Most people think that you only need quick reactions in skiing if you are a slalom racer or a mogul skier. Not true! At 30 mph on skis, which is relatively fast but not uncommon for free skiing and which is the average speed in a U.S. Alpine Masters–level giant slalom race, you are traveling 44 feet per second. That doesn't give you much time to react to something that you see ahead of you down the slope. One of the things that makes downhill ski racing so challenging is how fast everything goes by. When you see something 100 yards down the hill, if you don't react at that moment, it will be too late and perhaps catastrophic.

The best ways to improve your quickness and agility for skiing are sports that require quick changes in direction, especially if the change in direction is side to side. Tennis is great. Soccer is even better. Soccer requires not only quick lateral movements, but also precise eye-foot coordination. If you can dribble and kick a soccer ball without staring at it, chances are you will trust your feet on skis and be comfortable looking ahead down the slope.

Balance and Coordination

How many times have you heard the phrase, "balance over the center of your skis"? With the advent of shaped skis, you will hear it even more, because, in this era of simplified ski technique, the only two things you need to do to turn is balance in the middle of your skis and roll them on edge. Balance has always been the essence of skiing. Everything you do on your skis is aimed at staying stable and upright. Those who maintain balance at the fastest speeds and in the most demanding conditions ski the best.

Balance training for skiing can be as simple as walking a balance beam in your back yard, as exhilarating as windsurfing in a 20-knot breeze, or as adrenaline-pumping as running whitewater in a kayak—all activities that rely heavily on balance and coordination. Of course, as with agility, most sports require a certain degree of balance, but some require it more than others. For example, at face value you might not think fly-fishing has much to do with balancing on skis. Casting from a boat may not, but wading along the edge of a river does, especially if the bottom is uneven. As you work your way along the shoreline, you must walk over slippery rocks and logs while counteracting the flow of water against your legs. Your feet and ankles never land the same way twice; this strengthens them for skiing. If you don't develop good balance for fly-fishing, you will be emptying your waders more often than hooking a fish.

One of the best ways to develop skiing-specific balance is to cross-train with in-line skating. Turning on in-line skates is as close as you can come off the snow to turning on skis. In fact, skating can improve your skiing. If you have a problem of sitting too far back on your skis or putting too much pressure on your tips, you will correct it immediately on skates—or risk road rash. Skates are short, only slightly longer than the length of your foot. Unlike skis, they do not provide a long platform in front or behind, so they do not tolerate much variation in your fore-aft position. In addition, you can only carve turns on skates, they do not skid. If you have never felt a true carved turn on snow, you can on skates. If you try to turn skates with a skidding technique, ouch! Also, take heed, what looks like a beginner slope on skis is closer to a black diamond trail on skates.

In-line skating, however, is not a torturous sport. If you wear a helmet, knee and elbow pads, and wrist guards and skate within your ability, it is really very enjoyable. You may even find the same turning, gliding, wind-in-your-face freedom that got you addicted to skiing in the first place. Best of all, turning on skates uses the same muscle groups as turning on skis. For the perfect

GATE TRAINING ON SKATES

Gate training on in-line skates is an excellent way to improve your balance and ability to carve turns. It also teaches you how to look ahead and judge your line.

On a slight incline, set a course using pylons, cones, or paper cups. At first, start with an even rhythm all the way down the course. As you become more confident, vary the pattern of the cones to help you master rhythm changes on snow.

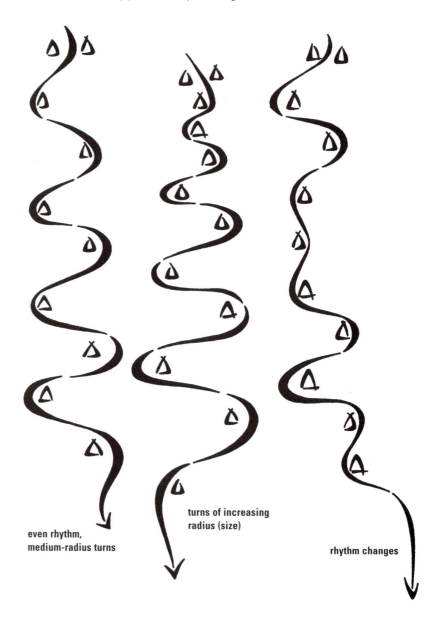

even rhythm,
medium-radius turns

turns of increasing
radius (size)

rhythm changes

Course patterns for in-line skating.

skating workout, plan a 10-mile skate (about an hour of skating). If you cruise on the flats, pump up the hills, and turn on the downhills, you will achieve an excellent skiing workout, covering four of the five areas of fitness (all but flexibility). Skating with ski poles is even better, because you can work on your pole plant as you turn.

Although in-line skating is certainly an excellent cross-training activity for skiing, it does have its pitfalls. Skating helps most in practicing C-shaped, short-radius turns. In-line skates do not allow hard-hitting J-shaped turns, as commonly occur when a skier goes too straight at a gate, then jams the skis sideways at the end of the turn to stay on course. Nor do skates allow a lot of knee and hip angulation. Giant slalom turns usually result in a skating version of *boot out*. On skis, boot out refers to having the ski so much on edge that the boot makes contact with the snow, lifting the edge of the ski off the snow. In skating, the wheels are tipped so far on edge that the skate chassis makes contact with the pavement and the wheels lose their grip. If you use in-line skating to cross-train for skiing, concentrate on short, round turns.

Flexibility

Flexibility training is more than just a quick stretch at the end of a workout to prevent muscle soreness. It is a concerted effort to increase your range of motion. In skiing, flexibility plays a much larger role than just helping prevent injury. It is critical to high performance and should be an integral part of your off-snow training program.

Skiing demands athletic prowess in extended positions. Picture in your mind angulation at mid-turn, in which the body looks like a comma. The torso is upright but the legs go out to the side. The faster you ski, the greater the degree of angulation that is required to turn and therefore the more extended your position. Even in short, quick turns, you need to be flexible. The knees are designed to bend forward with limited side-to-side motion. (They will rotate only about 20 to 25 degrees inward and outward as they flex to 90 degrees.) Thrusting your knees rapidly into the hill multiple times requires all five areas of fitness: strength, quickness, balance, endurance, and flexibility.

Like any workout, flexibility training should never be done with cold muscles. Warm up first by jogging easily, riding a stationary bike, or some other activity that will elevate your heart rate enough to break a sweat. There are several techniques for stretching. The simplest involves pressing into a position and breathing in a specific pattern. Hold a position for at least 30 seconds. Exhale as you press (*never* bounce). As you inhale, come up slightly, then, as you exhale again, press a little more. Repeat the process three times total, concentrating on relaxing the muscle as you stretch it.

Since skiing is a full-body sport, flexibility training should be a head-to-toe proposition. Work on all of your major muscle groups. If you don't have the discipline or desire to stretch on your own, try yoga or dance class. Many people avoid stretching because it is difficult or uncomfortable. Stretching should never hurt. It should only pull a little. Never force a stretch. Start slowly but be persistent. You may never touch your toes, but if you get closer to them, you'll ski faster.

Below Left

Standing quad stretch. Balance on one foot as you pull the heel of your other foot toward your buttocks. It helps to put the other hand (same side as your supporting leg) forward for stability.

Below Right

For more stretch, bend forward at the hip and pull up gently on the leg you are stretching.

Left

Forward lunge. Lunge forward, using your hands for support. Your forward foot should be parallel with your hands, with your knee bent approximately 90 degrees. Make sure your bent knee points forward, in the same direction as your toes.

Below

For more stretch, clasp your hands and lower your shoulders and chest until your elbows touch the ground. Your leg positions should not change.

Above

Standing, feet apart, opposite hand to foot. Reach toward one ankle with both hands, then try to pull your chest toward your leg.

Right

For more stretch, add a lunge to the opposite side and raise the arm in the air on the same side as the leg you're stretching.

Left
Standing Achilles stretch. Press the heel of one foot down behind you. If you have trouble balancing, hold a chair or place your hands against a wall.

Below
Modified hurdler's stretch. Tuck one foot into your groin, then reach toward the toes of your extended leg. Pull your chest toward your knee.

Below
Butterfly stretch. Sitting on the floor, bend your knees and let them fall apart to each side. Place the soles of your feet together and hold onto them. Then pull your chest toward your feet.

Above
Emily's stretch. Lie on your back with your knees pulled up toward your chest. Open your arms, shoulder height, out to each side, then roll your knees to one side.

Endurance Training

Endurance, or aerobic fitness, was once considered the foundation of conditioning for skiing. Today, endurance training has a much lower priority. Yet many aerobic activities benefit other areas of fitness, and although becoming aerobically fit is not the main focus of off-snow training, aerobic fitness still has an influence on your skiing. Having good endurance allows you to maintain good technique longer, ideally all day, which is becoming more and more challenging with the proliferation of high-speed chairlifts.

An aerobic activity is any activity that increases your breathing and heart rate for 20 minutes or longer. Running, hiking, biking, and in-line skating are the most common, particularly among good skiers. Each of these endurance sports can be made more skiing-specific with just a small change in focus.

If you are a runner, try to run on a trail rather than on pavement. Better yet, run through a glade of trees or through the woods. Run around the trees, as if you were in a course for ski racing. Leap from rock to rock across a stream and jump over logs. It not only makes your run more interesting, but it also adds balance, agility, and ankle strengthening to your workout.

Hiking is an even better way to improve your endurance. The key with hiking is to maintain a steady pace. Don't move so fast that you go past your anaerobic threshold into your anaerobic zone and have to stop every few hundred yards. If you can carry on a conversation while you hike, you are hiking at an acceptable pace for endurance work.

Hiking is good for skiers in other ways, too. It takes place in the mountains, making you more at home in that environment. It is also an excellent strength workout. Ascending works your butt, hamstrings, and calves. Descending works your quadriceps and shin area. Both ascending and descending help your feet and ankles, which become more aware of the texture of the terrain and stronger because they land differently with every step. Hiking is also psychologically rewarding. Standing on top of a peak invigorates, despite the fatigue of the climb. The self-confidence

ANAEROBIC THRESHOLD AND ZONE

The harder you exercise, the more oxygen your body takes in and the faster your heart pumps to deliver that oxygen to your muscles. At the same time, your muscles produce lactic acid, which initially is removed through the blood stream as quickly as it is produced. At a certain exertion level, your muscles are working so hard that your blood system can't keep up, and lactic acid begins to accumulate in your muscles. That exertion level is your *anaerobic threshold.* You can identify it by your pulse. When you reach your anaerobic threshold, your heart rate (number of beats per minute) is typically above 80 percent of your maximum, which is roughly calculated as 220 minus your age. Note that, in addition to your age, your level of fitness, your medical history, the altitude at which you exercise, and other factors contribute to your personal anaerobic threshold. Once you exceed this threshold, you are exercising in your anaerobic zone. This is the realm of sprinters. It doesn't take long before your legs feel like lead.

and sense of accomplishment carry over to winter. If you can hike up a ski slope, all the better. The imagery on the way down is a powerful reminder of your goals once the snow falls.

If you live in an urban or suburban area where hiking is not an option, try golf. A golf swing has little to do with skiing, but walking 18 holes is a viable substitute for a hike. The terrain might not be as vertical, but it is usually hilly and uneven, and the effort can be just as tiring.

If you have a choice between road biking and mountain biking, opt for the latter. Both types of biking help develop leg strength. The footwork for peddling a bike is similar to that for making short turns on steep slopes on skis. However, mountain biking is more skiing-specific by virtue of the fact that it is done on a trail, often in the mountains. Single-track mountain biking and turning a bike on downhills require agility, balance, and even angulation similar to that needed for skiing. There is only one problem with mountain biking: it is too much fun. "Mountain biking is good if it's not taken to an extreme," say Ron Kipp. "It appeals to a skier's mentality. It takes place outside. You can go fast and make turns going down hill. However, if you ride for two hours several times a week, you are probably not spending enough time in the weight room."

PRO TIP: RUN DOWNHILL TO GET IN SHAPE FOR SKIING

Ron Kipp, Director of Athlete Preparation for the U.S. Ski Team, recommends running downhill in short, choppy steps to improve your ability to control your skis. "It mimics the low-amplitude, high-frequency vibrations in skiing every time your foot lands," says Kipp, "When you arc a turn, you need to maintain consistent pressure on your skis, despite the vibration." Like skiing, running downhill is an eccentric exercise. The muscles lengthen as soon as your foot makes contact with the ground, similar to when you start adding pressure to your skis. If you can't find a hillside, Kipp recommends running down stairs.

Planning Your Off-Snow Training Program

If you are wondering how you're going to fit all of this training into your life, don't worry. You don't have to do everything at once. The following program is not as intense or as specific as the program of a World Cup racer, but it will put you in good enough shape to win a national title at the Alpine Masters level. It assumes that you can work out 5 days per week.

June–July

Assuming you have an active lifestyle, play a variety of sports during the summer. Enjoy yourself. By the end of July, you should feel generally fit and healthy.

August–September

Time to start focusing on skiing! Try to pick sports that are the most related to skiing, particularly those that incorporate lateral movement and eye-foot coordination, such as tennis, soccer, and in-line skating. Spend about 80 percent of your effort on strength training, primarily in the weight room.

October–November

As the ski season approaches, split your training about 50-50 between agility and strength. Add plyometrics into your strength routine. Maintain your aerobic base by going for a long run, hike, or mountain bike ride once a week.

Ski Season

Off-snow training should not stop when you start skiing. It should continue throughout the winter. If you ski exclusively, even if you ski every day, you will be less fit at the end of the ski season than at the beginning. If you can only ski on weekends and holidays, an off-snow maintenance program is even more important. Assuming you want to save your best skiing for Saturday and Sunday, when most competitive events are held, use the following schedule:

Monday: An easy day to help you recover from the weekend: Warm up plus flexibility routine.

Tuesday: Hit the gym! Strength maintenance routine. Stretch.

Wednesday: Have fun! Play tennis or basketball, take a step-aerobics class, go ice skating.

Thursday: Hit the gym again! Strength maintenance routine. Stretch.

Friday: Rest! Travel to the slopes.

Other Off-Snow Training Considerations

In this high-pressure world of overachievers, it is easy to get caught up in your training to the point where it is doing you more harm than good. Don't forget to rest at least one day a week.

THE "NO-TIME" WORKOUT

If you are just too busy to do anything else besides a few calisthenics, here are a few key exercises that, if performed at least three days per week, will go a long way toward getting you ready for the slopes. You won't mow down gates like Herman "The Herminator" Maier and you may still need to find your ski legs, but you'll be much closer to being fit for skiing than by doing nothing at all:

1. Sit-ups with bent knees, alternating elbows straight ahead, left elbow to right knee, and right elbow to left knee.
2. One-leg knee bends
3. Forward lunges
4. Lateral jumps
5. Push-ups

Your body needs a break to repair itself. Every time you lift a weight or play a sport, your muscles tear slightly, then mend so they are stronger than they were before the exercise. Good coaches and trainers preach alternating hard workouts with easy ones and alternating upper body sessions with lower body sessions to facilitate this recovery time. The older you are, the more recovery time you need.

Working out should invigorate you. If you begin to suffer from chronic exhaustion, low energy, loss of appetite, sleeplessness, or a lack of motivation, you are probably over-training. It helps to keep a training log; record not only your workouts, but also how you feel during them, how much sleep you get, and your weight. The log will serve as a progress report and as a reference for your shortcomings if you suspect you are over-training.

Be advised that you should never begin an exercise program without first consulting your physician. Also, always warm up and cool down properly to help prevent injury.

Selecting Equipment

Zen and the art of faster skiing: when your feet are one with your ski boots, and your ski boots are one with your skis, you are one with the mountain.

Skis

Your skis probably will be the most expensive component of your ski equipment, costing upward of $500 a pair. There are less expensive skis, but a high-performance skier needs high-performance skis. The right skis can enhance your ability. If you have not yet made the switch to shaped skis, a new pair could boost you to the next level of ability. Likewise, incorrect skis hold you back. Skiing on inadequate skis is like using an old-fashioned typewriter to write a book. You get the job done, perhaps quite elegantly, but it takes three times as long and it's painstakingly difficult to correct your mistakes.

The key difference between skis at the high end of the price spectrum and lower priced skis is that high-end skis provide more stability at higher speeds. Stability is a function of construction. Most high-end skis contain a lightweight metal alloy, such as titanal, which dampens vibration. The top of the ski may have additional vibration-absorbing devices built into or attached to it. Other aspects of the ski, such as the amount of fiberglass used to make it and whether it has a wood core or a foam core, affect its stiffness, weight, and rebound. (*Rebound* refers to how springy a ski feels when you release the pressure on it at the end of a turn; it literally rebounds from reverse camber back to its normal shape.)

In general, if you prefer a lightweight, lively ski, a foam core is for you. Heavy, powerful, or frequent skiers, who often prefer a stable yet responsive ski, will find a wood core more to their liking. However, keep in mind that attitudes about foam cores versus wood cores have changed recently. A short time ago, few high-end skis, except for a couple of slalom models, were made with foam cores, because foam cores had a reputation for quickly losing their life. Today, foam core skis are enjoying a resurgence because advances in technology have increased their durability and stability.

Titanium is the latest in a long line of special materials that have been integrated into the core of high-end skis. Titanium adds torsional stiffness to the ski, particularly in the tip and tail. You can quickly test the torsional rigidity of a ski by trying to twist its tip like a bottle top. A ski must be torsionally stiff to hold an edge on icy slopes and at high speeds. Shaped skis, which are exceptionally wide in the tip and tail, benefit from reinforcement in those areas. In addition, titanium is very light in weight, adds vibration dampening, and enhances rebound.

Another compelling reason to upgrade to a high-performance ski, if you haven't done so already, is that the base material, or P-Tex, is designed for better glide and wax absorption. A black base means it contains graphite, which reduces friction with the snow even further, particularly on dirty snow and in low humidity. See chapter 9 on waxing skis: the layer of wax on a race-prepped ski is so thin that it is almost imperceptible. As a result, it doesn't last long. Graphite is also used as a wax additive, for the same reason as a base material.

In truth, there is no such thing as the perfect ski. Everyone has a personal preference

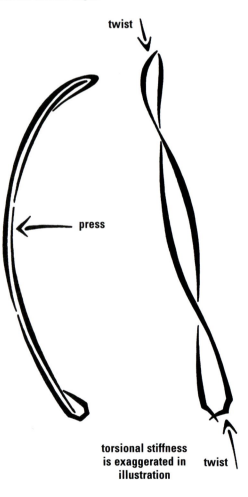

How stiff are your skis? **Longitudinal stiffness** (left) and **torsional stiffness** (right).

twist

press

torsional stiffness is exaggerated in illustration

twist

resulting from variations in physical size and skiing ability. In addition, conditions vary day to day, sometimes from slope to slope, and the shape of turns varies from slope to slope and from race to race, even in the same discipline. The turns in some giant slalom races feel very tight and slow, the turns in others feel wide open and fast. Since most people do not have an unlimited supply of skis, only a pair or two, selecting the right ski can be a stressful decision, but it is nothing a little research cannot overcome.

There is no single infallible source of information when it comes to selecting your ski equipment, particularly if your goal is faster skiing. To ensure you purchase the best ski for your needs, you should collect information from a variety of sources. As you explore these sources, the right ski will emerge.

Magazine Reviews

A good place to start is magazine reviews. The two most popular ski-oriented magazines, *Ski* and *Skiing*, either include a racing ski category in their tests or include racing skis among the high-performance skis they review. Lately, the trend has been to test primarily giant slalom skis, because the market for slalom skis is so tiny. (Super G and downhill skis are never included in magazine ski tests.) The issues with ski test results usually hit the newsstands by mid-September. These tests are reliable because, as a rule, the testers are top skiers. If the giant slalom (shaped) ski you are considering is not mentioned in any of the magazine test results, it should serve as a red flag. Magazines only mention the models that performed well. Omission does not necessarily mean that a ski is terrible, but it does infer that either it was not a top choice among the testers of a particular magazine or it was not tested. (Sometimes a magazine limits the number of skis a manufacturer may submit for testing.) In any case, you should seek additional information.

Advertising

When manufacturers have a hot ski, they want people to know it, usually by touting which World Cup stars have won on its product. As you would expect, these athletes are paid endorsers.

Because of their strength and the extreme demands that top-level racing puts on equipment, they are usually not on the same ski that is available in stores. The World Cup is also the proving ground for technology, so a top racer's skis may have the same paint job as a current model, but underneath the paint could be a prototype for the future. Do not base your ski purchase only on an advertisement. Ads, however, often do impart the key features and benefits of a ski. Plus, if a company shows a racer in its ads, then it is committed to faster skiing.

WORLD CUP RACERS

A manufacturer whose skis consistently put racers on the podium is onto something, especially if more than one racer is frequently in the medals. It is also a good sign if athletes win year after year on a particular brand of ski. Although an elite racer's skis might be different from "rack" skis, ongoing excellent results are additional proof of a company's commitment to faster skiing. Don't look only at American racers. Members of the U.S. Ski Team are limited to skis from manufacturers that have paid to join the U.S. supplier pool. Team pools are an expensive proposition. Also, ski manufacturers cannot be official suppliers to every national team. A company might sponsor the formidable Austrians and the Swiss, but not the Americans, or vice versa.

SKI SHOPS

Not all ski retailers are created equal. The employees of a specialty ski shop, especially one located near a ski area, tend to be more reliable sources of equipment information than employees of mass merchandisers of sporting goods. Although you might find a better deal at a large urban chain, know what you want before you put your credit card on the counter. Big stores near the city have higher employee turnover. The farther from the mountains and the larger the store, the less likely the salesperson skis, let alone skis well. Ski shop employees near a ski resort often not only ski more, but also try more new products. Skiing is their passion, hence their choice of location, lifestyle, and occupation. Eager to try the latest technology, they are more apt to attend on-snow demo days and hang out with trendsetters to check out the latest equipment.

If you do not have a long-standing relationship with a store, interview the salesperson. Ask how long he has worked there and where he likes to ski on the mountain. Does he race in a town league? Does he ski fast? Try to determine how sincere he is. Ask not only what ski he uses, but also why he uses it. Keep in mind that ski shop salespeople are courted by manufacturers, who offer them sales incentives and freebies—shirts, hats, stickers, posters, even free equipment and trips—to win support for their skis on the sales floor. Sometimes the store management has certain inventories that it needs to move. Also keep in mind that a store cannot carry every brand. Unless you know the person, and he has made excellent recommendations in the past, shop around. Get a variety of opinions.

COACHES

Coaches of junior racing programs are very influential when it comes to the skis that their athletes use, but equipment knowledge varies from coach to coach. In general, experienced coaches in the established programs are the most equipment-savvy. At the same time, they often have alliances with specific manufacturers. The job of soliciting sponsorships or special discounts for young racers typically falls to the coach. No doubt, a coach is most loyal to and most familiar with the companies that work with the coach's program. This is not necessarily bad. If you trust the way a coach imparts training, and if the racers on that team get good results, the equipment advice is probably sound. Feel confident in the fact that a coach needs to stay on top of ski technology to ensure that the racers on the team have every advantage, but remember that the coach is familiar with some brands more than others.

SKI LENGTH

Ski length has more to do with your weight, strength, and ability than your height. Today's top skiers are using skis that are about 10 centimeters shorter than what was used a decade ago, particularly in giant slalom and speed events. This is possible because of the advent of shaped skis. Here's a look at what World Cup racers used in 1998 compared with top Alpine Masters racers. Generally, Alpine Masters racers use slightly shorter skis because they are not as strong and do not go as fast as World Cup racers. Also, many Alpine Masters racers use their giant slalom skis for Super G races, partly because Super G skis are not available to the general public and partly because the Super G events at the Alpine Masters level tend to resemble fast giant slalom rather than true Super G.

Average Ski Length (cm)

Event	World Cup		Alpine Masters	
	Men	Women	Men	Women
Slalom	198	190	193	187
Giant Slalom	201	193	202 (1998)/ 191 (1999)	185
Super G	212	207	201	190
Downhill	212–17	212	na	na

All data are based on author's questionnaire for the winter 1998 and 1999 seasons. In general, the trend is toward shorter skis at every ski-racing level and in every event. By winter 1998, virtually all World Cup racers had switched to shaped skis for giant slalom, whereas Masters racers, particularly younger top men, had not. (By winter 1999, even these racers had switched.) For those who made the switch to shaped skis, their giant slalom and "unshaped" slalom skis were about the same length, because shaped skis typically are 5 to 10 centimeters shorter. Even Super G and downhill skis at the World Cup level are now shorter, with more pronounced sidecuts (see chapter 1). And for slalom, many racers are now experimenting with very short (160–170 cm) shaped skis.

HOW TO TEST SKIS

Taking a few runs on a pair of skis, then switching to another pair is one way to test skis at an on-snow demonstration day, but this is not the most effective way. Accurate ski comparisons require accurate methodology.

Seven Rules of Ski Testing

1. Ski the same trail each run, ideally a long trail with varying terrain and conditions.
2. Vary the radii of your turns, but try to make short turns and long turns in the same spot on each run.
3. Vary your speed during a run, but ski the same speed in a particular section of trail each time.
4. Unless you are at a ski area with less than 1,000 vertical feet, take only one run on each pair of skis. After the first run, you begin to adapt your technique to the ski, instead of the other way around.
5. Write down your impressions of the ski model on a test card or a pocket-sized notepad before taking a run on the next pair.
6. After you have tested all the skis that interest you, ski the first pair one more time. The first ski is your benchmark, yet you may not have been warmed up when you were on it. A second run should confirm your first opinion. If not, adjust your written comments accordingly.
7. Take a few more runs on your top pick on a variety of trails. Find a giant slalom course, such as a NASTAR (National Standard Race) course, and put the skis through their paces. By the end of an hour, you should know if they are the skis for you.

MANUFACTURERS' REPRESENTATIVES

The representatives of manufacturers are the most biased sources about ski brands. No surprise! However, they are also an excellent resource when it comes to selecting your skis. If you run into a rep in a ski shop, ask him the features and benefits of the brand he represents. Have the rep recommend the right ski and length for you, or explain why his brand is better than similar skis from other companies. In a best case scenario, ask several reps the same questions for a broader scope of the market.

Ultimately, if you decide to buy the ski that a company rep has recommended, then you will know exactly what to purchase, but try the ski first. If the shop doesn't have a particular ski for use as a demo ski, find out where on-snow demo days will be held in your area. Ideally, several manufacturers will attend, allowing you to compare models side by side. If a demo ski disappoints you, don't give up on it right away. Check the tune of the ski. If it's difficult to steer, it may be *edge high* (*railed*), the tips and tails may be too sharp, or the representative may have made a mistake with the wax. The skier that tried them before you may have hit a rock, or the edges may be dull. Bring the skis back to the company's van and try a similar pair. If the second pair feels just as bad, then the ski is probably not the best choice for you.

FRIENDS

Not all friends who ski are good equipment consultants. When it comes to advice on purchasing skis, choose your friends wisely. Talk to people who ski at the level to which you aspire. They should be about your size and ski with a similar style, only faster. If a friend outweighs you by 50 pounds and skis with a gritty, powerful style compared to your graceful, precise touch on the snow, that person's ski of choice is probably too beefy for you.

Ski Boots

The right skis won't help you ski faster unless you also have the right ski boots. Even if you have a high tolerance for pain, if your feet are miserable, you can't perform at your peak. Your feet and lower legs will be too tense. Your sense of the external forces and snow texture through your feet will be diminished. You will react slower and fatigue more quickly. Compromise on your choice of ski boots and you compromise your skiing performance as well.

You might wonder how humans can put someone on the moon but not be able to make comfortable ski boots that also perform well. For many skiers, comfort and performance seem mutually exclusive. To transmit energy efficiently from your flesh and bones through your bindings to your skis, a ski boot must wrap closely around your foot. This close wrapping also allows you to feel the snow and precisely control your skis. The trick is to fit your foot snugly inside the boot without cutting off circulation or causing pressure points. Your foot should feel supported, yet relaxed.

At one end of the spectrum, ski boots designed for novice skiers have lots of cushy padding and a soft flex, which makes them comfortable but too mushy for anyone with high-performance ambitions. All that cushioning requires more space between your foot and the shell. This sacrifices a close wrap around your foot. Don't lose hope. Ski boot *lasts* (the form around which a ski boot is shaped) and construction materials differ from manufacturer to manufacturer and sometimes from model to model within one brand. It may take some help from a master boot fitter, but a pain-free high-performance boot exists for your foot. To find it, make sure your ski shop is capable of custom fitting ski boots and then consider the following:

Stiffness

To ski faster, you should be able to flex your ski boots forward smoothly without any bulging of the lower boot, but they should still support your foot and lower leg. You will know boots are the right stiffness when you can flex them forward without collapsing them. After that, stiffness becomes a personal preference. Some racers prefer extremely stiff boots. Others like their boots soft. However, even the boots of those racers who prefer a softer flex will be stiffer than most "sport" or "carving" models available in ski shops.

Some companies have introduced *carving boots* to go with shaped skis. These are not racing boots. There are specific models for each level of ability. In general, carving boots have a soft forward flex, but are reinforced laterally. Many carving boots have an asymmetric cuff, which is higher on the inside of the leg for additional support while you are angulating to the side. Carving boots are designed on the theory that shaped skis require less steering (which is done by driving the knee forward and into the hill) but more hip angulation. In some models, you can see the reinforced areas because the shell is *bi-injected*. The bi-injection design and construction incorporate two different plastics into the shell, one stiffer than the other, each a different color.

Some racing boots are asymetric and bi-injected, too, with the stiffer plastic in front as well as to the inside and back of the boot. If you are already an expert skier, a racing boot is a better choice if becoming a good racer is your goal or if you ski varied terrain and conditions. If you are a carving purist who sticks mostly to wide-open groomed runs, then a carving boot is fine. Intermediate skiers and many women usually find a full-blown racing boot to be too stiff. For those people, manufacturers usually offer a softer version of their racing boots. A high-end carving boot works well, too, unless you are planning to ski a lot of slalom events. Slalom technique still demands a lot of steering with the knees and feet, which in turn requires more support in the front of the boot. Whatever the case, be sure the boot is not too stiff or too soft when you flex it forward. It should support you laterally, and it should never flex backward. If you are exceptionally strong, heavy, or tall, consider a slightly stiffer boot because you have more leverage over it and therefore can flex it more easily.

Heel Pocket

Your heel and ankle should nestle snugly into the heel pocket of the boot and, once the boot is buckled, should stay there. If your heel and ankle have any movement, up and down, or side to side, you will have less control over your turns. In fact, most of the boot should fit snugly. The toe box is the only area where a little extra space is okay, particularly if you have extra-cold feet.

Your toes should come to the front of the boot but still be able to wiggle. Be sure your toes are not curled or pinched in any way, or you will surely lose a toenail or two.

Closure System

Most ski boots today come with a power strap across the top of the boot. This secures the cuff and tongue in place while providing additional support. Micro-adjustable buckles also help you fine-tune the closure of the boot, so it is just tight enough for support, but not so tight that your circulation is cut off. The most critical buckles are at the ankle and over the instep, that is, the second and third buckles on a four-buckle boot. These should be tight, but not so tight that the buckle over the instep compresses the boot down on your foot, hindering blood flow. Your feet will fall asleep, if they don't freeze first.

The tightness of the top buckle is a personal preference. Some racers keep that buckle on the loose side, particularly if they ski in a stiff racing boot. A loose buckle allows them to flex forward more easily. If you do the same, be sure the top buckle is at least tight enough to prevent it from opening.

The tightness of the toe buckle is also a personal preference. It mostly serves to keep out snow. Don't make it so tight that it immobilizes your toes.

Custom Liners

One way to guarantee a perfect fit is with a custom boot liner. Stock liners have some ability to form to your foot, but a better choice is either an injected foam or an injected silicone system. Foam is the most common among elite skiers. The foam is injected into the liner as you stand in your ski boots. Gone are the days when the liner foam took 2 hours and a full dose of pain before it set up. Today, it takes less than 30 minutes for liner foam to harden, and the process is relatively effortless.

A few manufacturers also offer injected silicone liners. The silicone is similar to the material that dentists use to make molds of teeth. Silicone has slightly more give to it than foam, which is rather firm when it hardens. Although most World Cup racers prefer foam, silicone is a viable choice for most skiers, particularly if you plan to keep your boots for several seasons, because it won't pack out or compress, making the boot feel bigger over time.

Each year the number of high-end women's boots on the market increases, but unlike running shoes or tennis shoes, women interested in faster skiing should not assume that they should be in a women's ski boot. Top women racers ski in customized unisex boots. If you are a woman and find women's boots too soft, choose a unisex racing boot with the right stiffness and with a custom liner for the best fit.

Footbeds

Whichever type of boot liner you choose, definitely opt for a custom footbed. Ski boots come with little arch support. With the footbed that comes in the boot, your arch must collapse in order to apply pressure to the ski edge, which takes an extra split second every turn. Those fractions of a second add up quickly. With the right amount of arch support, your skis respond immediately when you roll them on edge. In addition, your foot is more relaxed in your boot. If you clench your toes, it is difficult to keep pressure on the tongue of the boot and therefore to start each turn. A footbed that is formed to your foot relaxes it, slowing fatigue and allowing you to ski better.

The footbed is also the place where corrections to your lower leg alignment take place. If you have a mild amount (2 degrees or less) of pronation (your foot rolls to the inside when you step) or supination (your foot rolls to the outside), the footbed can handle the adjustment. If you have extreme degrees of pronation or supination, then you may need to have a cant placed between your binding and your ski. Never try to cant your boots yourself by grinding your boot sole! This not only voids the manufacturer's warranty, but messes up the boot-binding interface, which affects the release system of the binding. There are only a handful of boot technicians in the country who can properly grind a boot sole while adding reinforcement to the toe and heel of the boot to keep the binding interface intact; these master fitters are few and far between.

Heel Lift

Ramp angle refers to the height of your heel relative to your toes inside your ski boot. Most unisex boots have minimal ramp angle. If your natural position in your ski boot places your weight over your heels, if you tend to sit back a lot, if your ski tips float and wobble a lot, or if you have trouble starting your turns because of a lack of tip pressure, consider adding a heel lift to increase the ramp angle of your boot.

Heel lifts don't seem high, only 4 millimeters or so, but they can make a big difference in your balance, particularly for women. Women carry most of their weight between their knees and their waist, whereas men carry most of their weight between their waist and their neck. As a result, compared with men, women have a lower center of gravity that is situated farther back, making it more difficult for women to stay centered over their skis. A heel lift often solves the problem. However, if you are a woman who already skis in a woman's boot, a heel lift may not be the solution. Increasing the ramp angle is one of the ways manufacturers make ski boots women-specific. Adding a heel lift may push you too far forward. If your binding and your ski also have some ramp angle

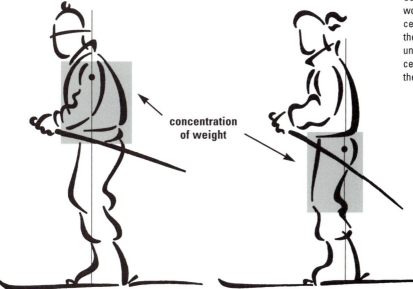

concentration of weight

Center of gravity, man versus woman of similar height. Man: the center of gravity is higher and over the balls of the feet. Woman (in unisex ski boot, no heel lift): the center of gravity is lower and over the heels.

built into them, you could be going downhill before you go up the chairlift. When you stand on your skis, you should stand at your natural balance point over the center of the ski. If you are too far forward, you may have good pressure on your ski tips at the start of your turns, but the tails of your skis will skid at the end of them.

More Ski Boot Advice

Customizing your ski boots takes time! If a ski shop does not offer customized liners and footbeds, then they do not cater to true high-performance skiers. Selling injectable liners is a good clue that the salesperson will take the extra time to work with you. Beware of the quick sell. It is a lot easier to put you in a ski boot that is a half-size too big. It feels good out of the box, but your foot will be swimming in it after a day or two.

Try on a lot of ski boots! If you have an effortless time buying shoes, you will probably find the same with ski boots. However, if shopping for shoes is a challenge, then be prepared to invest some time in shopping for your ski boots to get them to fit correctly.

Bindings

Of the triad of boots, bindings, and skis, skiers typically give the least amount of thought to their bindings. Yet bindings contain the most complicated technology. Consider that bindings must release easily when you want to take off your skis or when you fall, yet hold your boots to your skis at 75 mph.

Edgar Pollman, General Manager of Tyrolia Worldwide, compares a ski binding to the suspension system of a Formula 1 race car. "If the skier is the engine, then the boots are the steering, the skis are the slicks [tires], and the gearbox and the suspension are the bindings," says Pollman. Following Pollman's analogy, bindings handle three issues: energy transmission from the boot to the ski, snow handling, and safety. The system is adjustable to the ability and weight of the skier, and in some cases, the snow conditions.

Despite the complexity of a binding, most skiers, even high-performance skiers, pay them little attention. They think that as long as a binding does not pre-release (open in the middle of a turn), it is fine. However, given the critical functions that bindings perform, their purchase certainly deserves more thought. Just the fact that a set of high-end bindings costs over $200 should get your attention; then it is up to you to make the right choice.

Selecting the Correct Binding

The most important feature of a binding is its DIN setting. *DIN* stands for Deutsche Industrie Normen (German Industry Standards), which is loosely translated and understood as standardized spring tension. For practical purposes, it is the numbered scale in the window on your binding's toe and heel pieces that determines how tight the binding is set. DINs start at less than 1 in a young child's binding and go as high as 16 on over-the-counter racing bindings. World Cup downhill racers may use much higher DIN settings, but these bindings are not available to the general public. Top Alpine Masters racers rarely need a DIN setting over 15, and then only in speed events.

Your DIN setting is determined by your skiing ability and your weight. Be honest about your weight. If you tell the binding technician that you are 10 pounds lighter than you really are, the technician could set the bindings with too little tension, causing your bindings to prerelease at inopportune moments. If your bindings don't keep your ski boots attached to your skis on a regular basis, your confidence and your body could be unduly bruised.

When you do fall, you want your bindings to release. You want your skis as far away from you as possible. Skis that remain attached to your boots during a fall can twist your joints—the knee is particularly vulnerable—or increase the chance of a broken tibia or fibia in the lower leg. Bindings should not be the cause of a fall, but they should release when a fall occurs.

To ensure that your bindings work correctly without placing long-term stress on the spring, select a binding for which your personal setting is about halfway on its DIN scale. If your personal DIN setting is at the lower end of the range, the binding may be too strong for your weight and ability. If your personal DIN setting is at the top of the scale, you should consider a higher performance model, otherwise the spring may fatigue more quickly because it is at maximum tension all the time.

Select your bindings after you have chosen your skis and ski boots. Your bindings should be mounted on your skis using your ski boots as guides. After the binding technician sets everything up, check that your DIN setting is correct and that the boot-binding interface is snug at all points of contact. If the binding is loose laterally or if the forward pressure—that is, the amount of pressure the bindings exert from heel to toe—is not correct, the bindings may not function properly. When the binding is closed against the boot, it exerts pressure against the heel (back) of the boot, pushing it forward against the toe piece. This helps keep the boot in the binding when the ski is on edge, absorbing vibration as it carves through the snow or ice. If you get a new pair of boots, even if they are the same size as your old ones, have your bindings checked to be sure they are set properly for those boots.

Effects of Bindings on Ski Flex

Finding a binding with the correct DIN range is only the first step in choosing a binding. All bindings use the same DIN scale. A setting of 10 on a Tyrolia binding is the same as a 10 on a Marker binding or a Salomon binding. This standardization encourages people to think all bindings are created equal. They are not, especially at the high end. Some are light in weight. Some are heavy. Some have more ramp angle than others. Some have built-in vibration dampeners. Some have more lift than others. One releases diagonally as well as forward and side to side. Of all the features that make each binding model unique, however, the binding's effect on the ski's flex pattern is among the most significant.

Some high-performance bindings allow the ski to flex into its natural arc, instead of having a flat spot under the boot. Other bindings might have settings that change the characteristics of the ski, making it feel softer or stiffer. The former binding is beneficial to everyone. The latter is a matter of personal preference. When your ski boot is in a standard binding, it creates a flat spot in the middle of the ski when the ski is in reverse camber during

PRO TIP: HOW MUCH SHOULD YOU CRANK 'EM DOWN?

Most racers don't think about bindings releasing. They just want their skis to stay on. The tendency is to crank the bindings to a much higher DIN setting than the ski shop suggests. "Don't do it!" says Edgar Pollman, General Manager of Tyrolia Worldwide. "World Cup racers have special needs, due to their superior strength and their highly demanding courses. If you prerelease too often, then you may need to increase the setting by one or two, but don't crank down anything." Pollman advises skiers to look at their bindings when they prerelease. In general, the setting on the toe and the heel piece should be the same; however, if the heel piece prereleases several times, have a binding technician set it one point higher than the toe, making sure that it does not affect the binding's forward pressure.

a turn. Some bindings "float" the ski boot over the ski, allowing the ski to bend naturally (no flat spot), thus allowing a better carved turn. It may prevent prereleases, too. As you ski, vibrations go through the ski, causing the ski to flex and straighten over and over again in rapid succession. This creates slight variations in forward pressure. In theory, if you set an edge of the ski at the exact moment that the forward pressure is slightly looser, the binding is more apt to prerelease. If the boot is not directly connected to the ski, the ski takes vibration and stays on, because the binding's forward pressure is consistent.

What about bindings that make skis feel softer or stiffer? Some industry insiders believe that is the future of ski bindings. Some day in the future, we will step into our bindings and they will automatically calibrate themselves for the skier and the snow conditions. For now, a few models offer a manual adjustment, a lever or a dial in the front of the binding with three settings. The "stiffer" setting makes your skis feel more rigid, which may be helpful at faster speeds or on icy conditions. The middle setting allows you to feel the skis as they were made. It is the typical setting when conditions are perfect packed powder. The "softer" setting allows the skis to bend easier in a turn, which may be helpful in soft, new snow or springtime conditions. Some skiers love the versatility. Other skiers pick one setting and leave it there 99 percent of the time.

Plates and Lifters

You would be hard-pressed to find a good racer, or even an expert skier, who doesn't use some sort of a *plate*, a *lifter*, or both between the ski and the binding. If you want to ski faster, you should use these devices. Plates and lifters come in a range of heights, but they all serve two functions: they prevent boot out; and they give you more leverage over your edge. The difference between a plate and a lifter is that a plate also dampens vibration significantly.

With shaped skis, you angulate to the side much more, which means the angle between the snow and your lower leg is more acute. A shaped ski for racing has such a narrow waist, approximately 62 millimeters, that your ski boot is wider than your ski. During aggressive turns, which require the most angulation, the boot may touch the snow, causing the ski edge to lose its grip. By lifting the boot off the ski with a plate or lifter, the boot is less likely to touch the snow. You would have to angulate much farther, extremely far, for the boot to touch the snow in the middle of a turn.

Because lifters increase your stand-height off the snow, they not only help prevent boot out, but also give you more leverage over your edge. You can transfer more power to the edge, resulting in better edge grip.

Finally, most lifters dampen vibration at least a little, because you have put additional material between your boot and the ski. However, a high-performance skier should look for a plate that is specifically made to dampen vibration a lot. These plates typically use a combination of rubber and metal to absorb various frequencies. As your speed increases, it is these vibrations that start to affect your confidence and control. "I'm going too fast" starts to flash through your mind, not because you have reached a spe-

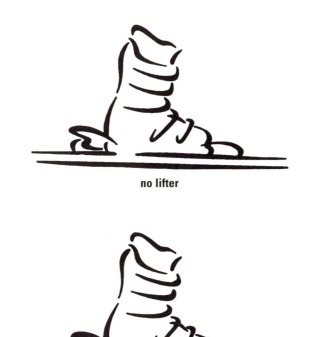

no lifter

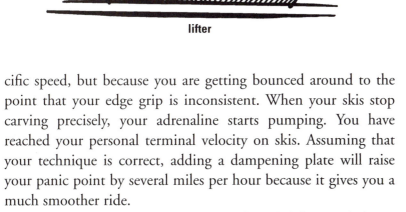

lifter

max. 55 mm

Lifters between your ski and binding increase **stand-height**, or the distance between the snow and the bottom of your boot.

cific speed, but because you are getting bounced around to the point that your edge grip is inconsistent. When your skis stop carving precisely, your adrenaline starts pumping. You have reached your personal terminal velocity on skis. Assuming that your technique is correct, adding a dampening plate will raise your panic point by several miles per hour because it gives you a much smoother ride.

Don't be fooled by the thought that if a little lift is good, then a lot of lift is better. There are limits. How high should you go? The Fédération Internationale du Ski (FIS), the international governing body of competitive skiing, has set the limit at 55 millimeters from the bottom of the ski to the bottom of the boot. With most ski-binding set-ups, that leaves room for approximately 15 millimeters of plate or lifter. Heavy, strong, aggressive skiers should take full advantage of every millimeter. Lighter or less aggressive skiers may be happier with a 10-millimeter plate or lifter.

Binding Care and Maintenance

It is not necessary to loosen the tension in your bindings at the end of the ski season, although it cannot hurt. It is more important to have your bindings checked at the beginning of the season to be sure the springs are still in good shape.

Bindings get more abuse in transport to and from the ski area that in actual use. If you carry your skis on a roof or trunk rack, road dirt, salt, and grime get into your bindings, which can affect them over time. Be sure to keep them clean. If possible, travel with your skis inside your car, or at least put them in a bag. It will preserve your bindings and bases.

Even if you only ski ten days a year, get new bindings every three or four years. If you have had a pair of bindings for a long time and ask a ski shop to check them only to find they won't, don't argue, get a new pair. The springs may fatigue over time whether you use the bindings or not. After a period of time, the manufacturer will no longer indemnify them. Your bindings are your insurance policy. They help prevent injury. Take care of them and never settle for second-best!

Ski Poles

Like bindings, ski poles are frequently relegated to commodity status, but there are a few things to consider when selecting a ski pole for faster skiing.

To determine if the ski pole is the correct height, turn the pole upside down, put the handle on the floor, and grasp the pole under the basket. Your elbow should form a 90-degree angle. Many racers prefer a slightly longer pole (an inch or two, but no more), because it gives them more leverage when pushing out of a starting gate. However, given the increased amounts of angulation and emphasis on lateral rather than up-and-down movement, don't select a pole that is too long or planting the pole for a turn will be impractical.

Bent poles are a must for downhill and Super G races because they allow you to assume a more aerodynamic tuck. World Cup racers have their poles bent to their body for minimum wind drag. Some racers like them for giant slalom, too, but they are not necessary for that event, since the time you spend in a tuck is a small percentage, if any, of your total time on the course. When it comes to the length of your poles for downhill racing, start with the same length as your regular poles. Try the poles in a tight tuck. Then, see how they feel if you drive your hands forward, a common move in speed events. If the poles seem short, go for poles that are one size (2 inches) longer.

The poles for downhill racing are not the only poles that have an unusual shape. Some regular poles are pencil thin or shaped like a long skinny airplane wing for less wind resistance. Some are bent at ergonomic angles to make the pole plant more efficient. Whether you opt for any of these innovations is a matter of personal preference. In any case, be sure the ski pole doesn't flex too much when you push with it. Not only is it annoying, but it will also cost you time in the starting gate.

More important than shape is the swing weight of a ski pole. To judge the swing weight of a ski pole, flick it forward in a planting motion, then back to its original position. Do this several times. The pole should swing effortlessly but still have enough weight that it can be controlled comfortably. A pole that is too light isn't as maneuverable at speed.

A closing thought on ski poles: Most elite racers prefer a small basket on the bottom of their poles, approximately 2 inches in diameter, to cut down on wind resistance. A small basket also reduces the swing weight of the pole. If your ski pole baskets are big, there is no need to buy an entirely new pole, just trim the baskets down to the desired diameter with a sharp knife.

Helmets

Racers are required to wear helmets in all USSA-sanctioned giant slalom, Super G, and downhill races. Most local and charitable events do not yet require helmets, but it is probably a good idea to wear one while skiing in general and certainly while racing. Thirty miles per hour is not an unusual speed in a GS race. If you wear a helmet to ride a bike or for in-line skating, where

Slalom helmet (top) and multiuse skiing helmet (bottom).

speeds rarely exceed 20 mph, then why not for skiing? It may sound like common sense, but be sure your helmet is made for skiing. A helmet won't necessarily prevent a head injury, but it can lessen the severity of one in the event of a bad crash. Be sure your helmet fits snugly, for both comfort and better protection.

Helmets are not yet required for slalom racing, but specialized slalom helmets that are designed to deflect slalom poles are available. These slalom helmets have a short visor over the brow and a half-circle of plastic in front of the mouth (see also chapter 5, page 89, for a discussion of slalom helmets). They are usually not designed to protect against blows to the head, but they do help prevent cuts to the face, and a broken nose or teeth.

Some manufacturers sell one helmet for all events. These multiuse helmets usually come with removable accessories to make them either slalom- or speed-specific. Helmets are a good idea, not only for racing but for all skiing. Today, they are available in a myriad of styles, with venting and better ability to hear clearly. They may not save your life if you hit a tree (you could snap your neck or sustain internal injuries), but they improve your odds if you hit your head.

Goggles

There's an old saying in skiing, "if you can't see, you can't ski." It's unthinkable to ski fast, let alone enter a race, without wearing goggles. Goggles prevent your eyes from watering, or worse (especially for contact lens wearers), from drying out. They also protect your eyes if your face hits a gate, the snow, or some other object.

Goggle selection need not be complicated. The first concern should be fit. Do the goggles hug your face securely with no gaps? Does the strap stay in place? (A wider strap is usually better.) Does it fit around your helmet? Check that your goggles fit properly on your face with your helmet on. They should have both a coating on the lens and good venting (which isn't blocked by your helmet) to prevent fogging, and they should offer excellent peripheral vision.

If you are skiing on a blue-bird day, a dark lens is a good choice, particularly if you are skiing at high altitude, such as in the Rockies, and if that lens offers both ultraviolet (UV) and infrared (IR) protection. If you are skiing at night, a clear lens is the best choice. If the light is flat, such as when it is overcast or snowing, most racers prefer a pink (*vermilion*) lens or a yellow-orange (*citron*) lens, which helps brighten the terrain and give it some texture.

If your vision is not 20-20, one of your biggest dilemmas will be whether to wear glasses or contact lenses when you ski. There is no definitive answer. If you are comfortable in contacts, they give you the best peripheral vision and ensure the least amount of fogging. They are a must for slalom racing, where a gate could hit you in the face. However, at faster speeds, your eyes are more susceptible to drying, since you don't blink much while racing. If you tend to have dry eyes, glasses under your goggles, prescription inserts, or a prescription lens for your goggles are a better bet for giant slaloms or speed events on an average winter day. The problem with glasses under your goggles, and with goggle inserts, is fogging. The problem with a prescription lens for your goggles is cost. The possibility of scratching and breakage from high-performance use is high, as well. When it is bitter cold, snowing hard, or wet—conditions in which goggle fogging is more likely—you may want to stick with contacts. In the end, you will have to experiment to see what works best for you.

When your goggles do fog or ice up, be sure to clean them only with a soft cloth or chamois, not a tissue or napkin. Paper products scratch the lens, especially on the inside where the antifog coating has been applied.

Performance Equipment for Kids

Kids want to ski faster, too, and as with adults, equipment makes a big difference in their performance.

In general, three factors differentiate young people, who are not fully developed, from adults. First, they are not as strong muscularly. Second, they still have a lot to learn technically.

Third, they are lighter in weight. All of these factors influence equipment selection.

Kids' Skis

Rossignol has been a front-runner in the development and testing of performance equipment for kids, particularly shaped skis. Their first formal test took place over a 10-day period at Mt. Hood, during the summer of 1996. Six to seven kids participated each day. Each child took eight timed runs, alternating two runs on shaped skis and two runs on straighter skis, on short 30-second courses. The courses were purposely short to factor out fatigue. Over the course of the test, Rossignol gathered data on a total of 600 timed runs. While the company continues to test equipment for kids on a worldwide basis, the results of the 1996 test remain conclusive. Kids who want to ski faster should be on shaped skis.

"There isn't a good racer under age 14 that Rossignol works with who isn't on a shaped ski at this point," says Thor Verdonk, Director of Rossignol's race program in the United States. "Kids can feel the ski carve without as much steering and forward movement. It helps them tactically, too. Before [shaped skis], they would typically skid their turns on a low line. Now, they carve on a higher line and go faster."

Regardless of age, the lower the technical ability and the less strength a child has, the more shape the skis should have. Also, like adult skis, shaped skis for kids should also be about 10 centimeters shorter. However, Verdonk advises juniors not to get hung up on the exact dimensions of a ski. "Shape is only one aspect," he says. "Look at the whole ski, including the length and construction. The core is still the heart of a ski."

Kids' Ski Boots

Kids' ski boots are typically too stiff. All the benchmarks for fit and performance in adult boots apply to boots for kids, too, especially the ability to flex the boot forward without collapsing it. Some ski boot manufacturers now make bi-injected boot shells (combining softer and stiffer plastics) for junior racers. Even with bi-injection technology, a kid with fast ambitions should not be in a junior race boot if the boot cannot be flexed. Tall kids have more leverage, so they can often handle a stiffer boot better. "Lower leg length is key," explains Verdonk. "The top of the liner should come up just past the bottom of the calf muscle."

Kids also tend to have smaller leg dimensions. Be sure the cuff of the boot fits snuggly around the lower leg. There should be no gap in the back when the boot flexes forward. If there is a gap, have a boot-fitter fill the space between the liner and the shell with a wedge or shim, commonly called a "spoiler."

What about the tiny 12-year-old with full-sized feet? This kid is about to do some growing, but in the meantime, the boot sole length should be as short as possible, without pinching the toes. The same is true for the 90-pound beanpole. Neither of these kids has the strength to match the body's dimensions. Their skis are already relatively short, commensurate with their light weight. A smaller boot length decreases the flat-spot on the ski under the boot. The smaller the flat spot, the truer the carve of the turns. Choosing the right binding and plate helps, too.

Kids' Bindings and Plates

Assuming the binding is mounted directly on the ski, to produce the smallest possible flat spot, Verdonk recommends looking for bindings with the least distance between the screws for the toe piece and the heel piece. Adding an antivibration plate between the ski and binding eliminates the issue.

If you decide to add a plate to the top of a junior racer's ski, be aware that the rules for stand-height are as much an issue for kids as they are for adults. The current rule limits the height from the base of the ski to the bottom of the boot sole to 50 millimeters for racers aged 14 years and under (versus 55 millimeters for racers aged 15 years and over). The FIS is debating whether to ban plates for racers under age 14. In truth, unless a nonteenage skier frequently "boots out," he or she probably doesn't need a plate.

"If a kid is under 100 pounds, then only use a lifter," advises Verdonk. "If a kid weighs between 100 and 130 pounds, select a softer, polyurethane plate, not a metal one. If the kid's over 130 pounds, an adult plate is fine, unless he or she is not very aggressive. And if the skier is age 12 or younger, and a one-ski rule is in effect [a kid must use the same skis for slalom and giant slalom], it is okay to use a pair of plates or a lifter in slalom."

With kids' bindings, elasticity is the biggest issue. Binding *elasticity* refers to the amount the binding gives to the side when shocked without releasing. When a ski is on edge, carving a fast turn, the binding is designed to open slightly to the side, then close, then open slightly, over and over again, as it receives vibrations. You don't feel it. However, if the shock is great enough, such as when you hook a tip, the binding goes past its elastic point and releases completely. More elasticity is better, particularly for racing where snow conditions can be icy or chattery, because it prevents prereleasing.

Kids' Helmets

As soon as a child can ski, she should wear a helmet—long before she has any desire to pursue faster skiing and racing. Small children are difficult to see behind bumps and knolls on the open slopes. They are like hidden obstacles, easy for other skiers to hit accidentally. Children also have little fear, so they tend to ski faster than others might deem prudent. When a child gets old enough to join a racing program, a helmet is required (same rules that apply to older racers). They must wear one for training and racing.

Giant Slalom Racing

To stand on top of the winner's platform is to stand on top of the world.

Giant Slalom Defined

Of the four ski-racing disciplines—slalom, giant slalom, Super G, and downhill—giant slalom, or "GS," is the most common. Most coin-operated and NASTAR courses at ski areas—those open to the public (usually on a daily basis)—are giant slalom courses. The same is true of most charity and promotional events, corporate outings, and town races. Among more serious ski racers who participate in competitions sanctioned by the U.S. Ski and Snowboard Association (USSA), the national governing body for ski racing, GS is considered one of two "technical" events; the other is slalom. Super G and downhill are considered speed events.

In general, most recreational GS courses are short in length, that is, they can be run by experienced racers in under 30 seconds. Even though they are fairly straight, skiers rarely go faster than 30 miles per hour because the terrain is usually moderate. GS courses sanctioned by the USSA and the Fédération Internationale du Ski (FIS), the international governing body for skiing, are much longer, 1 to 2 minutes, and faster, sometimes 45 mph or more. In addition, after the first run, the course is reset and racers take a second run. The combined time for both runs determines the winner.

Giant slalom seems like the easiest of the ski-racing disciplines because you feel speed without the intimidation of a downhill or

GIANT SLALOM AT A GLANCE
Average number of gates per run: 30 to 60 (World Cup format), 15 to 25 (NASTAR and pro formats)
Average time per run: 45 to 90 seconds (World Cup format), 18 to 35 seconds (NASTAR and pro formats)
Average speed: 25 to 35 mph (World Cup format), 15 to 30 mph (NASTAR and pro formats)

COURSE VARIABLES

The FIS rules for course length and number of gates are the accepted guidelines at USSA-sanctioned events. Here are the ranges by discipline from regional to World Cup-level competition. In some cases, the number of gates is a percentage of the vertical drop of the course. In slalom, GS, and super G, the colors for gates alternate red, blue, red, blue. In downhill courses, the gates, which are farther apart and function more as guides to the terrain, are only red.

Vertical Drop and Number of Gates by Event

Event	Vertical Drop		Number of Gates	
	Men	Women	Men	Women
Slalom	140–220 m	120–200 m	55–75 gates	45–65 gates
Giant Slalom	250–450 m	250–400 m	12–15% of vertical drop	
Super G	500–650 m	350–600 m	minimum	minimum
	(maximum of 2 jumps)		35 gates	30 gates
			(maximum = 10% of vertical drop)	
Downhill	500–1,100 m	500–800 m	number as required by terrain; red only	

SOURCE: "The International Ski Competition Rules," by the Fédération Internationale du Ski (FIS), 1996.

In GS, the gates are set so that the racer makes medium- to wide-radius turns back and forth across the fall line. The gates must be at least 10 meters apart. The radius of a typical GS turn is approximately 25 meters (inset).

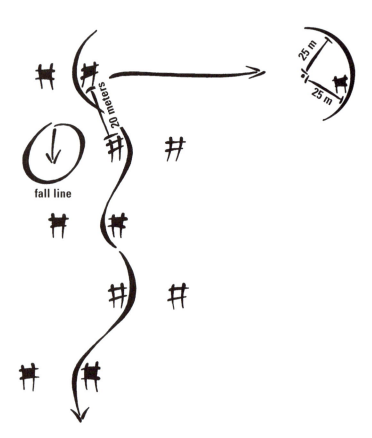

the sprint-like quickness of a slalom. The gates are at least 10 meters apart and set in a pattern of medium to wide-radius turns that crisscross the fall line. Although GS is the easiest type of race to finish, it is arguably the most difficult to ski well. In fact, GS can be maddening. It is common to have a relatively slow time even though you feel you skied well. Skiing GS well takes a combination of technique and tactics.

Equipment Considerations for GS

Most skis will work in a NASTAR-style GS course, particularly shaped skis, whose sidecuts are usually designed with a GS-sized turn in mind, but for a real edge over the competition, it helps to have the real McCoy (skis designed specifically for GS racing), or at least a slightly more forgiving version of the real thing, along with plates under your bindings. Both the skis and the plates are designed to smooth out your ride. Less vibration reaching your legs means better edge grip at higher speeds.

Skin-tight speed suits are the norm for USSA-sanctioned races. The hot shots at other events and at town races wear them, too. Functionally, they are more aerodynamic. Are they necessary? Only if you expect to win or lose by a second or less. Otherwise, wear the least baggy ski attire you own.

Helmets are required in all USSA- and FIS-sanctioned races; for a discussion of helmets, see page 61.

Giant Slalom Technique

Of the four racing disciplines, the turns in GS are the closest to those in free skiing, which is a reason why GS courses are the easiest to finish. As with any carved turn, you must angulate to the side against centrifugal force in a GS turn, increasing your angulation as the pressure builds on your skis, then decreasing it as your skis finish the turn and come back under your body. As illustrated in chapter 1 (item 6 in "The 10 Secrets of Faster Skiing"), angulation refers to the angles that your body forms in a turn. Your feet travel out to the side as the turn progresses, as your body leans down the hill. Angulating

Angulation in a GS turn. Notice the positions of the skis and the body in relation to the gate. The body is almost leaning away from the gates. The feet are out to the side, not under the body. Although angulation increases as the turn progresses, at any point in the turn lines through the shoulders, hips, knees, and feet are all parallel to one another.

allows the edges of your skis to dig into the snow or ice, with most of your weight on the downhill ski. The faster your speed and the tighter the turn, the more angulation you need.

In GS, you have to be precise to be fast. You must have excellent balance, and your feet need to be ultra-sensitive to what your skis are doing. You also have to let your skis run as fast as you dare.

It helps to free ski a lot at race speeds while practicing angulation and precision in your turns. Skiing a course magnifies flaws in your ski technique because you have to turn where the gates dictate. If you try to cheat by skidding your turns or by taking an unorthodox line, you will either fall or be very slow. If you perfect your turns on the open slopes first, where you can concentrate on your skiing without the course or the clock as a distraction, you will improve your performance in the gates.

The most common mistake in GS and in the other ski-racing disciplines is leaning toward the pole as you pass it by tilting your head, dropping your inside hand, or tipping down the shoulder closest to the pole. For many, it is a subconscious move, but the immediate result is a skidded rather than a carved turn. When you lean toward the gate, your weight moves to the uphill ski. You incline, banking against your skis, rather than angulating around the turns. As a result, the downhill ski stops carving. Your skis dump speed rather than maintaining or gaining speed.

As with free skiing, even though your torso travels a smaller radius around the gate than your skis, your body must still main-

PRO TIP: WHEN TO WEIGHT YOUR HEELS

Horst Weber, Program Director of the New York State Ski Educational Foundation at Whiteface Mountain, New York, who periodically works with the U.S. Ski Team, has trained ski racers of every age and ability. When it comes to GS technique, Weber warns racers not to force weight onto their heels to gain speed. "Riding the back of the ski at the end of a GS turn is the result of a good turn," he says, "The turn has to be clean to begin with. If the turn is clean, the g-forces [the increase in gravity caused by acceleration] of the turn will pull you onto your heels. It's a total misconception to push to your heels. It's an effect, not a cause. You can't ski clean on your heels." According to Weber, gravity and the g-forces of the turn determine the right place to be over your skis, which differs from person to person. A taller person will have a different body position than a shorter person.

Reprinted from Lisa Feinberg Densmore, "Technique and Tactics in Giant Slalom," *Ski Racing International*, 20 Jan. 1995.

Angulating versus inclinating. Skier A is angulated (body in comma shape). Her skis are on edge, carving a turn; Skier B is inclinating toward the pole. While her feet may be out to the side, her torso is tipped toward the gate (body forms a straight line), which pulls too much weight onto the uphill ski. Her skis are not only skidding but also heading more across the hill rather than down it.

tain a comma shape. In other words, the upper body is relatively upright, oriented down the hill, with the feet out to the side. To break the habit of leaning into the poles, overemphasize leaning away from them, and you will probably be in the right position.

Many racers concentrate on their hand position in GS, as well as in the other racing disciplines, because hand position is directly related to your balance over your skis and often to technical flaws, such as leaning in too much or rotating into the gates. However, some coaches believe that your arm position comes as a result of good balance, not vice versa. Whatever

Hand position. As the author angulates, she presses both hands forward. Her downhill hand also presses down the fall line (see definition page 74).

Deborah Compagnoni (Italy) during the 1998 Olympic GS race in Nagano, Japan. She drives her hands and her body mass forward as she comes over a knoll.

the case, skiing is a sport that deals with velocity. Your hands should be forward, in the bottom of your peripheral vision, for stability.

It helps to drive the downhill hand down the fall line, so that it feels slightly lower than the uphill one. This pulls you over your downhill ski. Be careful not to press the downhill hand directly forward or directly to the side, rather, it should be part way between the two. Another way to think about it is to slightly lift your uphill hand, the one closest to the gate, in effect tipping your torso down the hill as you pass by each gate. This is particularly helpful if you tend to drop the uphill hand.

Don't forget your pole plant! Even at faster speeds, you should still plant your pole as you finish your turn. The touch of the pole tip to the snow should always be down the hill, not toward your ski tips. By reaching down the hill to plant your pole, not only do you draw your weight over the downhill ski, but you also make it easier to roll your skis from one edge to the other into the next turn.

As you try to master angulation and hand position in GS, be careful not to "assume the position." In other words, do not simply drop the hip into the hill and freeze your hands in place. First, there is no such thing as instant angulation. If you only drop your

---

FIRST PERSON: MY FIRST CARVED TURN

I began skiing as soon as I could walk. My father, Philip Feinberg, an avid skier, would steer me down the hill or carry me on his shoulders, depending on my mood.

I remember learning to ski with my skis parallel sometime around age five. I was following my father down Whiteface Mountain, New York, near where I lived. Although I had made a turn here and there with my skis together, I had never linked consecutive short turns. Back then, in the mid-1960s, the style was called *wedeln*. The wedeln may have been quick, but it was not carving with the skis on edge. It was more of a pivot with the lower body.

At age 6, I started racing locally in a series called the Candy Bar Slaloms. The premise of the races was simple, the fastest racer in each age group got a free candy bar at the concession stand. What a motivation for skiing faster! Although I was fearless, carved turns were still not in my inventory of skiing skills.

By age 8, I had joined the junior racing program. We trained after dinner, under the lights, at a small area called Mt. Pisgah. A compact, quick-witted German guy named Horst Weber was our coach. He could turn faster than anyone I had ever met. I was awed by his finesse on skis. Unfortunately, he did not hold the same awe of my technique. Luckily, he still thought I had talent.

Weber tried everything to get me to carve a turn. After several weeks of encouragement, drills, and advice—all unsuccessful—he decided to take drastic measures. About ten turns into our practice course, he stuck a large crowbar that was used for setting the gates (about an inch in diameter and about four feet long) into the snow about 2 feet away from the pole. He told me to hike up to the start and ski the course as fast as I could. "You will either carve a turn or break your leg," he said matter-of-factly.

As I started my turn toward the crowbar, the space between the bar and the gate pole seemed more like 6 inches than 2 feet. I may have closed my eyes. I cannot remember for sure. But I do remember the sensation. My edges bit into the snow. My skis started to turn, and suddenly I sprang forward into the next turn. Wow! I will never forget the energy that my skis generated. The rebound from my skis made me feel like I was on a trampoline. I didn't exactly control that first carved turn, but I didn't hit the crowbar either. And Horst, he had a grin from ear to ear.

---

hip, your weight will land on the uphill ski, and you may end up sitting back too much. Second, you should flow down the course. If you are static, your turns won't flow from one to the next.

Fluid motion in GS, which refers to the increase and decrease in angulation from turn to turn, is a big issue, particularly as skiers age, because their joints become stiffer. Among Alpine Masters racers over age 50, maintaining flexibility in the ankles, knees, and hips is often the key to a national championship. To compensate for joint stiffness, most older racers bend up and down at the waist, while letting nothing happens in the hips, legs, and ankles. If the muscle is there, try to stay loose and feel your skis extend out to one side, then the other. And as you angulate, think about your hip position. The uphill hip should be slightly ahead of the downhill one, and your feet should be out from under your body.

GS Tactics

Once you understand angulation and hand position, you have overcome two big obstacles toward improving your course times in GS. If you add proper balance to those two key components of technique, you will feel some incredible turns (if you haven't felt some already). However, it is not enough to know how to turn. You must also know where to turn. In most cases, the right place is known as the *rise line*.

If you stand at the turning (inside) pole of a GS gate and roll a snowball down the hill, the path the snowball follows is called the *fall line*, a common skiing term. It is the path your skis would follow if you pointed them down the hill and let them run straight. On a slope with an even pitch, if you were to extend that line uphill from the gate, the portion of the line above the gate would be the rise line.

If the terrain is rolling and variable, you can still determine the rise line above a gate by looking ahead. If you let your skis traverse the course until the next turning pole lines up with the turning pole after it, then you have found the rise line. In general, you should start your turn at the rise line above each gate. How high or low on the rise line depends on the terrain. In general, the steeper the slope, the higher the start of your turn should be.

In truth, top racers do not think about finding the rise line for every turn. It becomes second nature. By looking several gates ahead, they judge the best line, plus they feel as if they have more time to react to the combination of gates. For example, in GS, if you only look one gate ahead, you only have as little as 10 meters to react. Assuming the terrain allows you to look three gates ahead (which is not always the case), you have at least 30 meters. This extended reaction time also helps raise your speed threshold, the rate of speed at which, if you went any faster, you would feel out of control. When you look two or three gates ahead, even though you may travel faster down the slope, you don't feel as rushed. As a result, you feel more comfortable and in control, even though you are moving more rapidly over the snow.

Looking ahead is perhaps the most important skill in ski rac-

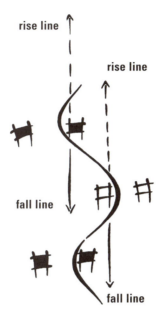

rise line

rise line

fall line

fall line

In general, start a GS turn when you reach the rise line above the turning pole of a gate. How high on the rise line you begin depends on the terrain.

ing, not just in giant slalom, but in all the racing disciplines, yet it is far from innate. Many racers, even at the highest level, have to concentrate on looking ahead all the way down a course. If you have trouble in the middle of a course, the natural reaction is to shorten your view to the immediate gate. Keep reminding yourself to look ahead!

Theory holds that GS races are lost on the steeps and won on the flats. "On the steeps, if you turn a hair too much, you will be slow," says Horst Weber, Program Director for the New York State Ski Educational Foundation at Whiteface Mountain, New York. "On the steeps, you have to have a very quiet [upper] body and a high line. On the flats, you have to risk more and take a lower line."

In steeper sections of a GS course, most racers intuitively understand that they have to maintain a high line, starting turns well above the gates and finishing turns just as they pass them. A high line allows you to set up your turns so that they flow down the hill. Most of the turn is finished by the time your skis leave the fall line, which is an advantage not only because of the pitch of the slope, but also because the gates tend to be set more tightly back and forth across the hill for speed control. When your line is low on the steeps, too much of your turn occurs at or below the gate.

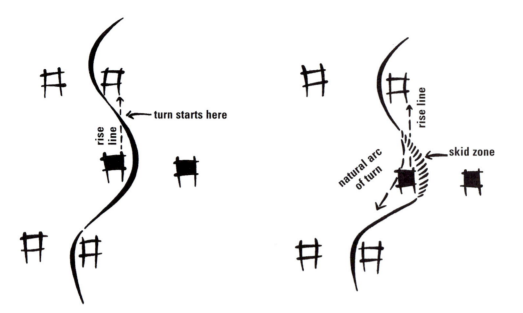

turn starts here

rise line

rise line

natural arc of turn

skid zone

With a **high line** (left), your turn begins at the rise line, just higher up the hill from the gate. If you turn too early (right), you start your turn before the rise line, which forces your skis to skid. If you maintain a turn that starts too early, you would either hit the panel or end up on the wrong side of it.

You have to stand harder on your edges and perhaps skid your skis sideways to make the next gate. This is a much slower method.

Beware! Many skiers confuse a high line with turning too early. Turning too early means starting your turn before you reach the rise line above the gate. Ironically, turning too early will ultimately cause your line to be low and late. If you start your turns too soon, it has the same affect as going too straight at the gates. It is impossible for the skis to carve a continuous arc, because that arc would lead you into or to the wrong side of the turning pole. To compensate, you have to let up on the pressure, then apply it again, perhaps more than once. Every time you make a slight adjustment, less total pressure builds on the skis, decreasing the energy you generate in the turn. It may only mean a tenth of a second in each gate, but over the course of 40 gates, that's a 4-second deficit.

The only way to cure turning too early or heading too straight at the gates is to delay the start of your turns. Sounds simple, but in practice it is one of the most difficult things to master, particularly when the clock is ticking and you are trying to ski aggressively. Giant slalom racing is an exercise in patience. Wait for the rise line. Until you can easily find the correct line, wait a fraction of a second longer than you think you should before starting your turns.

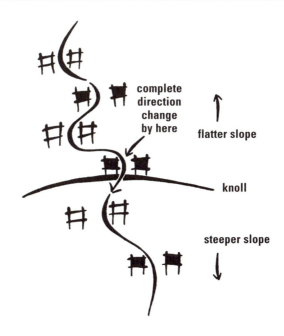

complete direction change by here

flatter slope

knoll

steeper slope

Adjusting your line for a knoll. When the terrain goes from flat to steep, such as when you ski over a knoll, your change of direction should be finished before going over the knoll.

In addition, be sure to finish your turns. In an effort to get to the next gate quickly, it is easy to end the turn too soon. Although you don't want to bring your skis across the hill any more than you have to, if you don't finish each turn, you won't generate as much power and you will end up turning too early (before the rise line above the gate).

As the course flattens out, it is okay to take a lower, straighter line, letting your skis run more and turning as little as possible. On the flats, the gates are usually set straighter. It helps to keep your upper body low and your hands forward, perhaps even tucking, for less wind resistance. Part of skiing the flats well is sensing when to tuck. If your skis skid at all while tucking, get out of your tuck and carve your turns. A carved turn is always faster than a skidding tuck.

In general, you know your line is good when you feel as if you are constantly on the edge of control. Take as low a line as you can handle, fighting to stay there without scrubbing speed. If you think you had a perfect run but were slow, your line was probably too high. A line that is too high feels comfortable, but a line that is too low leaves you either out of the course or poling to the next gate.

In addition to the steeps and flats themselves, the transitions between the two, particularly blind knolls or compressions, deserve extra attention during course inspection. Most racers who fall in a GS race do so where the trail goes from flat to steep. Finish your turn before you crest the knoll; as you come over the knoll, drive your hands and body mass forward, otherwise you will sit back, lean in, get launched, be very late for the next gate, or all of the above.

The transition from the steeps to the flats is less risky but just as crucial to a fast time. If the transition is severe enough to result in a compression, it is critical that you press your hands forward to keep your weight forward, or you may end up sitting on the tails of your skis. If you ski with a low position, rise up a little so that your legs have more room to absorb the compression. And as with a knoll, try to finish your change in direction and let your skis run as much as possible before the transition. You cannot win on the flats unless you carry as much speed as possible onto them.

"Fall-away" gates and "delay" gates also deserve some extra attention. A fall-away gate occurs over knolls or rolls in the terrain or if the fall line changes in the middle of the slope. In other words, if the fall line in a gate is different from your general direction of travel, it is considered a fall-away gate. Fall-away gates are unmarked traps. Sometimes a gate looks easy enough, but sud-

Fall-away gates. In a fall-away gate, the hill falls away from your direction of travel. To stay on course and to continue carving, you must angulate. Notice the high edge angle of the author's skis. Fall-away gates require that you tilt your skis on edge more than in normal fall-line turns.

DO'S AND DON'T'S OF FASTER GS SKIING

The following is a list of ten ski-racing principles that apply to GS. Most of them apply to the other ski-racing disciplines (slalom, Super G, and downhill) as well.

1. *Look ahead!* It's the only way to judge the correct line. If you were to pick one thing to think about during a race, this is it!
2. Try to correct problems while free skiing first, at race speeds. Whenever you free-ski, do it with a purpose.
3. Free-ski in varied conditions and terrain to improve your agility, your feel for the snow, and your ability to handle diversity. You never know what race day will bring.
4. Delay your turns. Most racers start their turns too early.
5. Examine the terrain, particularly the transitions, rolls, and fall-away gates. It is not necessary to memorize every gate in a course, but you should know the tricky ones.
6. Keep your hands forward.
7. Don't go straight at the gates. Approximately two-thirds of the turn should be made above the gate, more on the steeps, less on the flats.
8. Don't fight a low line. It might be faster, especially on the flats. And if you get a little lower than you want, don't try to recover all at once. Spread it out over two or three gates to prevent jamming your edges and dumping speed.
9. Don't look for the line a World Cup skier would take. Top racers have much more strength and experience, so they can handle a more aggressive line. Ski the course for yourself, not Hermann Maier. Know your strengths and weaknesses.
10. Don't over-turn. Turn just enough to stay on the correct line. Keep your skis heading down the hill as much as possible.

denly you are sliding on your side, out of the course. If you don't make a decisive move to lean down the hill, away from the turning pole, in a fall-away gate, your edges will stop gripping, and you will end up leaning into the hill, resulting in a skidded turn or your feet slipping out from under you, simply because of the change in terrain.

A delay gate, sometimes called an "under" gate, is precisely what its name suggests. You have to delay the start of your turn even more than usual. It signals a change in rhythm. Delay gates are nonexistent in most recreational races, in which only one gate panel is used to designate a turn, but they are common in USSA-sanctioned technical events, where two gate panels are used to mark each gate (a gate panel consists of two poles with a colored panel stretched between, as opposed to a single slalom pole, which might have a small, colored flag at its top). Given that GS courses cover a variety of terrain, delay gates are often used by course setters to traverse the hill, accommodate a bend in the trail, or otherwise keep racers thinking. Whereas most gates are "open," with a panel on the left and a matching panel on the right, delay gates are "closed," with a panel above and its mate below. The entire

Open gates are set horizontally across the slope, perpendicular to the fall line. **Closed gates** are set vertically up and down the slope, parallel to the fall line. Some closed gates are slightly offset; however, one panel is still higher on the hill than the other one.

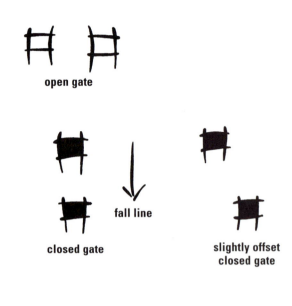

open gate

closed gate

slightly offset closed gate

fall line

Line through an "under" gate. Here, the "under" gate is the closed gate 3, but the three-gate combination begins at gate 2. You should make only two turns through the three gates 2–4. Rather than starting at the rise line above gate 2, delay the start of the turn so that the middle of the turn is between gates 2 and 3 (turn A). As a result, you'll be about one third of the way across gate 2 when you ski through it, not right next to the inside panel. Likewise, the middle of the second turn (turn B) will be somewhere between gates 3 and 4. The exact arc of the turn will be determined by the position of gate 5.

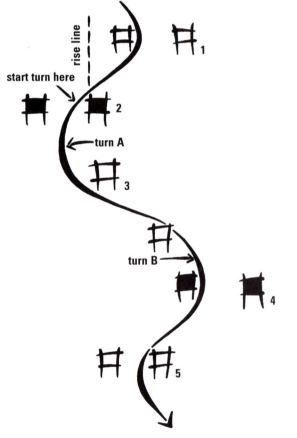

combination is actually three gates in a row—an open gate, a closed gate, then another open gate—however, only two turns are necessary. The first turn should be roughly between the first (open) gate and the second (under) gate. The second turn should be roughly between the second (under) gate and the third (open) gate. The most common mistake with delay gates is double-turning rather than making one long, smooth arc between the first two gates in the combination. In a race, it is critical to look farther ahead as you come to a delay gate. The only way to judge where to turn is by focusing down the hill at the exit gate (the third gate of the combination) and the next gate beyond that.

Amateur versus Pro Formats

Although USSA-sanctioned GS races follow an amateur format, i.e., one racer goes out of the starting gate at a time and there is only one course on the hill, the pro, or dual, format has become common for all other types of GS racing. In dual races, two skiers usually start at the same time, although sometimes the faster racer has a handicap and has to start slightly later. Skiers race side by side, one on a red course and the other on a blue course, which are theoretically identical. After that, the protocol varies from event to event.

Usually, each racer takes two runs, one on each course, because the two courses are never exactly the same as a result of variations in snow conditions and terrain. It is always a good idea to take both runs, even if only one run counts. If your first run was on the "faster" course, running the slower course is good practice, and the more you ski the courses, the better your chance of acing them. In addition, snow conditions often change as the race progresses, sometimes making the slower course faster during the second run.

Pro racing uses differential timing. In other words, the clock starts when the first racer crosses the finish line and stops when the second racer finishes. It is not top-to-bottom timing, only the difference between the two racers. Then, racers switch courses and race again. If you are in a race in which differential timing is

Common GS course formats. (A) The **NASTAR or coin-op format** has a single panel per gate; gates alternate two colors down the hill. (B) The **pro or dual format** has two identical single-panel courses set parallel to each other, each course with gate panels in one color (usually blue on one side and red on the other). (C) In the **World Cup format**, each gate has two panels; gates alternate red and blue down the hill.

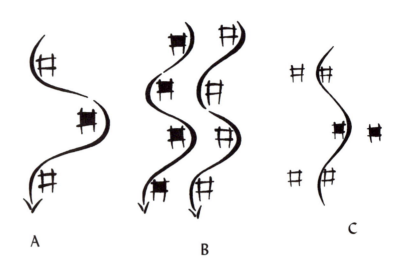

A

B

C

used, having the faster start is often the key to winning the race. If each course is timed top to bottom, then being the first out of the start is not critical. You still need to have a powerful start, but you can go when you want within a 5-second window, since you start and stop your clock. However, it is still a good idea to get a jump at the start.

One of the most difficult aspects of dual racing is having someone next to you, or worse, in front of you. You must remember to ski your own race. Try to avoid being distracted by the other person. Look down the hill at your own course. If you watch the other person instead of the gates ahead of you, you could easily make a mistake.

Slalom Racing

To some, slalom is a matter of survival. To some, it is
a blur of poles. But to the fastest skier, it is a daring dance,
fast and exhilarating.

Slalom Defined

In the 1930s and 1940s, alpine ski racing had only two disciplines, slalom and downhill. Slalom was a test of quickness and agility on a man-made course; downhill was a test of guts and speed dictated by the terrain. The same is true today, although both disciplines have evolved considerably since those early years, particularly in the case of slalom. In the mid-1970s, the introduction of hinged slalom poles (also known by brand names, such as Rapid Gates or Break-Away Gates), which bend at snow level if hit, had a profound impact on technique, tactics, and equipment. Instead of skiing around the gates, brushing them with the side of the body, usually the shoulder and upper arm, slalom racers began to go straighter at the poles, skiing "through" them, with only the racer's skis and feet on the turning side of the pole.

Whereas slalom racing was the common format for the general public 40 years ago, it is difficult to find a slalom race that is not part of a formal racing program today. Slalom racing is rarely used in town race leagues and never in promotional events, fund-raisers, and other recreational competitions. If you are 21 or older, the best way to experience a real slalom race is in the U.S. Alpine Masters program. Masters slalom races tend to get equal billing, but smaller attendance, than giant slalom (GS) races. At face value, slalom seems more challenging because it requires quick reactions and

SLALOM AT A GLANCE
Average number of gates: 45–75
Average time: 35–65 seconds
Average speed: 10–20 mph

agility just to finish, let alone win. On the other hand, your technique doesn't have to be as refined as in GS. The "bull in the china closet" approach can be effective up to a point.

Slalom is a sprint, both in terms of foot-to-foot movement and overall course length; a run typically takes anywhere from 35 seconds to just over a minute (see table, page 68, for comparison with other racing disciplines). Aggressive skiers who ride the straightest line bash a lot of gate poles on the way to the finish. In many instances, slalom could be considered ski racing's version of a full-contact sport. As with any contact sport, having the right equipment helps tremendously.

Equipment Considerations for Slalom Racing

True slalom skis are becoming difficult to find in ski shops because they don't have much appeal to the free-skiing public. As a result, they're relegated specialty status. Although manufacturers have experimented with more pronounced side cuts for slalom skis, the first slalom skis to be considered "shaped" are just becoming available in stores and only in those with a large ski-racing clientele. For younger racers, if true slalom skis are not available, shorter giant slalom skis will work just as well, because their main focus should be perfecting carved turns, not skiing the straightest possible line. The same is true for adults until they reach a fairly high level of proficiency, when subtle nuances in their line have a big impact on their results.

Traditionally, straight slalom skis had a soft tip and a snappy tail. The tail was also quite narrow, for quick release out of a turn. Currently, many junior racers and masters racers are switching to the latest shaped slalom skis, which have a more even, giant slalom-like flex, and which are very short (160 cm to 180 cm). Although World Cup skiers are more resistant to this change, adhering to the old principle, "if it isn't broke, don't fix it," even these elite racers are testing these ultra-short, shaped slalom skis.

Do you need a true slalom ski to run slalom? Maybe. The majority of people who raced at a national level as juniors still opt

FIRST PERSON: A MEMORABLE VICTORY

Although I had competed at the national and international levels both as a junior racer and as a pro, my only win at those levels before 1991 was in the 1977 Junior Olympic giant slalom. Talk about a dry spell! Sure, I had won races during those 14 years and had many top ten finishes, but no important titles.

In 1991, the year after I retired from the Women's Pro Tour, I joined the Alpine Masters circuit. My husband, Jason, had been a Masters racer for years. Even though I was tired of the ski racing scene—the pressure, the travel, the constant promotional appearances—if I wanted to spend a weekend with Jason in the winter, I would have to go to Masters races.

I'm not much of a spectator, so I entered the first race on the 1991 New England Masters Skiing calendar. I had so much fun! I enjoyed seeing many old friends and was instantly hooked on the challenge of skiing long World Cup-style courses. (Pro courses are short, usually under 30 seconds per run, and are always in a dual format—see page 82 for a description.) In addition, there was no pressure, no prize money, no head games, only an inner desire to ski faster. My passion for ski racing was renewed.

After a successful season at the regional level, we traveled to Vail, Colorado, in late March for the U.S. Masters Championships. I had not run a downhill course in several years, but it all came back after a couple of training runs. I won the downhill in Women's Class 1 (then ages 25–29, now ages 21–29). Next I won the giant slalom race. Then, on the last day of the event, I posted the fastest time for the first run of the slalom.

In junior and World Cup racing, combined medals are awarded based on results in the slalom and the downhill. At the Masters level, the combined medals are based on the slalom, the giant slalom, and a speed event. Until 1996, the speed event was downhill. Now, it is Super G. With so much specialization at the World Cup level, combined medals have been downplayed over the last decade. Not so on the Alpine Masters circuit! A combined medal at the nationals is the most coveted of all. Suddenly, it was mine to win or lose.

As I inspected the second run of the slalom, my stomach was in knots. I had trouble concentrating. After 25 years of ski racing, one would think that I could handle the pressure. The problem with slalom is that so much can go wrong, no matter how good you are. I could easily hook a ski tip on a gate or make some other common mistake. What's more, my slalom career had had its inconsistencies. Many coaches thought I was most suited to slalom, but my results were more consistent in downhill and giant slalom. (Most of my ski racing career preceded the invention of Super G.) Could I do it? Although I didn't need to have the race of my life, I needed to do more than just stand up. I needed to have a solid, smart run.

In slalom, when you enter the starting gate, there is no count down. The starter simply gives you a 10-second warning, then says, "Go when ready." I wasn't ready. Somehow, I knew I would never be ready. Then, with a final silent reminder to myself to look ahead, I blasted out of the starting gate.

I remember feeling the rhythm of the course. I remember crossing the finish line and gasping for air as the wave of relief at having survived the course with no major problems washed over me. I looked for Jason, but he was hugging me before I saw him. By the time I had regained my composure, the four racers who were within striking distance had finished. I had won. Not only had I won the slalom, but also the combined, and every gold medal in that championship, a clean sweep. I had never skied so consistently in my life.

In retrospect, that run was a significant turning point in my ski-racing career. I felt like a true champion. I knew that I could win under pressure. I knew I could ski like a winner when I needed to, no matter the discipline. My only regret was that it didn't happen about 10 years earlier.

for true slalom skis at the Masters level. Those who started racing as adults may be just as successful on their GS skis, at least in the beginning. For example, Glenn McConkey, two-time Masters Skier of the Year, used the same shaped GS model for both events when she swept Women's Class 6 (ages 50–54) at the 1997 U.S. Alpine Masters National Championships. A year earlier, Bode Miller of Franconia, New Hampshire, won the GS and took second in the slalom at the Junior Olympics on the same pair of shaped skis. A few weeks later, he placed third in the slalom at the U.S. Alpine Championships. A member of the U.S. Ski Team and the 1998 U.S. Olympic Team in Nagano, he was the first World Cup competitor to use shaped skis successfully in slalom.

Selecting a shaped ski for slalom is a safe bet, but whether you will ski faster on a true slalom ski is a personal matter. Remember, although shaped skis are becoming widely accepted for slalom, the actual shape will vary from brand to brand. The amount of sidecut and the length that work best for you are on skis that allow you to carve the best turn.

Although the top GS racers in the world have the strength to crush a GS gate panel as they pass it, in general, slalom is the only event in alpine skiing in which most people purposely ski through the poles. Typically, your feet are on one side of the turning pole and your upper body is on the other side of it, while one hand blocks it. However, the odds are high that you will whack the pole with other body parts along the course. It is a good idea to cover these primary targets, particularly the shins, knees, and knuckles, with hard plastic pads. Be sure your pads have a plastic exterior. The friction created when you hit the plastic poles will burn a fabric-covered pad after only one hit and shred it after only a run.

Shin guards should cover your legs from the tops of your ski boots to the tops of your knees but not restrict knee movement. Most have two Velcro straps, one below the calf and one above the calf. Check that the straps are wide enough (at least an inch wide) so that the Velcro will hold securely in the heat of battle and that they are not too long. Loose straps are distracting and impede agility. When you try on a pair of shin guards, move your knees from side to side in a skiing motion. The shin guards should not catch on each other or your equipment. Petite women have the most difficulty finding shin guards that fit. If you cannot find shin guards that are short enough, you can always trim the plastic to size.

There are two ways to protect your knuckles, either guards on your ski poles over the grips, or special gloves with plastic pads built into them. Both are effective. The guards that attach to your ski poles are easier to find and cheaper, but they are not something you would put on and take off regularly. Once on your poles, they are likely to stay there. Slalom guards are a little awkward for anything but slalom racing. Unless you are willing to designate a pair of ski poles just for slalom, you may prefer protective gloves.

Although not required, a slalom helmet has become standard equipment for many racers. The main purpose of a slalom helmet is deflecting slalom poles, not preventing head injuries. It also helps keep your goggles on straight. A slalom helmet has a short visor over the brow and a half-circle of plastic in front of the mouth that is situated farther away from your face than the visor.

Some manufacturers sell one helmet for all events. These multiuse helmets do help protect you from serious head injury. They usually come with removable accessories to make them either slalom- or speed-specific.

Speed suits similar to those worn in GS have become fairly common in slalom, too. Many racers wear the same speed suit for all events, adding a padded top under the suit for slalom and GS. Slalom suits, or separate tops and bottoms, are also available. These have padding on the shins, knees, thighs, and arms. As with GS, unless your races are decided by very close margins (under 1 second), the only advantage of a speed suit is less luggage. Padded pants and tops are bulkier, but as long as they fit snugly and don't inhibit your mobility, they are often warmer and make you less self-conscious, if you are the modest type.

Slalom Technique

Skiing a slalom course is like making quick, carved turns down the fall line on an open slope except that the gates dictate where you must turn. A slalom course covers half the distance of a USSA-sanctioned giant slalom but has about the same number of gates (see page 68). The average distance between slalom gates is

Opposite Page
Annemarie Gerg (Germany) at the 1999 World Championships in Vail, Colorado. She blocks the gate with her inside (uphill) hand.

Through two slalom turns, Pernilla Wiberg (Sweden) maintains a level upper body at the 1999 World Championships.

about 10 meters, or five ski lengths. GS gates are often twice that distance. A 60-second slalom run is considered a leg burner, whereas giant slaloms are often over 70 seconds per run.

For most of the 1980s and the early 1990s, top slalom racers perfected a *J-shaped turn;* a racer headed straight at the gate, then made a crisp edge set to change direction, left or right. The current trend is back to a *C-shaped turn*, which is less jamming, yet still quick, with the straightest possible line. In effect, there is no middle phase of the turn. You initiate it and complete it immediately.

Assuming your weight is forward, the initiation of the turn is the easy part. The finish of the turn is tougher. Gravity is a powerful force, which gives you speed when your skis are heading down the fall line, but takes it away when your skis go against it. The secret in slalom is to feel gravity pull through your feet, rather than against them. To do this, you must have a strong center: your feet should be spaced the width of your shoulders apart, and you should not stand too upright. "The biomechanics of a slalom turn come from your middle," says Pavel Stastny, Head Coach at the Stratton Mountain School, Stratton Mountain, Vermont (a ski racing academy that has developed many U.S. Ski Team members), and former Head Coach of the Czechoslovakian National Team. "If you watch good slalom skiers from behind, they look like a pendulum. The lower body moves side to side and forward at the same time, while the upper body just moves forward in the same plane." According to Stastny, your body position and balance have to be such that gravity pulls through the center of your body to your feet. If your skis are chattering, you are standing too upright relative to the incline of the hill. You are bracing against gravity, instead of working with it.

Stastny also tells racers that the shoulders should be inside the arc of the skis during a turn. In other words, when the body is angulated correctly, the head and torso are inside the pole. "Your feet should be next to the base of the pole. Your knees should be next to the base of the pole or just inside it, and your head should be inside the pole," says Statsny.

To prevent getting whacked in the face or the chest, you have to block the pole with your hand. This is commonly called *cross-blocking*, which is a misnomer. In reality, the hand punches forward, not sideways. It should never move across the vertical axis of the body. If your hand literally crosses your body to hit the gate, it will likely rotate you onto your uphill ski, causing you to skid, or worse, to go off the course. "With cross-blocking, there's little mar-

To pass legally through a gate, only your feet need to be inside the turning pole. Although your body's path will still follow an arc, it should be less of an arc than that of the skis, and ideally on the other side of each pole. During the transition between turns, when the skis come under your body, the paths cross.

gin for error," says Peter Dodge, coach of the Dartmouth Men's Alpine Ski Team. "A simple mistake, like leaning in, can quickly end your run. It isn't very dramatic. To everyone else, it looks like you just gave up, but it is impossible to make the next gate."

In addition to no edge grip, leaning into the hill or over-rotating also decreases your agility. Slalom racing is one of the few situations in modern skiing where no weight should be placed on the uphill ski. The movement is foot to foot. "You should always be in a position to get to the outside [downhill] ski," continues Dodge. "Even if you finish a turn on the inside [uphill] ski, the outside one should be immediately available in case you slip. On a good day in slalom, you feel light on your feet and totally agile. On a bad day, you feel as if you have two left feet and can't get out of your own way."

Another common mistake in slalom is too much hand and shoulder movement. Cross-blocking requires only a slight movement of the hands. The hips and shoulders remain level. The upper body should not move at all. The hands should be higher than in giant slalom, comfortably extended in front of the chest. Cross-blocking results from wanting to ski the tightest line while keeping your face intact. It is not only performed by the downhill hand. Sometimes, the uphill hand does it. Sometimes, your shins or knees move the gate out of the way. Sometimes, no blocking is required. It depends on the gate and the individual style of the skier, but regardless, you should never reach across your body for the pole.

When it comes to cross-blocking, getting your head on the other side of the pole is the hardest part for psychological reasons. No one wants to get hit in the face. When your brain says "flinch" every half-second, it is difficult to think about skiing faster. Learning to cross-block is a case of matter over mind, but it is not intuitive. What a dilemma! If you think about each block, you

SIX STEPS TO CROSS-BLOCKING

Learning to cross-block takes lots of practice. It is a technique so fraught with bad habits that most junior racing programs don't introduce it until age 12 or 13. Don't try to figure it out on a full-length slalom course. You will end up slow and late before you have skied ten gates. If you follow this progression of drills, you may not see a real slalom course right away, but you will cross-block spontaneously sooner.

1. **Modified wedge turns.** On a slalom hill (not too flat), press around the turn aggressively with your knees while keeping your upper body quiet and your hands forward. Concentrate on carving each turn with precision. Feel the energy of the ski. You should carve with the outside ski and wedge with the inside one, not vice versa. In other words, don't push the downhill ski out to the side. Instead, roll it on edge, pressure it, then turn.

2. **Foot-to-foot turns.** Using a similar knee action to the modified wedge turn but with your skis parallel, make turns just shy of jump turns. Your turns should be so quick that you have to move from foot to foot, but your skis remain on the snow. Your torso and hands should face down the hill, regardless of what your feet are doing.

3. **Modified ski poles.** Hold your ski poles parallel to the snow, chest-high, away from your body, as you make quick slalom-like turns down the fall line. After ten turns, hold your ski poles above your head. After another ten turns, bring them back to the position in front of your chest. Continue the pattern all the way down the trail, letting all the work happen below the waist.

4. **Stubbies.** Stubbies are hinged poles that only come up to knee-level. Using stubbies, set a short slalom course, only 10 to 15 gates, that has a regular rhythm. Try to get your feet as close to the base of the pole as possible while making carved turns. Don't go totally straight at the stubby, then jam your skis sideways to make the next one. This drill allows you to figure out the correct line without worrying about blocking something away from your face. You don't have to do anything special. Your knees and shins hit the gates out of the way as you angulate. When you get comfortable, add a rhythm change to the course, such as a straight section in the middle or a slightly tighter turn near the bottom.

5. **Half-and-half slalom.** Set a slalom course that alternates, three or four stubbies then two or three full-height gates, then three or four stubbies, and so forth. At first, the courses should be short, under 15 gates, and have a regular rhythm. As you get better at blocking the full-height poles, experiment with longer courses and rhythm changes. This is a good time to use video analysis, if you haven't done so already, to be sure your technique is correct and consistent between the stubbies and the longer poles. Gradually decrease the number of stubbies until you are ready for the real thing.

6. **Real slalom.** Use regular slalom poles for the entire course. Set short courses at first, concentrating on looking ahead, not at the pole you are blocking. Gradually increase the length of the course until you are able to run a full-length slalom smoothly.

PRO TIP: THE ABCS OF CROSS-BLOCKING

Peter Dodge, a former U.S. Ski Team Member and pro racer, is now the highly respected coach of the Dartmouth Men's Alpine Ski Team. During his tenure at Dartmouth, he has helped guide a number of athletes to All-American or U.S. Ski Team status. He offers this advice about slalom technique:

- **Accelerate.** To ski slalom well, you must feel the momentum created by your center of mass moving down the hill. Dodge compares it to putting in the clutch of an old VW at the top of a mountain pass. "Let the speed come," he says. "Experiment while free skiing to see how long you dare go with your skis in the fall line. It's surprising how quickly you accelerate. Skiers like Tomba keep the clutch in longer, even on the steepest hills and toughest turns. Mere mortals brake early."
- **Be alert to your body position.** Dodge finds that one of the most common mistakes in slalom is leaning forward too much as you try to cross-block. "Don't go fast with your head and hunch," says Dodge. "Do it with your center. Imagine a rope pulling you forward from your belly button. You go fast with your hips and feet. They should lead the way down the course. Your upper body should be relaxed, which helps clear your vision."
- **Make C-shaped turns**. Dodge warns slalom racers not to push their feet quickly out to the side to start their turns. "Even though slalom turns are fast, you still have to put the ski on edge, then pressure it, then turn," he says. "This slows the start of the turn, which shapes it into a C. Straight is late! If you go too straight, you will have to drop your hips as you duck under the gate, which improperly releases the ski. Fast slalom racers feel like they are coming up through the gate by extending their legs as they resist the pressure of the turn."

Opposite Page

In this **cross-blocking** move, notice the position of Natasa Bokal's (Slovenia) feet, knees, hips, shoulders, arms, and eyes as she hits the pole. Her feet are just inside (next to) the pole. As she blocks the pole with her outside (downhill) hand, her shoulders remain level, with her torso facing down the hill. She is looking well past the gate she is hitting, down the course.

will be slower than skiing completely around the gates without touching them at all, yet it is not an innate skill. As with any learned movement, there will be a period in which you feel slow and awkward, but once you become comfortable with the technique, it becomes second nature. You can stop thinking about it, and, as in GS, start to look two to three gates ahead, rather than staring at the pole you are about to block. If you commit to the technique, eventually you will ski aggressively again, letting your eye-hand coordination and reactions take over.

As with any ski-racing technique, it helps to master the movement pattern and rhythm of slalom turns while free skiing first. Also, when you start to cross-block in a course, don't worry about your speed. Once you master the technique, the speed will come.

Slalom Tactics

In slalom, you want to make each turn as close to the pole as possible. If your feet are a mere 6 inches farther away from the pole than your competitor's feet, it will cost you 5/100ths of a second per turn. Over a 40-gate slalom run, that adds up to a 2-second deficit. The ability to cross-block gives you the confidence to ski closer to the gates, often by a foot or two. If you have to reach for the gates, your line is too wide, even though you are hitting them. And worse, you are probably making a poor turn. Remember, cross-blocking is a function of line, not vice versa.

Getting close to the poles also ensures that your skis move down the hill as much as possible rather than across the hill. Skiing the straightest line is usually the fastest, as long as you are not late for a gate. Even though a slalom turn is quick, it is still a complete carved turn. As in GS, you should generally make about two-thirds of the turn above the gate, and you should complete your change of direction before going over a bump or a transition onto the steeps or flats. Your turn is basically finished when you cross-block a gate. "You should always ski ahead of the course," says Peter Dodge. "If you block a pole with your boot top, that's okay, but only if you are looking ahead, and your direction change is complete at the point of contact with the gate."

One of the things that differentiates slalom racing from GS racing is the variety of gate combinations. While both have open gates, closed gates, and under gates, slalom also has flushes, hairpins, and elbows (for a discussion of open and closed gates, see pages 79–81). A *flush* is three or four closed gates in a row with almost no space between the gates. Flushes are usually placed down the fall line. They are a test of quickness. Good racers use them to pick up speed and make time. When you come to a flush during course inspection, first determine on which side of the first gate (entry gate) you should enter the flush, to the left or to the right, in order to exit the flush correctly. Usually, the entry gate follows the rhythm of the course. In other words, if the turn above the flush was to the left, the turn into the flush will be to the right (but not always!). In the rare instance when both turns are to the right, similar to an under gate, make only one turn through both gates, with the middle of the turn about midway between them.

The key to making time in a flush is letting your skis run as straight as possible. Get through the gates with a light touch on your edges. Don't over-turn! As you enter the flush, look at the exit gate (the last gate in the flush) and the next one after it. The trick is to take advantage of gravity for a split second without getting trapped. A common mistake is to go straight for too long. If the turn after the flush is a tough one, you have to set up for it by making more of a turn for the exit gate. Be sure to complete most of the turn above the gate, otherwise you will have to jam your skis, losing whatever advantage you may have gained in the flush and more.

Another common mistake in flushes is letting your hips drop back a little, which also pulls your weight back. It feels fast for a split second, but it wrecks your timing. You can't be quick and proactive if your weight is not centered over your skis and you are not in balance. As you enter the flush, keep your hips over your feet. Don't admire your speed, even for a moment; rather, keep looking for more, which will keep you oriented down the hill, both physically and mentally.

Many flushes are not set straight down the fall line but diagonally to it. Although it is not as easy to pick up speed in a diagonal flush, it is just as easy to over-turn in one. The turn on one ski goes easily down the hill, whereas the turn on the other ski resembles a fall-away turn. In addition to not over-turning, you must also be careful to not lean into the hill or your skis will skid and possibly go out from under you. Have a light touch on the easy side and a crisp, forward-moving edge set on the difficult side to get the most out of the combination. As with regular flushes, look at the exit gate and beyond as soon as you approach the entry gate to set up for whatever awaits you afterward.

Hairpins and elbows are both two-gate combinations. *Hairpins* are two closed gates, one above the other, similar to a flush only shorter. In *elbows*, one gate is open and the other is closed to some degree. The angle between the two gates may be anywhere from 90 to 179 degrees. Like flushes, hairpins and elbows may be set down the fall line or diagonally to it. Also like flushes, the key to skiing hairpins and elbows well is looking beyond the exit gate before you enter the combination. Hairpins and elbows can be good places to pick up a few tenths of a second, too. Although the

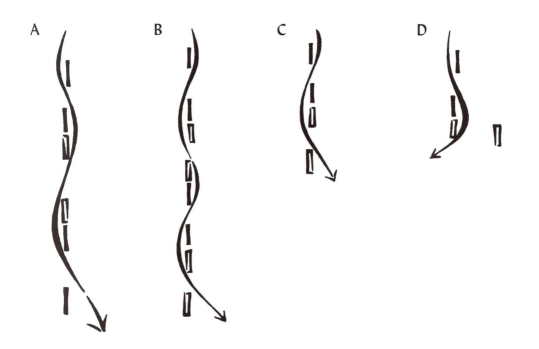

A   B   C   D

Four gate combinations unique to slalom: **(A)** three-gate flush, **(B)** four-gate flush, **(C)** hairpin, and **(D)** elbow gate.

gate after the exit gate is usually a tight turn, the gate above the combination is sometimes fairly straight. Inspect the combination from above and below. If the gate before the combination lines up with it, ski the three gates as a flush, letting your skis run straight earlier.

One of the most common causes of a fall in slalom racing is hooking the tip of your uphill ski on a gate. It is also the most common way to injure yourself. If your bindings are set correctly, your ski should come off instantly. If it doesn't come off, you could pull a groin muscle, tweak your knee, sprain your ankle, or incur any of the host of battle wounds that guarantee you a toboggan ride to the bottom. It happens before you know what hit you. Your brain is already several gates down the hill, when suddenly you cartwheel out of the course. A hooked tip is the result of either a line that's a micrometer too straight or a turn that is too early. It happens to everyone, even at the World Cup level. Tip deflectors, which are plastic accessories that attach to the tips of your skis, extending the tips and curving them away from the gate, are helpful, but if the mistake becomes chronic, you will have to make a conscious effort to ski a slightly rounder, wider line.

If you aren't catching tips or falling but you can't seem to finish a slalom course, you need to look ahead more (see also page 79, "Do's and Don'ts of Faster GS Skiing"). In slalom, you may only travel 20 mph, but there are a lot of gates. As in other events, you have to look at least two to three gates ahead. This gives you more time to judge the correct line and execute it. In practice, slow down a little and relax. Take a couple of runs on the course as if you are free skiing instead of racing. If one particular section is causing the problem, just run that section until you get it right. Then go back to the top.

Finally, remember to keep your skis on the snow, as if you are massaging it. There are no jumps in USSA-sanctioned slalom races. Any air time is the result of the misdirected rebound of your skis. Slalom skis are lively by nature. When you pressure a slalom ski aggressively in a turn, it gives back a lot of energy when you unweight it. If left uncontrolled, you literally pop into the air slightly. It may feel good, but it is slow. The key is to channel this energy forward, down the hill, toward the next gate. Then you will be fast!

Super G
and Downhill Racing

Speed, the ultimate adventure . . .

Super G versus Downhill

For most of the 20th century, Super G racing did not exist. Downhill was the traditional and only speed event. By the late 1970s, ski racers had become specialized to the point that few racers at the World Cup level who raced downhill also raced slalom and GS. Even regional teams had become segregated. Once a racer, man or woman, was singled out as a downhiller, that person rarely made runs on skis shorter than 210 centimeters (men) or 200 centimeters (women)—the lengths of long GS skis.

In 1987, in a successful attempt to give downhill racers and technical (slalom and GS) skiers a common event, the FIS instituted Super G. Today, many gate skiers, usually those who favor GS, participate in Super G, but not downhill. Super G is a hybrid event, mixing skills from downhill and giant slalom. Compared with a downhill course, a Super G course is not quite as long, fast, or straight, and it has guaranteed limited air time.

At the World Cup level, the maximum vertical drop of a Super G course is 650 meters, versus 1,100 meters for downhill (see page 68). Speeds for Super G top out around 65 mph, versus 80 mph in downhill races. (At the regional and Masters levels, speeds rarely exceed 55 mph in Super G and 75 mph in the downhill, respectively.) Super G gates can be spread out, but the colors of the gates still alternate red and blue, like the technical events, and may be set so that you must make turns, even though a section of trail is straight. Contrary to popular belief, there are turns in downhill, too, but they are usually dictated by the terrain. In downhill courses, the gates are all one color (red) and act more as guides than as indicators for a turn. In addition, a Super G course has a specified maximum of two jumps, whereas a downhill course may have more or less, depending on the terrain.

Compared with giant slalom, Super G is undeniably faster—65 versus 40 mph—and longer. In terms of vertical drop, the longest, leg-burning giant slalom, at 450 meters, is still shorter than the shortest Super G race, at 500 meters. Super G courses vary greatly. If the trail is wide open and steep, they seem like fast giant slaloms. If the trail is relatively flat or if it has a large number of rolls, knolls, and doglegs, it tends to follow the terrain, like a downhill. The best Super G events offer a mix of fast, straight sections and turns on the steeps.

When it was first introduced into ski racing, Super G was criticized by traditionalists as an unnecessary event, an easy downhill. Now, more than 10 years later, it is an accepted and valuable ski-racing discipline. It gives junior racers an opportunity to train and race in a speed event at a younger age. This is mostly because of accessibility. Only a handful of ski areas in the United States can or want to hold downhill races. For both disciplines, the minimum vertical drop at the regional level is about 500 meters, which is top-to-bottom skiing at many resorts. A 500-meter downhill would require two runs to meet the necessary length for an official race. Two-run downhills are rare because most downhill courses are significantly longer. In a typical downhill, racers cover over 2 miles of terrain in under 2 minutes. Few ski areas are long enough to host such a course.

Because of the required length of the course, a downhill course usually takes over a portion of a ski area's favorite runs. All intersecting trails are blocked off. The course is closed to the public for a week or more, first to prepare the snow, then for course inspection by officials, coaches, ski technicians, and racers, then for training runs, and finally for the race. Not only must the hill be

SPEED EVENTS AT A GLANCE

Average number of gates: 30 to 65 (Super G); as dictated by the terrain (downhill)

Average time: 60 to 80 seconds (Super G); 65 to 90 seconds (downhill)

Average speed: 50 to 65 mph (Super G); 60 to 80 mph (downhill)

FIRST PERSON: THE CRASH

When a ski resort is awarded an Olympic venue, it typically designs its downhill courses—one for men and one for women—specifically for the big event. Sometimes that means cutting entirely new trails. Other times, it means modifying existing runs. The runs are usually completed two to three winters before the Olympics, which allows for several "test" competitions at the national and international levels. Whiteface Mountain near Lake Placid, New York, was no different. In the case of Whiteface Mountain, the main modifications included widening existing trails and putting up huge safety nets.

I grew up skiing at Whiteface Mountain. I knew every inch of the place. I ran my first downhill race there in 1973, at age 11. Although the women's course had been widened for the 1980 Winter Olympics, it was still familiar. In addition, downhills are unlike any other ski racing discipline. Perhaps it is the speed and the exceptional challenge. Perhaps it is the rush and the accompanying relief after surviving a run on the edge of control. Perhaps it is because, in downhill, every inch of the course is analyzed and memorized. Whatever the case, one never forgets a downhill. I had raced the downhill at Whiteface many times. I had the home hill advantage. I was supremely confident that I would ace the course during the pre-Olympic downhill in 1979.

After course inspection the first morning, I made my way to the start for my first training run. I delighted in the crisp, sunny day and the fact that all the ski instructors, ski patrollers, lift attendants, local coaches, and junior racers were cheering for me.

In the start area, my coach gave me a few last tips. I stripped down to my speed suit, did a few final stretches, had the manufacturer's representative check my bindings, then entered the starting gate. I wasn't nervous. It wasn't the race, it was only training, but I was determined to lay down a solid first run and begin the process of working up to 100 percent race speed.

Not that first-run training speeds are wimpy. My approach was to ski the turns conservatively but go for it on the steeps, partly because it is always safer to go for it on the steeps—if you hold back, your weight drifts back, which is dangerous—and partly because it is just plain fun.

The bottom third of the course was relatively flat, with a long straight section that even-

long enough, it also must be wide enough to handle big sweeping turns and to minimize the chances of racers hitting a tree or a lift tower in the event of a fall. Hazards along the course must be covered by safety nets, hay bales, or fences. Although there aren't many gates in a downhill course, the course requires a small army of people to maintain and police it over several days. The competitors are required to take at least two, and up to four, training runs during the two days before the race.

Downhill is arguably the most exciting, macho event in ski racing, but it also takes the biggest commitment on the part of everyone involved. And although you can severely injure yourself in any racing discipline, downhill racers are at the highest risk of a serious or life-threatening injury. If you fall at 75 mph with only a helmet and a skimpy speed suit to protect you, you probably won't bounce back as quickly as you would from a fall at 20 mph.

tually came to a drop-off near the top of a short chair lift. The section is known as *midstation* even though it is well below the midpoint of the course. To increase the difficulty level of the race for the international field, a large prejump (a bump over which racers catch air) had been built with the grooming machines there. The combination of the prejump and the drop-off made for a monster jump. It had never been remotely that big in previous downhill races.

As I made my *prejump* (literally jumping early to land on the backside of the bump, minimizing my air time), I heard a click. A split second later, I was in the air in my tuck, with only one ski attached to my feet. As I sailed over the ground about 15 feet up, I caught a glimpse of my other ski zooming into the hay bales on the side of the course. Suddenly, everything seemed to move slowly. My first thought was a nasty four-letter word. My second thought was, "This is gonna hurt."

There was no way I could ski away from a landing at 60 mph on one ski on that section of trail. It was just too narrow. As soon as my feet hit the ground, I skidded onto my side, then crashed into the hay bales.

When I came to my senses, I took inventory. Right ankle okay. Right knee okay. Right hip okay, and so on. By the time I got to my left knee, two ski patrol members were by my side. They quickly grabbed my foot and dragged me off the course. Racers were coming every 45 seconds, and the next one would be there soon. I vaguely remember one of the ski patrollers propping me on a hay bale and asking if I were injured. "I don't think so," I muttered, holding back the anger and frustration of not finishing the run. I was so dizzy. I sat there for almost 30 minutes, regaining my strength and composure.

In the final analysis, I only had a minor concussion. I skied to the base lodge, where my mother, who doesn't ski, had anxiously waited for me. When I saw her, I was holding the ski that had come off in one hand and was looking for my ski rep to tell him the bad news. My ski had delaminated into three slabs, just ahead of the binding. My mother looked like she was going to faint. I hadn't noticed, but I had shredded my speed suit, smashed my goggle lens, and dented my helmet (after all, I had just had my bell rung). I was a sight! I hadn't noticed because I was too distracted, trying to get my broken ski replaced in time for the next training run. My mother didn't watch another race of mine until my senior year at Dartmouth College, five winters later.

For all these reasons, Super G has become attractive. It offers thrilling speed but with slightly more control. The time commitment is much less, because there are no required training runs. Everything happens on race day. A Super G race won't paralyze a ski resort. Because less course preparation is required, athletes can train for Super G almost as easily as for GS, and usually on the same hill. In fact, periodic Super G training can help your GS racing, because it accustoms you to skiing faster. Most programs for junior racers at bigger mountains regularly incorporate Super G into their training regimens.

Super G replaced downhill as the speed event at the U.S. Alpine Masters Championships in 1996. The change meant that a number of excellent ski resorts, which could not accommodate downhill races, became eligible host sites for the nationals. In addition, most Masters racers do not have the opportunity to train for downhill. With two national titles at stake for their one downhill of the year (the downhill and the combined), many racers, especially the former hot shots turned doctors or business people, were pushing the envelope a little too far, sometimes with damaging results. Super G is a slightly tamer option that requires only one-third of the time commitment.

A separate downhill championship is still held at the Masters level, but it is not considered part of the combined results. It also is not a factor in the selection of the U.S. Alpine Masters Ski Team, an honorary team made up of the top-ranked man and woman in each age group based on results in three disciplines— Super G, GS, and slalom—at the national championships.

At the World Cup and national levels, combined medals are still based on two events, downhill and slalom. There aren't many combined events. The most notable are at the Winter Olympics, the long-standing World Cups at Wengen, Switzerland, and Kitzbühel, Austria (both for men only), and the U.S. Alpine National Championships. Combined downhills and slaloms are usually separate races from regular downhills and slaloms, and on shorter courses.

Although Super G and downhill are commonly referred to as "speed events," they are not "speed skiing." Speed skiing is a separate discipline that is no longer sanctioned by the USSA or the FIS. In speed skiing, athletes tuck straight down a steep, short, smooth track (no turns or jumps). The only goal is to go as fast as possible through a speed trap. At the world class level, speed skiers exceed 130 mph. At press time, the world speed-skiing record is 152 mph. The winner is the competitor who records the fastest rate of speed (miles per hour or kilometers per hour) for the day.

Equipment Considerations for Speed Events

Skis

If you think slalom skis are tough to find, try finding downhill or Super G skis. Even if a ski shop has a hard-core ski-racing clientele, they probably do not stock skis for speed events. Usually, such skis must be specially ordered, and even then, they might not be available. They are not mass-produced, but custom-made primarily for elite racers who are sponsored by manufacturers. A better source for downhill or Super G skis might be your local race program. Check with coaches or older junior racers who are on adult equipment and who specialize in speed events.

Lack of skis is not such a big problem for Super G. A pair of GS skis that are 5 to 10 centimeters longer than your normal GS skis will usually do the trick. Over half of the U.S. Alpine Masters Team members don't even bother to use a longer ski. They use their GS skis for Super G, too. However, if the course happens to be relatively fast and straight, they would be at a disadvantage to an equally good racer on a longer ski. You can go 55 mph on a pair of 190-centimeter skis, but you'll be hanging on by your toenails rather than looking for more speed. Although true Super G and downhill skis are designed for maximum glide and to hug the terrain, just having the extra length gives added stability and vibration absorption. If you don't know what the course will be like, prepare both types of skis and make a decision after inspecting the course.

On average, downhill skis are 5 centimeters longer than Super G skis. Although you may be able to get away with using Super G skis for easier downhills, real downhill skis are desirable at higher speeds. Downhill skis also have some shape to them now. Although 215 centimeters sounds long for a shaped ski, that is significantly shorter than the 225-centimeter downhill skis that were the norm for men (215 centimeters for women) just a few years ago, and shaped downhill skis are surprisingly maneuverable.

If you do acquire a pair of Super G or downhill skis, remember, they are sensitive beasts. They bend easily because they are long and contain a lot of metal. Their bases must be handled with tender loving care. They should be waxed frequently, whether you ski on them or not. Don't even think about skiing on them if there is a chance of hitting a rock. Every little scratch on the base slows you down. The edges are narrower than standard edges, so they take less kindly to nicks and burrs, and they don't tolerate excess filing. The kinder you treat your long boards, the faster you will ski. (See also chapter 9 for techniques of waxing and tuning.)

Ski Boots

In speed events, the lateral stiffness of your boots, particularly to the inside, not the forward flex, is the issue. Unlike gate skiers, many speed specialists feel less lateral stiffness is better. "At my peak, I didn't use overlap boots, because they were too responsive," says Hilary Lindh, 1992 Olympic Silver Medalist and 1997 World Champion in downhill. "I didn't want such a fine touch. I wanted to work into it. If a boot was too stiff laterally, I would suddenly be in a turn and too hard on my edges. A boot could still be stiff forward. That's a personal preference."

Shaped GS-type skis have ushered in an era of laterally stiff ski boots. Most skiers who carve normal turns at normal speeds like the extra lateral stiffness because they are angulating much more. It is unlikely that you would have a separate pair of boots for speed events if you only enter one or two per year. Don't sweat it, but be aware of how your equipment will react and plan accordingly.

Helmets

It almost goes without saying that a helmet is a must for speed events. You won't be allowed in the starting gate, even for a training run, without one. Although there are not yet specific standards for helmets, the helmet you wear should be designed for skiing, not another sport.

Apparel

What you wear can greatly affect your speed in Super G and downhill racing. In the technical events, a speed suit functions mostly as a fashion statement until such point as the competition gets within a second of your time. In Super G or downhill, don't bother showing up without one, regardless of how slow you are. Aerodynamics is the name of the game in speed events. On a long course, a speed suit can account for over 2 seconds, which means the difference between first and tenth at the regional level in the United States, and twentieth at the international level.

The same suit will work for both downhill and Super G racing. Your speed suit should not be padded, but it can be lined with something fleecy to help you retain your body heat. Speed

---

GEAR CHECKLIST FOR SPEED EVENTS

Super G and downhill races require virtually the same equipment, except for the skis (downhill skis are longer). Most of these items have been covered in previous chapters. Here is a summary of the basics:

1. Long skis for more stability.
2. Bent poles for aerodynamics and a more comfortable tuck.
3. Snug ski boots. Some speed event specialists prefer a boot with a softer lateral flex. Others keep the top buckle on the cuff relatively loose to allow their legs and feet to be looser and more sensitive to the terrain.
4. Bindings with a higher DIN setting to handle the extra forces at speeds greater than 50 mph.
5. A vibration dampening plate under the binding for a smoother, more controlled ride. The maximum height from the base of the ski to the bottom of

(continued on page 107)

suits are notoriously cold, particularly the best ones, which are made solely with aerodynamics in mind. They are very stretchy. Some look positively tiny on a hanger. To ensure that a speed suit fits properly, try it on. You should have full range of motion in all of your joints, and you should be able to stand up straight and bend over into a low tuck without noticing the suit. The ends of the arms should have loops that go around your thumbs to hold the sleeves in place when you thrust your hands forward. The bottoms of the legs should have wide elastic (about 1 inch) that holds snugly just below the top buckle of your ski boots.

It is okay to add layers under the suit, especially on cold days, but don't go overboard. A microfleece body suit or expedition-weight long underwear and a turtleneck are about as thick as you can go without either restricting movement or loosing aerodynamics. Bulk is bad. Think thin to win! In addition to a thin suit, thin ski gloves, such as "springtime" ski gloves or cross-country ski gloves, may be worth a couple tenths of a second.

Finally, don't forget to take off extra warm-up clothing before the start. A common mistake, particularly on cold days, is leaving on a neck gaiter. It is tough to see where you are going in a tuck if a neck gaiter prevents you from raising your head. As you cock your head up to see forward, the neck gaiter bunches on the back of your neck. Instead of lifting just your head, you must lift your whole torso, which catches the wind and slows you down.

Technique for Speed Events

Even at 75 mph, top downhill racers look for more speed. It is not recklessness. It is a deep-seated need, a single-minded will to win, that comes from the core of their being. Their superior strength and technique give them the confidence of a conqueror. Which isn't to say that downhillers don't get a little scared every once in awhile. After all, they are adrenaline junkies, racing on the edge of control.

There is nothing more thrilling than finishing a downhill run, particularly if you don't often have a chance to race downhill. But the edge of control is a precarious spot. When trouble strikes, the

(continued from page 106)
the ski boot cannot exceed 55 millimeters (50 millimeters for junior racers under age 14).

6. A helmet that is recommended by the manufacturer for downhill or Super G racing. Be sure you can get into a tuck with your head cocked up to comfortably see where you are going when you are wearing it.

7. A speed suit. The fabric must allow air to pass through. The fibers of the fabric may be smooth in one direction for aerodynamics, but slightly rough, as if tiny hairs are sticking up, if the suit is rubbed in the other direction. These small fibers help prevent an uncontrollable, accelerating slide in the event of a fall.

8. Goggles that fit comfortably with your helmet and that resist fogging. It is always a good idea to put in a new lens before a speed event to ensure the clearest possible vision.

9. Streamlined gloves.

reaction of a veteran is to thrust the hands forward. The veteran does not hesitate. The moment a downhill racer hesitates, she might as well pull off the course.

When you hesitate, you naturally pull back, both psychologically and physically. To pull back physically is downright dangerous when it comes to downhill or Super G racing. The cardinal rule of speed events is *press forward all the time.* If you think of nothing else except keeping your hands, and thus your weight, forward, you are more likely to finish the run and do well.

The first thing you notice when you get into Super G or downhill racing is the length of your skis. It is a good idea to free ski as much as possible on them before you try them on a course, even if you've only got an hour. Although long skis are surprisingly maneuverable, they feel longer and heavier than normal skis. Pick a groomed trail with no other skiers on it. Concentrate on driving your hands forward all the time as you carve your turns. Start fairly upright, in the same position as if you were on GS skis. As you get comfortable with the feel of the skis, wherever the trail flattens, try lowering your torso into a high tuck as you turn. Finally, try a lower tuck.

If you watch random skiers tuck across a flat section of trail, you notice a hundred different versions of a tuck. There is only one correct version. When you are in a perfect tuck, you resemble an airplane wing. Your back curves toward the sky, creating a longer surface area than your stomach, which is pulled up underneath you. Your shoulders should be lower than the center of your back. A common mistake is to drop the hips and raise the chest as you look ahead. In this position, you are more a wind sock than an airplane wing. If your chest is up, it catches the air, but if it is low, the air flows over your back aerodynamically.

Another common mistake is allowing your hands to drift apart, or worse, to drop in front of each knee. Kudos for keeping them forward, but you won't be happy when you see the time for your run. Your hands should be together, a comfortable distance in front of your face, so they slice, rather than drag, through the air.

Your feet should be under your knees and about the width of your shoulders apart. Your knees should be under your shoulders, almost in your armpits. Be careful that your feet don't drift too wide. When you go straight in a tuck, your skis must be flat on the snow for the best glide. If your feet are too far apart, you will be slightly on your inside edges. The same is true if you are slightly knock-kneed in your tuck. Riding a flat ski in speed events takes precise body position, balance, and a certain touch for the snow. It is not a secure feeling for the uninitiated, because your skis feel like they are floating or drifting rather than gripping. "You can't force your skis to swim," explains Lindh, a natural glider. "A lot of people describe the feeling of riding a flat ski as swimming. That's not really it, but the looseness has to be great."

Once you get a feel for a flat ski, riding it at speed takes strength and suppleness. Whether because of nerves or aggressiveness, many racers are too tense in downhill, especially from the knees down. As a result, they bounce around a lot. If you are relaxed, your skis hug the terrain better. Downhill and Super G skis are relatively flexible, allowing them to snake over slight washboard-like bumps. If your lower body is too stiff, however, you skim across the tops of the bumps. You feel less secure, even though you are going slower, because your skis constantly lose contact with the snow.

In speed events, racers fight to stay in their tucks as much as possible because a tuck is the most aerodynamic position on skis. You know you are going over 60 mph because it becomes more challenging to hold a tuck as a result of the intense wind and the vibrations. Put your hand outside your car window at 60 mph to get a sense of the wind on your body during a downhill or a fast Super G race.

At high speed, if you stand up quickly or if you get thrown up by a bump, your torso acts like a parachute, catching the air. It is a risky way to slow down. When the air hits your body, you can easily get pulled onto the tails of your skis and crash, especially if your hands drop to your sides. You are better off in a higher tuck, which promotes a forward hand position and allows you to better absorb variations due to the texture of the snow. If the speed becomes too intimidating, scrub it by skidding a few turns and separating your hands, not by suddenly standing up.

Two views of the perfect tuck, executed by Bibiana Perez (Italy) (top) and Lasse Kjus (Norway) (right). Perez is turning in a tuck at high speed. Although her torso is higher to allow her legs to angulate, her hands are still forward and together in front of her face. Kjus is in the air, but his tuck is still tight. His knees are near his chest, his elbows are in, and his back and shoulders are curved forward. He looks ahead over his hands.

Even though a key to faster skiing is holding the best tuck the longest, it is rare that you can hold your tuck for the entire course in a Super G or a downhill. "You have to be aware of what your skis are doing," says Lindh. "If they skid, then it is not appropriate to tuck." As in the technical events, the fastest turns are carved turns. If you can stay in your tuck while you carve, do it. Most likely, you won't really be turning, just making subtle changes in direction with edge pressure.

Turning in a tuck takes practice. Because your hands are forward and together, the most common mistake is initiating and steering around the turn with your hands. Just as if you were standing upright, you rotate onto your uphill ski and the tails of your skis slide. If a turn does lend itself to a tuck, you still have to angulate at the hip. If you have a low tuck, come up slightly to free the hip and leg joints. The lower your tuck, the more difficult it is to angulate. Instead of pointing your hands toward the end of the turn, keep them in front of your face, but oriented toward the outside of the turn. Feel your skis track cleanly in the snow.

In the downhill at the 1999 World Championships in Vail, Colorado, Anja Kalan (Slovenia) turns in a tuck.

Anja Kalan (Slovenia) about to land after a prejump during the 1999 World Championship Downhill at Vail, Colorado.

Sometimes a turn is too tight for you to hold a full tuck, but a "one-handed tuck" is possible. Every time you break your tuck, body parts catch air, slowing you down. Provided you can carve the turn, you create less wind drag by releasing only the downhill hand. It is critical to use the correct hand. By letting the downhill hand assume its normal turning position, pressing forward and down the hill, it helps pull the majority of your weight onto the downhill ski, promoting angulation. Although also releasing the uphill hand improves your stability, it increases your wind resistance. Never release just the uphill hand! You will lean into the hill, causing your feet to slide out from under you.

Another common mistake is tucking too far into a turn, which results in a poor turn and a low line because you started the turn late. Although it is important to stay in a tuck as much as possible, it never hurts to open up a split second early in preparation for a turn if it ensures a clean arc. It is easy to misjudge how far into a turn to tuck because the course comes at you so quickly. You are always better off erring on the side of early.

At high speeds, *g*-forces tug at every part of your body, trying to pull you out of position. Push back, and remember, if you have to get out of your tuck in a particular section of the course, chances are that almost everyone else has to also. In Super G, expect to constantly get into and out of your tuck. Skis, wax, and technical ability being equal, the fastest racer is the one who fights the hardest to stay in a tuck.

The most likely place to get out of position is in the air. Spectators love air time. Racers hate it. It is the moment of least control during a speed event, yet handling it well is critical to a fast time. The object is to spend as little time in the air as possible. You cannot accelerate in the air. Hopefully, you maintain your speed. You can certainly lose the race up there.

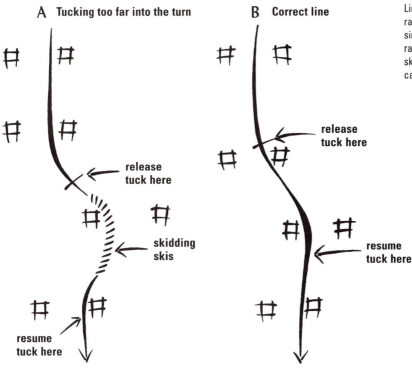

A Tucking too far into the turn

release tuck here

skidding skis

resume tuck here

B Correct line

release tuck here

resume tuck here

Line through a downhill turn. Both racers are out of their tucks for similar lengths of the course, but racer A is slower due to skidding skis. Note the smoothly arcing, carved turn of racer B.

There are different degrees of air, ranging from a light feeling, when your skis barely leave the ground, to a magnificent launch. The best way to handle the former situation is to complete your change in direction, if any, before whatever element of terrain—usually a subtle roll—causes you to catch air. Then try to hold your tuck by pressing forward aggressively as you contract your abdominal muscles. However, if the bump has any kick at all, just holding your tuck is not enough. You must make a specifically timed prejump or get rocketed into space.

Prejumps are so named because the move you make to minimize your air time is literally an early jump. By jumping early, you miss most of the kicker and land on the backside of the roll or bump. If the jump is big, you may still fly, but not nearly as far. To prejump from a tuck, make a quick powerful spring upward with your legs, not your upper body, as you drive your hands forward. Keep your chest low. The higher the speed, the more difficult it is to judge when to prejump. The common tendency is to wait too long. If that happens, and you are already in the air before you can make your move, press your hands forward and down like crazy, and try to keep your knees tucked to your chest.

Jumping too early is even worse. If you prejump too early, you may land on

Peter Rzehak (Austria) in a mid-prejump. Although one hand gets thrown to the side while he's in the air (1), he immediately pulls it forward as his skis touch the snow (2).

PRO TIP: HILARY LINDH

Hilary Lindh served notice to the rest of the ski racing world of her abilities by earning the 1992 Olympic Silver Medal in downhill. She went on to win several World Cups, capping her successful career in 1997 as World Downhill Champion and U.S. Champion in Downhill and Super G. Lindh broke through to the top by correcting one common yet nagging mistake in her technique. During high-speed turns, in an effort to keep all her weight on the downhill ski, she inadvertently allowed the tip of her uphill ski to drift up the hill. Her skis made a slight V as they traveled rapidly across the snow (or ice, as was more often the case).

"If the inside ski vees, it's not just the edge, but the surface area of the ski that's dragging." explains Lindh. "My inside ski was not on edge. I was using it as a crutch. It happened mostly at the end of the turn, when my hips were back. I used the inside ski as a platform for a balance." That extra drag on the snow cost Lindh a tenth of a second here and there, enough to mean the difference between first and somewhere in the middle of the pack.

"One of my coaches pointed it out to me," says Lindh. "Correcting it was tough. I watched videos, looked at split times, and tried to figure out what faster racers were doing. I couldn't correct it in the turn. I had to have my skis in the right position, parallel, before the turn started." Lindh constantly visualized her skis parallel and made a point of it during every run down a course. Eventually, she retrained herself to keep her skis perfectly parallel throughout her turns, leading to many top finishes before she retired.

To others who make the same mistake, Lindh advises, "You have to enter the turn with the idea that you are going to stay forward for the entire turn. By staying forward, you are not as likely to go to the inside. Think of your skis as railroad tracks. If you feel forward pressure on the tongues of both boots, your skis will be parallel."

Hilary Lindh keeps her skis parallel during a high-speed turn.

Right: Air—the winning way. Werner Franz (Austria) during the 1990 World Cup at Whistler Mountain, British Columbia. His form is excellent. Notice how compact his body is, still in his tuck. His hands are pressing forward and down. This is the most confident, stable, fast way to take air in a speed event. He won't lose any time to other racers in this position.

Left: Air—the slow way. Chad Fleischer (USA) during the 1998 U.S. Alpine Championships at Jackson Hole, Wyoming. His hands are out to the side like wings, rather than forward, and his torso is upright, rather than in a tuck. In this position, his body is catching air, slowing him down.
Below: Air—the scary way. Kristian Ghedina (Italy) during the 1991 Hannenkahm downhill in Kizbuhel, Austria. Notice his hand position behind his hips. His weight is back and the tips of his skis are higher than the tails. You can bet he's not looking forward to landing like this at 80 mph.

the crest of the knoll and get launched before you drop into a low, stable stance. Your only chance of recovery is to fight for your equilibrium and press, press, press your hands forward!

The best skiers in the world can hold their tucks in the air. It takes superior stomach muscles, because you must hold up not only your legs, but also your skis, boots, and bindings. Most likely, one or both feet will drop down. Even if you cannot hold a tight tuck in the air, remember (you guessed it!) to press forward and down with your hands to stay in balance. Never open up like a parachute! When the wind suddenly hits you, it will push you backward, maybe so far that your skis are the last part of you to land.

Tactics for Speed Events

Super G and downhill races are two and three times faster, respectively, than you usually ski. Everything happens much quicker. At 60 mph, a common speed in both events, you are traveling 88 feet per second. That means, when you see a gate 88 feet in front of you, you have about a half-second to decide what to do about it. That's right, a half-second. As in the technical events, you usually make most of your turn above a gate. If you use up a full second reacting to the situation, you will already be at the gate, too late to start your turn. If you go too straight at the gates in turnier sections of a course, your speed will bleed away as you jam your edges into the snow and skid. Turns in speed events should respect the rise line, too.

The first thing to learn about tactics in speed events is that the straightest line is not always the fastest line. It depends on what lies ahead. As a rule of thumb, the faster you go, the more detrimental and potentially disastrous going straight at each gate becomes to your run. As speed picks up, the need to hit the poles declines. In slalom, the slowest of the ski-racing disciplines in terms of miles per hour, your line is the straightest, and you hit almost every gate. In GS, you may brush the gates with your shoulder or side, but only the strongest World Cup racers can ski so tight a line that they hit the gates without getting knocked off

In speed events, you have to perform at speeds two to three times faster than you normally ski. As a result, visualization and recognition of the subtle variations in the terrain are the keys to a fast race. Here are four tips for more effective Super G and downhill course inspection:

1. Agree on a name for key turns and bumps in the course, so you can talk about them with your coaches and the other racers. If the trail has been used for a speed event in the past, these names may already exist.

2. Visualize your skis on the snow at speed as you ski through sections of the course. Remember that your skis react differently at higher speeds.

3. Note minor terrain changes as much as the major ones. It is the minor ones that can throw you when you least expect it. It is also the minor ones where, with just the right line, you can put a few tenths of a second between yourself and the competition.

4. Predict how the course will deteriorate. The places where people are most likely to skid are where holes and berms build up. They won't be there during inspection, but they will be by the time you take your run, especially if you have a late starting position.

balance. In Super G, you rarely touch the gates. In downhill, the fastest discipline, you make wide sweeping turns, touching a gate only when you have made a serious mistake or when it is in the path of a fall.

In downhill and in faster Super G races that follow the terrain, the gates are guides to the line, showing the corridor through which to ski, rather than poles at which to turn in the same sense as GS and slalom gates. In the technical events, the line is obvious based on the placement of the gates. The challenge is skiing it correctly. In speed events, there may be several gates in a row but no need to turn. In addition, a roll or bump that looks benign during inspection, which is always done by sideslipping, could be transformed into a monster prejump at high speed. The line is not always obvious. You have to look at the turns and terrain a little differently than in slalom or giant slalom. Recognizing the line during course inspection is the key to successful downhill, and even more so to Super G racing, where there are usually no training runs on the course before the race. At least in downhill, you can start conservatively and work up to your best run by race day.

The Start

In any ski racing discipline, a race can be won or lost in the starting gate. In slalom and giant slalom, it is not uncommon to push and skate aggressively to the first gate. In downhill and Super G, it is rare. First of all, in downhill and Super G, the first gate is usually much farther down the hill. Plus, because of the longer skis in speed events, it is much easier to catch an edge and end up doing an embarrassing face plant. A better plan is to make two to four powerful pushes out of the starting gate, then drop into your tuck. If you have waxed correctly, you will be up to speed almost immediately. (For more details on start technique, see page 198.)

High Speed Turns

The faster your speed and the less the sidecut of your skis, the wider the radius of your turns must be in order to carve. One reason why downhill turns are big sweeping arcs is that, while down-

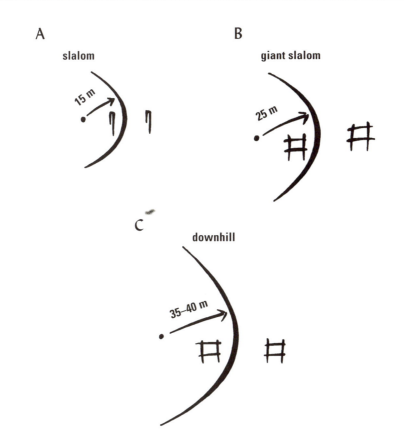

A
slalom
15 m

B
giant slalom
25 m

C
downhill
35–40 m

Radii of typical ski racing turns. The faster the event, the larger its turns. Downhill is the fastest event, so its turns are the biggest and the fewest. A downhill might have five turns compared with the forty turns in a slalom.

hill skis have more sidecut than they did five years ago, they still do not have as much as GS skis.

The first step in judging the line of a course in Super G or downhill racing is knowing what your skis can do. Before showing up at a race, free ski on your Super G or downhill skis to the point where you trust them. You must be comfortable on your skis so that you can focus on your line rather than making your skis work. In downhill, you can also experiment during your training runs until you find the right line. During training runs, when in doubt, take a high, wide line. Try a tighter line on each subsequent run until you find a reasonable one. During course inspection, it helps to look at the end of the turn, then work backward to figure out where to start the turn. The rise line theory applies to downhill and Super G, although it might be in relation to a terrain characteristic rather than a gate.

Bumps and Rolls

As in GS, you want to finish a change in direction before you take air. When examining a bump or even a small roll, the first step is to figure out where to start your turn. It will probably be much higher than usual, and it might not be next to the inside panel. Sometimes, the gate (two panels side by side) is not set on the lip of the jump, but back from it. Be sure to judge your turn so that your change in direction is made before the lip, not the gate. You may go through the middle of the gate or even next to the outside panel. The rules say that both feet must pass between the two panels of a gate, not that you have to pass next to the inside panel.

In slalom and GS racing, the gates are supposed to be set so that you can always see several gates ahead. In speed events, one gate may be all that you can see, particularly after a knoll. Sometimes you can't see a gate after a knoll, because the racer's view from a tuck is lower than that of the course setter, who is standing. It may take a training run before anyone figures it out and extends the gate panels upward. Always carefully examine a section where the trail goes from flat to steep or where there is a slight roll or a prejump, from the tuck position. If you cannot see the next gate, pick a point along the side of the trail or on the horizon or some object in the landscape, such as a tree, a boulder, or a sign. When your skis line up with that point, that is your cue to start your turn or your prejump. If you trust your landmarks, you can ski aggressively through blind spots looking for speed rather than holding back.

During course inspection, it is often difficult to determine how much air you will get off a bump because you don't know exactly how fast you will be going. In downhill, when you inspect the course between training runs, be sure to notice any change in the snow conditions. If the course gets icier, you will carry more speed into the jump and therefore go farther after lift-off.

In addition to picking the position of your turn on the snow, look at the shape of the lip of the bump. Get low, on the snow if you have to, so that you can see the profile of the lip as a horizon. Bumps are rarely flat across. Use the lowest point within a reasonable line as your point to go off the jump to help minimize your air time.

Finally, check out your landing zone. What is the texture of the snow? Does the terrain fall away to one side? What comes next? The answers to these three questions contribute to your tactics in preparing for the bump. Ruts or a hole may form if the snow is soft under the bump. If the terrain falls away to one side, you will have to land with more weight on the ski to that side to counteract it. If there is another bump or a turn immediately after this one, you may have to react as soon as you land. If it is clear sailing, you can drop into a tuck and enjoy the ride.

Compressions

Compressions are usually found at the bottom of a steep pitch. Older Masters racers are particularly vulnerable in compressions because their hips and knees lose flexibility with age and cannot absorb a strong compression as easily as the legs of a 15-year-old. As a result, older racers often get thrown into the back seat, which makes them more susceptible to a knee injury, or they fall, which is always chancy in speed events. Even if you are flexible, a compression will push your knees up to your ear lobes if it catches you off-guard. To avoid this awkward and potentially hazardous position, assume a higher tuck as you approach the compression; this gives you more room to absorb the *g*-forces. Also, be sure your hands are pressing forward.

The Finish

In speed events, the run is not over until you come to a complete stop. In fact, the finish corral is one of the most dangerous places on the course. Many injuries occur there. When you cross the finish line, the natural tendency is to relax, let up, and quickly stand up to relieve your aching legs. The snow in the finish area is often much rougher because many racers have slammed their skis sideways in the same place to stop. You are exhausted, yet you are going much faster than you usually ski. If you cross the finish line going 60 mph and suddenly stand up, the same thing happens as higher on the course. The wind catches your body and pushes your weight back, sometimes to the point where you lose control. A better technique is to release your arms from your tuck to catch the wind a little bit while keeping your chest relatively low. As your arms spread apart, keep them low and forward, as if mimicking a gorilla, as you push your skis sideways into a skidding turn. You may have to make several skidded turns, standing up a little more each time, until you stop. (For more details on technique for finishing a race, see page 207.)

Running the Course

In downhill racing, you can work up to race speed because of the training runs. If you rarely race downhill, pace yourself according to the number of training runs you think are likely. If the weather is uncertain or the snow conditions are soft or thin, you may only get the requisite two training runs. If the snow is firm and a high pressure system is stuck over the ski area, you may get more. Whatever the case, there is no need to push it the first run.

It's a good idea to strip down to your race suit, even for your first run. Your warm-up clothes slow you down dramatically compared with a speed suit, often to the point where you do not get a true idea of the way your skis will react to the terrain. The primary goal of training runs is to find the right line. For the first run, give yourself an assertive push rather than a power blast out of the starting gate. Get into a tuck for the straight sections to get a feel for the speed you will be carrying. Break your tuck early for turns. Get a feel for the bumps. Start slowing down before you cross the finish line. You should feel like you gave an effort of 60 to 70 percent compared with an all-out race run.

Assuming your second training run is your last one, up the ante about 20 percent. Push out of the start gate as you would for the race. Try a tighter line through the turns. Fight to stay in your tuck as much as possible. Make your best effort to minimize air time. Then, stand up early to ensure that you come to a safe stop in the finish area. After you catch your breath, you should feel like you gave an effort of 80 to 90 percent.

Everyone's time and sometimes their speed (obtained with a radar gun) is posted after each run, as if it were the real race. Most people get too hung up on training run times. The only time a training run counts for anything more than practice is if it becomes a qualifier for the race itself. For example, the Austrian Ski Team, which has many top downhill racers, is notorious for using downhill training runs to determine who gets to race in those big events in which each country has a quota of racers, such as the Olympics. The Olympics allow only four skiers in each discipline per national team. This can be a tough decision when any of ten racers have the potential to win a medal on a given day. The Austrians aside, keep in mind that your time only counts on race day. At most, use training runs as a reference. With each training run, you should get closer to the fastest time on the course. If you are the fastest, try to up the ante a bit with each training run, assuming snow conditions remain the same.

As training progresses and you feel more comfortable with the speed and the line of the course, one way to trim time is to let your skis run more. "Let 'em run" is a common sideline cheer in all ski-racing disciplines and good advice if you want to ski faster. However, an equally common reaction is, "How? I'm trying my hardest already." Letting your skis run means giving them some freedom. Training, concentration, technique, and strength can only get you so far. You must then stop thinking so much and not be so mechanical. Start on the flatter, straighter sections of the course, where you can flatten your skis on the snow. As that floating feeling sets in, allow your skis to drift a little. Let your skis find the line of least resistance, within an acceptable range. In other words, don't fight the terrain. The shortest line is not necessarily the fastest if you have to edge more to maintain it.

In Super G, if your first chance to ski the course is the race, you have to go for it! Many racers at the regional and Masters levels mistakenly think Super G is easier than downhill because the speeds are more manageable. Super G speeds, however, are still very fast, which, in a way, makes Super G much more difficult than downhill. "In downhill, you have time to train and figure out the course through feel, not just memory," explains Hilary

Lindh. "In Super G, you really have to know what you are doing. It is easy to be too cautious in Super G. You have to run it as straight as you can and still make the gates."

Your personality has a great deal to do with whether you ski Super G better than downhill or vice versa. Many people have a hard time pushing it the first run in a speed event. "Super G is more reactive," says Lindh. "Things seem like they are coming at you much faster. It feels like there is more terrain because the speed is slower and there are more turns. You have to link the turns! Don't finish a turn, then wait for the next one. In inspection, you have to look at how you can link turns given the terrain, eliminating the 'dead spot.'"

On-Snow Training

Perfection is the Holy Grail of faster skiing.

Ask any superbly trained skier if they ski perfectly, and they would surely say, "No." It is that quest for perfection, turn after turn, that has led them to the peak of proficiency, but they are not flawless. If you want to improve as a ski racer, you need to do a lot of free skiing and train specifically in gates. Access to a suitable ski area is a prerequisite for regular training. Access to good coaching is also critical, perhaps more so than the terrain available to you on a regular basis. This chapter covers four elements of on-snow training: selecting the right "home" ski area, free skiing, gate training, and what to look for in a coach.

Selecting the Right "Home" Ski Area

You may have no choice about your "home" ski area, the place where you train regularly. However, if you do, there are several criteria to consider before buying your season pass.

Terrain

When considering terrain, you must look not only at the training slope or slopes, but also at the rest of the mountain. Ideally, the training slope should have a moderate pitch, with at least one transition from steep to flat and one knoll. It should also have enough length for at least a 45-second GS run. The training corridor should be closed to the public for safety reasons and to prevent some knucklehead from either cutting you off or knocking down half of the gates before you go.

Another consideration is the amount of snowmaking and grooming on the training slope. It is difficult to concentrate on your technique in the gates when you are concerned about wrecking your skis. Find out what priority that trail has in the snowmaking strategy of the ski area, particularly early in the season. If the priority is low, then be sure gate training is allowed on other trails. If good cover is likely, then find out about the grooming. The training slope should be groomed nightly. There is nothing worse than trying to run slalom down a mogul field or through day-old ruts.

Given the importance of free skiing, the rest of the mountain should offer as much variety as possible. Having a vertical drop of at least 1,000 feet, preferably more, is also a good feature. Long, nonstop runs build leg strength. If you only ski a maximum of 500 vertical feet per run (or between stops), you will suffer rubber legs at the end of a longer race.

Lift Access

Although it doesn't have to be a high-speed quad chairlift, the lift that serves the training slope should be quick and should not service a beginner area. There is nothing more frustrating than expecting to make four to six runs in an hour, but only getting two because of a slow line or a lift that stops frequently.

Course Maintenance

In most training programs, protocol calls for all racers to sideslip every course before they run it to remove excess snow and to smooth it out, and to sideslip it again after the course is closed also to smooth it out. Sideslipping can do only so much, however. Find out how many groups, and thus how many people, practice on a given course. If there are three groups with ten racers in each group, after three training runs, ninety people will have skied the course. Even with three coaches maintaining it, it

FIRST PERSON: BECOMING A "VERMONT" GIRL

From the time I was 11 years old, I was one of the top junior ski racers in my age group in New York State. By age 14, I was totally dedicated to ski racing. As I improved, the training and travel demands increased. I missed a lot of ninth grade, so much in fact that my local high school was considering having me repeat the grade because I had not fulfilled the minimum required school days. I was a straight-A student, with varsity letters in soccer, skiing, track and field, and gymnastics as a freshman, but the principal didn't seem to care. He was mostly concerned about the lack of state aid that would result because of my absences.

My parents appealed to the school board, but to no avail. It didn't make sense. Saranac Lake High School was adjacent to the winter sports capital of the country, Lake Placid. (Lake Placid was only four years away from becoming the first town in the world to host two Winter Olympics.) Thousands of athletes came to the area each year to train. But rules were rules.

One of my mother's sorority sisters at Syracuse University was among the original developers of Stratton Mountain, Vermont. Through this friend, my parents had met Don Taranelli, one of the founders of the Stratton Mountain School (SMS), a ski-racing academy. Suddenly, I had options. At that time, there were only two viable ski-racing academies, SMS and Burke Mountain Academy, in East Burke, Vermont. Two other academies, the Mountain House (now called the National Sports Academy) in Lake Placid and Green Mountain Valley School in Waitsfield, Vermont, were in their infancy and unproven academically at that point. We settled on SMS, because of Taranelli's influence and because I could walk from the school to the lifts. I started tenth grade at my home high school, but left after Thanksgiving for Vermont.

I remember arriving at SMS with great anticipation and anxiety. There was a saying in ski-racing circles, "if you could make it in Vermont, you could make it in the East, and if you could make it in the East, you could make it to the National Team." Over 60 percent of the U.S. Ski Team at that time were from Vermont. From my perspective, the Vermont girls were the stars. I was "nobody" from New York. They seemed so much stronger and faster than everyone else. Many of the students at SMS were on the U.S. Ski Team. I was in awe of their uniforms, their equipment, and their trips to Europe. They were all about my age, but they seemed to have so much experience. I listened to their war stories. I watched them on the hill like a hawk. And I took pride in the fact that I could do more sit-ups per minute than any of them.

I was assigned to the lowest level training group and spent most of my first month travelling to a series of races around Vermont. By the end of January, I had won a couple of them. I was happy, but still a minnow among sharks. However, my modest success was enough to qualify me for the Eastern Cup Series, the highest level of ski racing at the regional level. The first two races, a slalom and a giant slalom, were demoralizing. I started at the back of the pack and didn't finish much better. With each race, however, I gained more confidence and my results got better, including a few top ten finishes.

At the end of February, I entered an Eastern Cup downhill at Smuggler's Notch, Vermont, and, to my surprise, won! The next weekend, I was on my way to Sugarloaf, Maine, with only two other girls from SMS, both national team members, for a NorAm downhill. Everything was happening so quickly. The NorAm series, short for North American Trophy Series, was considered the highest level of competition in North America, just below the World Cup level. It was an international field, mostly Americans and Canadians. Many of my heroes were there. I remember meeting Tamara McKinney for the first time during a weather hold. We sat in the base lodge drinking hot chocolate and telling jokes.

I finished in the top 20, nothing to write home about now, but even that was a breakthrough for me. I was a NorAm racer! I no longer felt like a guest at SMS. It was my home. I was from Vermont. I was a Vermont girl! It happened by osmosis (and a few good race results).

will deteriorate quickly. Thirty or more skiers training on the same course is not unusual. In general, the course should be reset every 60 to 90 minutes. If the course deteriorates too much and too quickly beyond race conditions, you'll build more frustration than character.

Other Racers

Fast skiers are an obvious clue to the quality of the ski area as a training site and of its support of racing. Like a tennis match against a slightly better opponent, as long as the gap is not too large, training with skiers who are better than you boosts your skiing. They provide an excellent visual reference for technique and line, plus the psychological motivation to keep up. On the flip side, if you are the best in a particular program, it will be tougher for you to improve, because you won't be pushed constantly to ski faster.

Training Aids

Training aids are the bells and whistles that make a program complete. Video analysis is the most common one. Ideally, you should watch a video of your performance immediately after or at least by the end of the training session. In many resorts, the television monitor is an old hand-me-down. Check that the television is fairly new, with a clear, nongrainy picture, and that the viewing area is shaded enough to avoid glare on the screen.

Timed runs are another valuable perquisite. They are really the only way to find out if an adjustment to your technique or equipment is beneficial before you commit to it. It takes more than one run the "old" way and one run the "new" way to make a judgment. You should take several runs each way to take into account course deterioration, fatigue, slight variations in mental outlook (how much you "go for it"), and other variables resulting from human piloting. Over the course of several runs, look for the trend that emerges. If the "new" way is not significantly faster or slower, go with the newer technology in the case of equipment (that old ski design might not be available in a year), or with the recommendation of a coach or a trusted peer in the case of a tactical or technical change. As soon as you get more used to it, it will be the superior way.

Free Skiing

As soon as you get your first taste of gates, it is easy to get hooked. They are fun, challenging, and induce an adrenaline rush. They inflict a serious "golf syndrome" on you. In golf, if you hit a couple of good shots on a hole but miss par, you want to do it again, because you know you can do better. In skiing, most racers cross the finish line thinking, "I know I can go faster." Junior racers and Masters racers alike become "gate-aholics," especially Masters racers who were deprived of gates as teenagers. Do not fall into the trap of thinking that if you are not racing through gates every moment you are on the hill, you can't possibly perform well on race day. If anything, you should free ski more than run gates, particularly early in the season. Free skiing is training, too, particularly if it is focused skiing.

As mentioned in chapters 4 and 5 on giant slalom and slalom racing, whenever you want to learn a new skill, it is critical that you master it first outside of a course if you ever want to do it well in a course. This includes not only various shapes (radii) of turns at various speeds, but also such skills as cross-blocking, looking ahead, and absorbing rolls in terrain. Even though you may picture the gates in your mind's eye, you are free to concentrate on your technique, because you don't really have to stay on a particular line. You can experiment with hand placement and angulation, seeing how it affects your skis.

Most racers do not free ski enough. While some are fairly good about getting their ski legs early in the season, few continue to free ski much once the first race arrives. You should free ski exclusively for two to three weeks when you get back on snow. No gates! Concentrate on finding your balance over your skis and work on carving turns. Once you start gate training, free skiing should remain at least 50 percent of the mix, *every time you go out on the hill*, including race day. Even if your training time is severely limited, you should still spend half of it free skiing.

A TYPICAL TRAINING SESSION

The ideal training session has quick lift service to the top of the course, with only a short ski to the start. This would allow many runs in a short period of time. Here's how to plan your runs to get the most out of a 2½-hour training session, assuming efficient lift service:

- Runs 1–2: Free skiing warm-up. Concentrate on finding your balance and feeling the skis carve on the snow.
- Run 3: Sideslip and inspect the course.
- Runs 4–7: Train on the course.
- Run 8: Sideslip and inspect the course as it is reset.
- Runs 9–12: Train on the course.
- Run 13: Sideslip to remove the ruts as your coach or a training partner picks up the gates.
- Runs 14–16: Free ski. Time to decompress and think about what you did well.

In this typical training session, an athlete takes 16 runs! That is a lot of skiing. Only eight of those runs were in a course, yet the racer had excellent training.

If the ski to the start is longer, don't ski it obliviously. Make use of the hill by focusing on your technique. At smaller areas, consider taking a free-skiing run every fifth run. If you have recurring trouble in gates, go free skiing until you figure it out.

When you are free skiing, in addition to focusing on good technique, try not to stop during the run. "Nonstops" are commonly prescribed by coaches at larger ski areas, where there is enough vertical drop to get your attention. If you want to build up your ski legs, make several nonstops in a row. Do not stop halfway down. Some of your nonstops should be off the groomed runs, in rough snow or bumps. You will become a better all-around skier in addition to being able to handle adverse snow conditions in a course.

"It is super important, especially at younger levels, to be instinctive," says Felix McGrath, a member of the 1988 Olympic team in Calgary, who now coaches the formidable University of Vermont ski team, "First you need the basics, then you have to be athletic and natural. When I started coaching, my guys were too mechanical from the repetitive motion of gate training. Free skiing makes you not just the fastest, but also the best."

McGrath encourages free skiing even on race day. "When I was a kid, I skied all day on race day," he says, "Now, the trend is to only inspect and race. Go ski!"

PRO TIP: FELIX McGRATH

Felix McGrath never won a World Cup, but he came darn close. In 1988, during the peak of Alberto Tomba's ski racing career, McGrath placed second behind Tomba in a slalom in Are, Sweden, only 22/100ths of a second back. He finished the season ranked third in the world in slalom. McGrath's successful career also included competing in the 1988 Winter Olympics in Calgary, Alberta, winning five U.S. National Championships, and several seasons as the top-ranked American on the U.S. Pro Ski Tour. He is now the Men's Alpine Coach at the University of Vermont, a perennial powerhouse on the NCAA circuit.

Although McGrath skied through an infinite number of gates during his career, he remains a strong proponent of free skiing as much as possible. "Free skiing is the best way—the only way—especially in the beginning of the season to find your balance and to be efficient on your skis," he says. "Do it a lot, and fast where it is allowed."

While competing on the World Cup circuit, his quest for the elusive gold medal made him a keen observer of the training habits of the Europeans, who always seemed just a little bit faster. "In America, we may free ski fast, making big GS turns, but we don't do it enough over ripples, rolls, bumps, in flat light, and on ungroomed snow," he says. "You have to simulate race conditions when you free ski. A perfect 60-gate course doesn't happen very often. The Euro's have done it forever on the glaciers, which are ungroomed."

McGrath warns skiers not to fall into the trap of making only great turns on shaped skis on the groomed runs. "It gives you a false sense of security," he says, "It is a false sense of how good you are. A smooth course is easy, but most ski races are about adapting to different variables." This does not mean that a run on the corduroy is out of the question. McGrath suggests a mix, part of the day on the good stuff, and part of the day on the rest of the mountain. "You may feel like crap for awhile, but it will get better, and you will race faster," he says.

Basic Gate Training

When it comes to great gate training, quality, not quantity, is the rule of faster skiers. At the World Cup level, racers typically warm up by free skiing for about an hour, then take about eight runs on a course, then free ski for another 30 minutes. They don't take many runs, because gate training is tough on the body, but the runs they take are focused and energetic.

Of course, World Cup skiers have the luxury of training every day. That is their job. For those of us who have off-snow occupations, the natural reaction is to try to run gates all day long on the few days that you can train. Don't do it. You will beat yourself up, with little incremental gain. Instead, make fewer runs on a course, but with maximum effort each run.

There are two ways to approach gate training. You can try to correct a problem with your line or technique or you can simulate a race. Ideally, it is best to do a little of both, but not on the same run. The first time you take a run on a course, pretend it is a race. Ski as fast as you can, looking down the hill and not micromanaging your technique. In a real race, your first run down the course counts. If you also make your first training run count, you will be more comfortable pushing yourself on race day.

After your first "race" run, use subsequent runs to work on a problem with your technique or tactics, depending on the course. If the course is not very tricky, concentrate on your technique. Pick one error, only one, and work on fixing it. Too often skiers try to think of too many things as they ski down the course. The end result is a muddled brain, and thus, a muddled performance. Faster skiing comes by curing one bad habit at a time. Remember, getting rid of one habit usually gets rid of others as well.

Early in the season, have your coach set courses with an even rhythm from top to bottom. It is difficult to work on technique if you have to think about challenges on the course. The emphasis should be on carving every turn and accelerating. Many times, drill courses are set that are not a regulation format but that help develop certain skills, such as looking ahead or agility.

As the season moves along, put less emphasis on technique and more emphasis on tactics in your gate training. A problem with your technique may persist, which cannot be ignored, but tactical training becomes equally important. Ask your coach to set drills or courses that involve interesting gate combinations. If you have trouble in a certain section, ski just that section a few times until you get it right, then ski the whole course. While training on a section of the course, be sure to look uphill before entering the course, so you don't interfere with another racer's run.

Above all, don't give up during a training run. Push yourself to recover after big mistakes. Finish the course. The sole purpose of training is to prepare yourself for racing. Skiing out of a course sets a precedent that is easy to follow on race day. Even if a training run is not going well, stick it out and salvage what you can from it. You may surprise yourself. In ski racing, the fastest run is rarely a perfect run.

In addition to the quality of each run, try to find a balance in your training between slalom and giant slalom. Normally, training for one discipline is offered on a given day, but the discipline varies from day to day. Given the option, spend about two thirds of your time on the discipline that will be your next race. For example, if you have a slalom race on the coming weekend and can train Tuesday, Wednesday, and Thursday, train for the slalom on Tuesday and Thursday. Train for another discipline (GS or Super G) or free ski, on the day between, Wednesday. Although regular slalom training is valuable, a daily dose could be detrimental. By race day, you feel more bruised than enthused. Training in another event compliments your slalom training and it prepares you for future events. Take a long-term approach to your training. Set goals for the season, not just the coming weekend.

When it comes to training, everyone has good days and bad days. If you are tired, don't push yourself to ski two extra runs, even if everyone else is doing it. That is when an injury is most likely to occur. Ultimately, you are your own best coach in all aspects of your athletic endeavors. Listen to your body and pace yourself accordingly. Don't forget, overtraining makes you a dull ski racer. If you keep it fun, you will ski faster.

What Makes a Good Coach

If you want to ski faster, you need to do two things, spend a large amount of time skiing and find a good coach. Mileage certainly makes you a better skier, but having a good coach who analyzes your skiing and provides you with a thoughtful training program can greatly accelerate your progress. Even seasoned experts who can feel every nuance in their skiing need a second opinion now and then.

A good coach is also your friend, your confidante, your moral support, someone to pump you up at the start, and a source of encouragement after you have hooked a tip for the fifth race in a row. That is not to say that a good friend should be your coach. Best friends, spouses, and relatives often make the worst coaches, even if they are excellent skiers. In fact, the right coach might not ski as well as you do, but he or she understands what makes your skiing tick and can communicate it to you. You must also share respect for each other and work together to set attainable short-term and long-term goals. For example, if your goal is to win a medal at the U.S. Alpine Masters Championships within the next 3 years but your current coach is aiming for finishes in the top ten at the regional level, you must first be sure your goal is realistic and, if it is, find a new coach who shares your viewpoint.

Your personalities must mesh, too. If you are serious about getting better, you will spend a lot of time practicing under your coach's watchful eye. Even if your coach doesn't travel to your races—a traveling coach is common among junior racers but rare among adult competitors—you will ride a lot of chairlifts, set a lot of courses, drink a lot of hot chocolate, and thaw a lot of toes together. Being a tolerable person is a prerequisite, but teaching style is the most important criterion.

The most productive coach-athlete relationship is typically a function of teaching style. Do you learn best by example or through dialogue? Do you thrive on technical information or simple street talk? Do you need discipline or soothing encouragement? If you don't know anything about a prospective coach, ask the racers who have worked with that coach, not just the ones who have spent a long time in the program, but also those who have quit. Be sure to explore the bad traits as well as the good ones.

Self Test: What Teaching Style Works Best for You?

To determine what teaching style works best for you, circle the letter of the answer that best describes how you prefer to deal with each situation.

1. When I want to cook something I've never made before, I prefer to
   a. watch someone else cook it, discussing each step of the process.
   b. read a recipe.

2. In school, I was better at
   a. Math.
   b. English.

3. If I have a deadline at work, I tend to
   a. wait until the last minute to do the project—I work best under pressure.
   b. try to start right away and pace myself—I hate waiting until the last minute.

4. When I'm heading down a trail that I've never skied before, I like to
   a. follow someone else to get a sense of what's coming.
   b. go first—I don't want anyone to block my vision or risk interfering with my line.

5. When it comes to my equipment, I like to
   a. know about the latest innovations—I read the magazine reviews carefully and do a lot of research before purchasing my equipment.
   b. rely on the recommendations of people I trust and perhaps test a few models before making my decision.

6. When I'm learning a new skill (skiing or otherwise), I like my instructor to
   a. watch me all the time, giving me constant feedback.
   b. let me work on the task, giving me feedback now and then.

7. When I visit a new ski area, I tend to
   a. get on any lift and go explore—all trails eventually lead to the bottom, and I can ask directions if I get lost.
   b. find a trail map and use it—I like to know where I am.

8. After skiing with my friends, I enjoy stories about
   a. something that happened, such as a crash or a particularly hairy run, in great detail.
   b. an interesting person on the chairlift or where the best snow conditions were.

9. When I'm working on my ski technique, I tend to
   a. coach myself all the way down the trail—I may talk to myself, and I'm working on so many things that it's tough to remember them all.
   b. think of one thing—if I get that right, everything else seems to work.

Now circle your responses under the appropriate headings. For example, if your answer to question 9 was a, you should circle 9a under the column heading Drill Sergeant.

Example	Dialogue	Technical	Simple	Drill Sergeant	Nurturer
1a, 4a, 7a	1b, 4b, 7b	2a, 5a, 8a	2b, 5b, 8b	3a, 6a, 9a	3b, 6b, 9b

The column headings with two circles under them coincide with three coaching traits that work best for you. For example, if your double circles are under Example, Technical, and Drill Sergeant, you will relate best to a coach who speaks technically and who is demanding but who does the drills with you. Here are the descriptions that coincide with each heading.

Example. You learn by example. You are an observer. Your coach should ski better than you so that you can watch the coach's technique and try to mimic it. Follow the coach as much as possible, particularly free skiing, to absorb the image.

Dialogue. You learn best by discussing the problem, then assimilating what you discussed into your skiing. You may need the same information several ways before you discover what works for you. Your coach should be very experienced, with excellent communications skills. Your coach uses proven drills and other training techniques that may be old-fashioned but continue to work.

Technical. You are a cause-and-effect type of person. You grasp the chain reactions in ski technique, how one bad habit leads to several others. You are up-to-date on terminology. Your coach should be highly analytical about ski technique, able to explain the minute differences between top World Cup racers. Your coach should also be an industry insider who knows the latest equipment and training techniques.

Simple. You learn best by straight talk in layman's terms. Technoids are a turn-off. You abide by the KISS method (Keep It Simple, Stupid) in your pursuits, and your coach should, too. Your coach should help you find the mantra, such as "look ahead" or "hands forward," that cures several problems at once, without going into a detailed explanation.

Drill Sergeant. You need someone looking over your shoulder, constantly reminding you what to do. Although your coach shouldn't yell at you or teach by intimidation, he or she should believe in repetition and constant feedback.

Nurturer. You are a sensitive person; you may be too hard on yourself when you make a mistake. Your coach should balance the good news with the bad news, telling you not only what you did wrong, but also what was right. Your coach's enthusiasm is contagious. He or she has a way of making training fun while remaining a professional.

Once you find a coach who appeals to you, ask to join the program for a session or two to get a true taste of it. After that, a decision should be easy.

Coach Versus Ski School Instructor

Some ski-racing programs are run by local ski clubs. Others are part of a resort's ski school. In some cases, both options are available. Regardless of who runs the program, find out the attitude of the program's personnel toward training and racing. Ski club programs are usually more performance oriented, with longer practice courses geared toward USSA-sanctioned races. Ski

SAMPLE COACH'S INTERVIEW

If you are thinking of joining a training program, here are ten questions to ask your prospective coach to be sure the program is going to meet your expectations and to determine if that person is worthy as your coach.

1. *What is your background as a ski racer?* If the prospective coach has raced at a level that at least coincides with your goals as a ski racer, she will know what it takes to get there. However, do not disqualify a coach on this credential alone. Success as a coach is far more important than success as a ski racer. If her résumé has both, all the better.

2. *Why do you like coaching?* The possible answers to this question vary widely, but you should detect a strong passion for the sport and for teaching. Your coach should not only enjoy ski racing, but also helping people improve.

3. *How long have you been coaching this program? In general?* If a coach has less than

(continued on page 137)

school programs run the gamut from an introduction to NAS-TAR to a program similar to that of a club.

Also find out what kind of certification the coaches have. If they were not formerly nationally ranked competitors, they should have at least a level 2 (level 3 is the highest) certification from the U.S. Ski Coaches Association (USSCA). In many cases, ski coaches are also certified by the Professional Ski Instructors of America (PSIA). Likewise, some PSIA-certified instructors are also certified by the USSCA. The PSIA certification (also levels 1 to 3) is a bonus, not a prerequisite. Although both organizations endorse similar technique at the expert level, the PSIA tends to be more concerned with free skiing situations—tactics for crud, powder, bumps, ice, and steeps—with an emphasis on speed control rather than faster skiing in gates.

Ratio of Coach to Racers

Although ski racing is an individual sport for the 60 seconds you are on the course, the rest of the time it is a team sport. In ski racing, you must be either very wealthy or very fast to have a personal coach. Even at the World Cup level, personal coaches are rare. Most coaches are hired by a program and take care of many racers. Skiing with a group has its advantages, however. A conscientious coach still manages to give individual attention to everyone. In addition, training with others, especially if they are a little better than you, will push you to a higher level. The coach-to-racer ratio should be small. Ten to one is realistic. Six to one is better.

Big Name Pro Versus "Bo Know"

A big name draws attention to any program, at least initially, but another racer's success won't rub off on you unless that person is a good communicator, too. If you are attracted to a program because of a celebrity coach, determine how much that person will be on the hill. Cameo appearances won't improve your skiing. A World Cup winner only helps if that person takes the time to really coach you.

In many cases, coaches who were once middle-of-the-pack racers are better. They often get involved with coaching as a way

(continued from page 136)
5 years of experience, he should have the ski-racing background to make up for it.

4. *What is your level of certification?* If the prospective coach has not achieved at least a Level 2 certification with the U.S. Ski Coaches Association, she should have substantial ski-racing or coaching experience.

5. *Where have you coached?* Regardless of where the prospective coach is now, it is a good sign if he has worked for an established ski-racing program (usually a club) or one of the ski-racing academies.

6. *What is the highest level of ski racer that you have coached?* Success often breeds success, usually because the coach knows how it was achieved.

7. *What is a typical day on the hill like?* The program should be balanced between free skiing and gates with a schedule that works for you.

8. *Describe your coaching style.* See the Self Test in this chapter to determine what coaching styles work best for you.

to stay connected to ski racing. They think of coaching as a career, not a promotional program. Their dedication is the ticket to the most feedback because they truly care about your success. Which is not to say that all star racers make bad coaches. Quite the contrary. Just get the whole story before you sign up.

No Choice

All of this advice on selecting a coach assumes that you have some flexibility, the funds, and access to more than one ski area on a regular basis. More commonly, coaching options are limited to one, because of location, time constraints, cost, or any combination of these factors. It is the luck of the draw, so to speak. If you happen to respond well, no worries! If you don't, you can still learn to ski faster.

If your coach frustrates you, pursue other resources in the program. Talk about technique with other skiers. Watch each other. Make and accept comments. Don't forget to take advantage of video. Sometimes you may feel like everything is working correctly, yet you post slow times or you cannot grip on ice. When you see what you look like on video, you may suddenly realize what you are doing wrong, even though you could not feel it while skiing. You feel good on the hill, because your movement patterns are familiar or comfortable. As you try to improve your image on the video tape, you cannot help but improve your technique.

A coach is only part of the equation, albeit an important one, for faster skiing. Thoughtful mileage on the snow is equally important. Take advantage of the opportunity to run gates. If the courses are not set well, they will still help you develop correct body position, balance, a sense of line, and the ability to look ahead.

As time permits, try to supplement your ongoing program with training camps. Camps vary in length from a weekend to 2 weeks or more. Most camps involve travel to another resort, which offers different terrain as well as different personnel. Most take place in the summer, fall, or early winter (before Christmas). Even if you get along famously with your regular coach, it never hurts to attend a camp or two. A second opinion may be just what the ski doctor ordered.

Tomorrow's Race

8

Preparation is the antidote to anxiety.

Travel

Regardless of the type of race you plan to enter—fund-raiser, Masters race, junior race, or NASTAR—before you can test your newfound skills to see if you really can ski faster, you must travel to the event. Traveling to a ski area without a competitive reason is stressful enough, both physically and mentally. You pack, which can be a decision-making challenge. During the trip to the mountain, you lug at least a ski bag, a duffel bag, and maybe a boot bag wherever you go. If the weather is bad, the flight or the drive is rough or delayed. You unpack at your destination. You have less control over your diet because you eat out, often fast food en route. You sleep in a strange bed. Add the anticipation of a ski race into the mix, and it is no wonder you are exhausted before you've made it to the start! For these reasons, many coaches consider a long travel day as a maximum workout, despite the fact that you sit for hours without any hope of exercise.

Even elite racers, who are away from home up to nine months of the year, never become completely accustomed to the rigors of travel. A long-standing complaint of North Americans on the World Cup circuit is the amount of time they must spend on the road. Because most World Cup events are in western Europe, European athletes frequently go home to their families. Between races they drive their own cars, sleep in their own beds, change the clothes in their duffel bags, and eat their favorite foods. They definitely have a "home continent" advantage. Over the course of an entire season, it is tougher on the North Americans to stay sharp. Although they might not ski on their days off, they don't get to unwind in the comfort of their own homes, either. Constantly dealing with different cultures, languages, and currencies also takes its toll. An athlete may be technically and tactically the best, but if that person is travel weary, he or she won't win.

For the average skier, travel fatigue is a factor, too. Your trips may be much shorter in duration and within the United States, but they are often compounded by stress at work, school, or in your personal life. Managing your travel properly, whether it is by car or by airplane, has a great deal to do with your skiing performance. To feel pumped up rather than put down, you have to plan ahead and focus on your goals for the event. Let yourself become absorbed by the race. If you are prepared, you may still feel nervous and excited, but you won't feel negative stress.

Many people who don't have a hope or intention of qualifying for the U.S. Ski Team are passionate about ski racing because it demands a total commitment while it is happening. It offers an escape from other issues in life. Many races involve weekend excursions to a ski resort. If the trip goes smoothly, the fresh air, the beautiful scenery, the camaraderie, and the stimulation of the race are excellent anesthetics to an otherwise stressful world. However, if you expend extra energy running around, wound up like a toy robot, worrying about every detail of the weekend, you may run out of gas before it is time to hit the accelerator. While there is no guaranteed formula for a stress-free weekend at a ski area, the more prepared you are, the less your chances of something going wrong, the easier it is to handle mishaps, and the more likely you will ski faster.

Accommodations

Where you stay is one of the most important decisions of the weekend, not only financially, but also in terms of stress level. Whether you are reserving space at an upscale resort hotel or on a friend's floor, do it early. Most accommodations—deluxe and economy—fill up several months in advance of big events. Finding housing during holiday periods may require a lead time of up to a year, whereas for a run-of-the-mill weekend you might find a good place to stay only a week in advance.

If you are on such a tight budget that a sleeping bag on the floor of a friend's condominium is the only option, it is still possible to get a decent night's sleep. In addition to your sleeping bag, bring your own pillow and a mat for under your bag (you have to be either very tough or extremely exhausted to sleep soundly on a drafty hardwood floor without a pad or a pillow). Hopefully, the floor will be at least carpeted and warm.

If your friend's ski house has a guest room, staying there can be more enjoyable than staying in a hotel. After all, the socializing is a big reason to pursue ski racing. However, there may be several commonsense reasons to just get together for dinner. If your friend's house is "party central," your odds of getting a good night's sleep are slim, and there is nothing like the smell of stale beer to dampen your enthusiasm in the morning. If your dear friend has seven kids, even if you are crazy about kids, you will not have a relaxing evening. If your friend loves cats but you're allergic to them . . . you get the picture. The bottom line is that your friend may live slope-side in a multimillion dollar mansion, but if your friend's lifestyle is not compatible with yours, you are better off in a hotel.

If you opt for a hotel (in this context, *hotel* refers to any place where you have to pay to stay, including hotels, motels, inns, and bed-and-breakfasts, but not condominiums), proximity to the slopes is the first consideration. In general, the closer you stay to the lifts, the more expensive and more convenient it is. However, anything within 30 minutes of the ski area ensures a semi-reasonable wake-up call.

If you have to drive to the ski area, scout the parking situation. Your hotel may be only 10 minutes to the slopes, but on busy weekends, it may take an extra 15 minutes to get through the traffic jam on the access road and another 15 minutes to walk from an outer parking lot to the day lodge. In that case, your real time to the slopes is closer to 40 minutes.

In addition to drive time, find out the policy on equipment storage. Hotels rarely allow guests to store skis in their rooms for fear they will scratch the walls (they are right). Usually they have a ski room, sometimes with individual ski lockers and sometimes not. Be sure there is adequate security and that you can access your equipment quickly at an early hour. Smaller hotels often do not have round-the-clock bell service. Ski races start as early as 9:00 A.M., which means a 7:30 A.M. arrival at the area. Getting locked out of a ski room is a surefire way to raise your blood pressure on race morning.

You should also inquire about a waxing area. Although you should tune and wax your skis before leaving home (see chapter 9), your choice of wax is, at best, an educated guest. How often have you planned an outdoor activity based on the weather bureau's forecast for clear skies only to get caught in a torrential downpour? Mountain weather is unpredictable. Even if you can get a local forecast for the ski area before your trip, the difference between the base and the top of the mountain can be significant. You never know if (whether) you will have to rewax the morning of the event, and sometimes, you just don't have a chance to prepare your skis before you depart.

Another consideration is accessibility to food, particularly breakfast. If a hotel includes breakfast, check that it is served quickly and early enough. A quick glance at the dining room decor and menu is a clue to the service. Densmore's Law states that the more gourmet a restaurant, the longer it takes to toast an English muffin. A buffet breakfast is ideal.

A condominium is another common option at most ski resorts. The two most compelling reasons for staying in a condo are the extra living space and the kitchen. A hotel room is usually cheaper for a couple, but three or more people will be more comfortable in a condo and usually for less money per person. The kitchen is helpful if you have kids or to accommodate special dietary needs. If you drive to the resort, remember to pack food for breakfast. If you fly, look into quick breakfast options in case you cannot get to a grocery store the evening of your arrival.

Ten Ways to Desensitize Sensitive Sleepers

Nervous about your race the next morning? Many people cannot turn off their brain the night before a competition, even though they are completely prepared. If sound slumber eludes you, here are ten tips that might help:

1. Bring your own pillow, especially if you like a soft one. Hotel pillows usually are firm and unforgiving. Sleeping with your own pillow makes a strange bed feel more familiar.

2. If you are really particular or if you have a bad back, it is worth spending a few extra dollars for a newer, recently renovated, or high-end hotel. Such accomodations are more likely to have new, firm mattresses.

3. Find out who else is staying at the hotel while you're there. Hotel walls are notoriously thin. If 90 percent of the guests are college groups, you are in for a noisy night. The older the clientele, the better the chance of a peaceful slumber.

4. Use a humidifier. Heating systems lower indoor humidity levels. The problem is compounded in western states, where the air is generally less humid. If you have just traveled by airplane from the East to the West, a humidifier is critical because the dry atmosphere in the airplane has already left you dehydrated. Most hotels store a humidifier in every closet or provide one on request. Before turning it on, be sure it is clean to prevent flooding the air with germs.

5. Drink a lot of water. You should hydrate yourself from the inside, for the same reasons you use a humidifier.

6. Bring all of your normal toiletries. In an effort to travel as light as possible, many people bring only the bare necessities for toiletries on a ski trip. Humans are creatures of habit. It is important to follow your normal bedtime routine, including washing and brushing with your usual soap and toothpaste. You are more apt to drift off if that routine is unchanged.

7. Don't take sleeping pills! The ingredients typically linger in your system for 24 hours or longer. You may sleep soundly, but even a bottomless cup of coffee won't perk you up by race time.

8. Avoid consuming excess alcohol, caffeine, and sugar. Racing

with a hangover is not a joyous experience. At best, everything will happen in slow motion, including your run. Caffeine and sugar may rev you up, but if you are too jumpy, you won't find the state of relaxed concentration that is so critical to top performance. If you stimulate yourself too early, your body will infuse itself with insulin, the antithesis of adrenaline. In the starting gate, you'll feel more like a nap than aggressive skiing.

9. Eat mild food. Even if you normally ingest jalapeño peppers by the bushel, give your system a break the night before a race. A churning digestive system is not conducive to sound sleep.

10. As you lie in bed, visualize yourself skiing well. The image doesn't have to be ski racing, but it should be carefree and at speed. Fall asleep skiing fast and having fun.

Other Details before You Leave Home

Make a note in your appointment book to send in your registration form and entry fee so that the race secretary receives it on time. Some entries are due a month in advance or more. Some are due a week before the event. Some events do not require preregistration. The nagging notion that your entry may not have arrived in time won't upset your equilibrium, but it does add to your worries.

If you need daycare or ski school for anyone else in your party, reserve it at least a week in advance, 2 weeks or more if it is a busy ski resort or a holiday period. You can request that the paperwork be sent to you so that you can complete it before arriving. The more things you can check off your "to do" list before the morning of a race, the less hectic the morning will feel.

Pack clothes for all weather variables, including rain. A "January thaw" is just as likely to occur in February. Likewise, an Arctic air mass may descend in December or April. It takes the pressure off the departure day if you begin packing a day or two in advance. Many racers keep a bag of ski gear packed all the time so there is no risk of forgetting something critical, such as goggles, gloves, or ski socks.

SKI RACER'S CHECKLIST

Packing from memory puts you at risk of forgetting something important. Here is a checklist of the basic items.

☐ Skis

☐ Ski boots

☐ Ski poles

☐ Hat

☐ Two pairs of gloves

☐ Two pairs of goggles, one with a pink lens, one with a dark lens

☐ Ski socks

☐ Other socks to wear off-snow

☐ Jacket

☐ Warm-up pants with full side zippers

☐ Raingear

☐ Fleece pullover or vest

☐ Speed suit

☐ Shin guards (if the race is a slalom)

☐ Helmet

☐ Ski wax and tuning kit

☐ Clothes for après-ski

☐ Regular underwear

☐ Thermal underwear

☐ Turtlenecks

☐ Neck gaiter

☐ Toiletries

☐ Sunscreen

☐ Lip balm

☐ Sunglasses

☐ Baseball cap (for sun and rain protection)

☐ Money

☐ Lodging, daycare, and race registration forms

☐ Airplane tickets and ground transportation information (if flying)

☐ Map and directions (if driving)

Driving

Sometimes you cannot help but travel late at night because of work and other commitments, but if you are driving, try to leave as early as possible. The longer the drive and the later at night you travel, the more tired you will feel the next morning. If the drive is longer than 2 hours and you have a skiing mate, switch drivers at the halfway point. The short break also gives you a chance to stretch your legs. Make sure to get door-to-door directions before you leave. There is nothing worse than pulling into a ski town at midnight, only to spend another hour looking for the hotel or a friend's house.

To protect your skis and bindings from road dirt, transport them inside your car. If they must go on the roof, use a full ski bag, not just a binding cover. A binding cover helps prevent road grit from infiltrating the binding area, but does nothing for your precious bases. Dirt and road salt will slow you down.

Plane Travel

You may be a seasoned business traveler who logs 75,000 frequent-flier miles a year with only carry-on luggage (briefcase and garment bag), who uses priority check-in and electronic tickets, and who arrives at the airport as the flight is boarding. However, your travel savvy habits won't work when it comes to ski travel for one reason—a lot more luggage, particularly bags that are too large for the overhead bins. It's a good idea to arrive at least an hour in advance of your scheduled flight with a ski bag. Baggage handlers are not fond of ski bags, especially heavy ones. To ensure that a procrastinator gets your skis to the plane on time, check them in as early as possible and give the skycap a big tip.

A common dilemma among ski travelers is the amount of luggage they need. Many airlines are starting to enforce luggage limits of approximately three bags. A common ploy among seasoned ski racers is to put bulky ski clothes in their ski bags. It helps protect the skis and helps reduce the number of bags needed. If you use this technique, on the way home, repack your ski clothes in your ski bag or use it as a repository for your dirty laundry.

Regardless of your luggage situation, the cardinal rule for ski racers is always carry your ski boots on the plane. In theory, you can always borrow or buy anything else, but custom-fit, high-performance ski boots are impossible to arrange on short notice. The three easiest ways to tote them are in a boot bag, in a large backpack, or with a shoulder strap with loops that go around the top buckle of each boot. The advantage of a boot bag or backpack is that you also have room for other items. The disadvantage is that it counts as a bag. The strap system keeps your hands free and it may allow you an extra bag, because most airlines don't count two boots strapped together as a carry-on. On the downside, the strap doesn't hold additional stuff, and your boots tend to clank against each other, you, and those around you if you are in a rush or simply don't pay attention.

A final word on air travel: flying to a ski resort usually indicates an extended visit, not just a weekend outing. If it is a big race, try to allow at least a day of free skiing between your travel day and the race to recover from the travel and to become familiar with the ski area. If the race is at an altitude higher than 6,000 feet and you live below that level, three days would be even better. Although it takes two weeks for your body to completely adapt to a big change in altitude, the first three days are the most critical. A mild case of altitude sickness produces symptoms such as a headache, nausea, sleeplessness, and fatigue, which certainly won't make you feel like skiing fast, if you can bring yourself to ski at all. Acute altitude sickness can be life-threatening and is only curable by returning to lower altitude. Altitude sickness is exacerbated by dehydration, stress, fatigue, and overexertion. Being in top physical condition helps only a little. If you are worn out from work, get dehydrated on the airplane, and ski hard all day the first day, you are a prime candidate for altitude sickness.

FIRST PERSON: A TRAVEL NIGHTMARE

I've spent most of the last 20 years traveling, usually in pursuit of fast skiing. I'm often asked if I like to travel. The answer is "yes" and "no." I love being at a ski area, carving high-speed turns down snow-covered slopes, but I dislike the process of getting there. However, sometimes travel woes can work out in odd ways.

In 1988, while competing on the Women's Pro Tour, I had to fly from Denver, Colorado (we had just finished an event at Keystone), to Fresno, California, for a race at Sierra Summit. My itinerary involved one airplane change in Los Angeles. By coincidence, most of the ski-racing world seemed to travel through Denver airport that day. The racers on the Women's Pro Tour were heading to California. The U.S. Pro Tour for men was heading from Denver to New England, and many of the national teams on the World Cup circuit were connecting through Denver en route to Japan. Imagine the number of large ski bags in the bowels of the baggage department that day.

When I arrived at the Fresno airport, my duffel bag was waiting for me in baggage claim, but no ski bag. No problem. I filed the missing bag forms, figuring the ski bag would show up within the next 24 hours. It was often delayed because of weight restrictions or unwilling baggage handlers. I understood and planned accordingly. After all, five pairs of skis were not exactly a light load. In truth, I was grateful for the delay, because the airline would have to deliver the skis, saving me the chore of lifting the bag.

My gratitude was short-lived. When my ski bag didn't arrive the next day, I became concerned and began my phone vigil with the airline. Two days later, my ski bag still had not arrived at Sierra Summit, and the airline had no idea where it was. The first day of racing was only a day away. A perky customer service representative gave me permission to rent a pair of skis on the airline's tab. She didn't get it. This was not vacation. This was my livelihood, and the World Championships no less. I was discouraged, not only at the prospect of missing the race, but also at finding my skis at all. They were tuned to my exact specifications, perfect tools of my trade, and irreplaceable, particularly that late in the ski season (early March), when ski manufacturers' inventories were low on even regular "stock" skis.

On race day, I borrowed a pair of skis from a local junior racer. They were a different brand, untuned and unwaxed. I could barely turn them. In the finish area, as I despaired at my bad luck, a producer from the local television station in Fresno walked up to me. "Hey, Lisa!" he called, "I heard about your missing skis. Tough break. Any chance you could sit with one of our announcers and make a few comments over the air." Why not? It would take my mind off the situation. Little did I know that modest assignment would lead to several hundred hours over the next decade commentating at sport events, hosting shows, not to mention writing, producing, and directing a myriad of television segments and sports-related videos.

And my skis: the airline found them two weeks later at Narita Airport in Tokyo. Apparently, my bag got mixed up with about a dozen similar bags belonging to the Japanese Ski Team. My skis caught up with me at the next pro race in Squaw Valley, California.

A better tack would be to ski easily, drink a lot of fluids (cocktails and caffeinated beverages don't count), and go to bed early.

How Members of the 1999 U.S. Alpine Masters Ski Team Prepare for Big Races

In addition to the physical preparation—packing, preparing your skis, traveling—tomorrow's race can only be successful if you are psyched for it. You have to be in a frame of mind to ski faster. You should look forward to the race with great eagerness. Age, ability, experience, and the importance of the event all influence your mental preparation. Over time, you will develop a habit, a ritual, that helps you perform at your peak.

The members of the U.S. Alpine Masters Ski Team run the gamut from former U.S. Ski Team and pro racers to recreational skiers who got more serious about skiing faster as adults. Regardless of their backgrounds, they are considered the top-ranked racers in their respective age groups in the country. To reach that level of competitive skiing takes experience. To get experience, they had to attend many races, some just a few hours from home, others across the country. In their own words, here's how they recommend preparing for big races:

❋

"I watch World Cup videos."

—Susan Roberts (Women's Class 2, Ages 30–34)

Why it works: Although you might not ski as fast as World Cup racers, watching them frequently on videos plants an excellent image in your mind for you to try to imitate. It is also exciting, which helps psych you up for your own competition. Whether you are male or female, given a choice, watch videos of top women racers rather than of men for ideas on technique and line. Women tend to ski with more finesse and more technical precision. Men tend to ski with more power. In addition, the top men ski lines that are too aggressive for weekend warriors.

DEALING WITH JET LAG

It takes about three days for most people to get accustomed to a new time zone. The greater the differential in hours from home, the longer the transition. Assuming you can't fly to an event a few days early, here are a few tricks for getting your internal clock reset as quickly as possible.

1. Reset your watch for the new time zone on the airplane. The most important step to overcoming jet lag is to start living in the new time zone immediately. Don't translate the "new" time into what it would be "at home."

2. Drink lots of fluids throughout the trip to avoid dehydration.

3. Take a multivitamin to ensure you're getting a full complement of nutrients. Air travel is not known for its healthy cuisine. A healthy body adjusts easier to change.

4. Try to relax. Travel is stressful enough on the body. Adding internal stress to the trip only exacerbates your fatigue and difficulty sleeping. Even if you never take baths, only showers, sometimes a soothing bath after a long flight does wonders to rejuvenate you.

(continued on page 149)

❄

"I try to relax and visualize. The mental aspect is more difficult to prepare for than the physical. If you can maintain mental focus, the body will perform."

—*Charlene Braga (Women's Class 5, Ages 45–49)*

Why it works: The "mind over matter" argument is a strong one in skiing. Many people ski fast in practice but fall apart in a race. The atmosphere around the course is quieter and more personal during practice, making it easier to concentrate. On race day, in addition to your own nervousness and desire to do well, there are people everywhere—at the start, along the course, in the finish area—which creates a noisier, more chaotic, more social atmosphere. The commotion can start as early as a week before the event, and it is easy to get caught up in the energy of the day without channeling it into your race. Of course, you cannot know the exact course until race day, but if you know the trail, you can run an imaginary course in your mind. Concentrate on the tougher sections of terrain, such as the steeps and the knolls, until you imagine skiing them confidently. Then, try to imagine yourself making time on the flats or some other section. If you are working on a problem with your technique, picture yourself skiing your imaginary course correctly. When you see the real course, make any necessary adjustments in your mind and continue the exercise every chairlift ride. By the time you reach the starting gate, it will be much easier to find that state of relaxed concentration amidst the turmoil.

❄

"I tell myself I better do well, as it might be my last race."

—*John Woodward (Men's Class 12, Age 80+)*

Why it works: If your first reaction to this comment is "most of us will be pleased to ski at all, let alone race at a national level, when we are in our 80s," then you have missed the point. Ski racing provides people of all ages with motivation to stay in shape. When it comes to preparing for a big event, self-encouragement

(continued from page 148)

5. Try to get a good night's sleep for the two nights before your departure. If you start the trip fatigued, it will be harder to catch up, let alone adjust your internal clock.

6. If you have missed a night's sleep because of air travel, try to stay up throughout your day of arrival. It is okay to go to bed early, but not too early. Try to stay awake until the time is within an hour of your normal bedtime. For example, if you usually go to bed at 11:00 P.M., keep your head off the pillow until 10:00 P.M.

6. If you must take a nap after you arrive at your destination, limit it to two hours or less.

7. Get some light exercise, such as a short walk and an easy stretch. If you get your blood flowing, you'll feel more awake.

8. Don't skip meals. Try to eat your regular meals on time (the "new" time). Food intake is an important cue for your body's internal clock.

9. If you take medication, consult your doctor whether it matters if the dosage is delayed during travel because of the time change and plan accordingly.

1. Staying in a hot tub, steam room, or sauna more than 15 minutes. Relaxing is fine, but cooking yourself until you feel like a wet noodle is not conducive to quick muscle response. Plus, you risk dehydration.

2. Staying up late partying. You won't tolerate heart-pounding speed if your head is also pounding.

3. Staying up late because you arrived late at a long-lost friend's house, started to talk about the old days, and suddenly realized it was 2:00 A.M. Talk long enough to be gracious, then go to your room. A travel buzz subsides much quicker when you are alone.

4. Changing your evening routine. If you normally eat dinner at 7:00 P.M., then read for an hour, then get ready for bed, do it on the eve of your race, too.

5. Waiting until the last minute to make travel plans, to pack, and to prepare your skis. Plan

(continued on page 151)

is critical. The reason for success varies from racer to racer, but in every case, the desire to ski faster has to come from within.

❄

"Physically, I train, train, train. Mentally, I realize it is just a fun endeavor and really no big deal."
—Bob Bernard, Men's Class 10, Ages 70–74)

Why it works: You derive confidence from training. First, training not only helps you correct errors, but also makes more things automatic. For example, while standing in the starting gate, instead of thinking about how you are going to do your start, you look ahead to the first few gates. More gate combinations and terrain changes look familiar. In addition, you feel strong, on top of your game. With that confidence, you can enjoy yourself and still ski fast, especially if ski racing is a recreational outlet. Many people get far too uptight about doing well. They put enormous pressure on themselves, to the point where it works against them. Some people claim that they have to be "mad" to win. Others feel emotion more akin to glee with a "go-for-it" attitude. If you can adopt the latter frame of mind, you will stay with ski racing much longer.

❄

"I get some training in 2 days prior to the event, "carb up" at dinner the night before, then, on race day, try to stay loose and relax!"
—Greg Sarkis (Men's Class 3, Ages 35–39)

Why it works: The average person, with a full-time job or school, travels to a race the evening before, so practice is not an option. A few lucky people take an extra day off to ski, usually the Friday before a weekend race. If you have this opportunity, by all means, take it! But don't train per se. Take a few runs. Loosen up! Don't ski from the moment the lifts open until the moment they close, and don't pound gates until your legs beg for mercy. If this is your only chance to run gates, take a half-dozen runs or less, concentrating on looking ahead or some other basic skill. If you train in gates regularly, free ski and have fun!

✳

"I have proper sleep, nutrition, and the attitude that I'm not an also-ran. I'm going to win." —Joan Skiff (Women's Class 9, Ages 65–69)

Why it works: Assuming you are in shape and ski well, being well-rested, eating right, and having self-confidence are the magic triad for faster skiing. It is a common sense approach that is more difficult than it sounds. Fate may deal you a blinding snowstorm during the drive to the mountain. You arrive at 11:00 P.M., famished, with only the local greasy-spoon diner open for dinner. In this all-too-common scenario, you have already voided the first two parts of the triad. The trick is to get proper sleep and eat right all the time, not just the day before a race. Think of it as building up credit. The better you take care of yourself over the long term, the less likely one snafu will have a detrimental effect.

✳

"I try to eat right and get plenty of sleep. I spend a lot of time and effort preparing my equipment so that I don't have to worry about it on race day. I also follow a physical conditioning program throughout the year."

—Margaret Vaughn (Women's Class 4, Ages 40–44)

Why it works: As mentioned in Chapter 2 on off-snow training, staying in good shape throughout the winter is a key ingredient of peak performance. Skiing is not enough. And ski racing is even worse. On race day, unless you are diligent about free skiing a lot, many racers take as little as six runs during the entire day, four of which are side-slipping for course inspection. If you feel strong and flexible, you will have more confidence in your ability to ski faster.

(continued from page 152)
ahead to avoid a hectic departure and late-night chores on arrival.

6. Getting dehydrated. Resort water is notoriously bad, but that's no excuse. Buy bottled water and drink up!

7. Drinking too much wine, or any alcohol for that matter. Après-ski time (Happy Hour) is one of the more enjoyable traditions in skiing. Save it for after the race.

8. Training hard the day before the race. By then, it's too late. The net result is the same skiing ability but more fatigue. If you want to exercise the day before a race, keep it low key and fun.

9. Dining at the Spice Garden, an exotic new restaurant in town. Heartburn and ski racing don't mix.

10. Leaving your ski boots in the car. It is nearly impossible to get your feet into ice cold ski boots. If you do manage to get your feet in them, it's difficult to have a sensitive touch for the terrain when your feet are frozen.

Preparing Your Skis

Fast skis are a prerequisite for fast skiing. You can hone your mind and body, but if you miss the wax, your effort is for naught.

Why You Should Prep Your Skis

Besides moving faster, a well-tuned ski is much easier to control. It enters and exits turns with ease. It glides smoothly. It is more responsive and maneuverable. Some people love to tune their skis. It is cathartic, relaxing. Like a master mechanic working on a prized Ferrari, they tweak, wax, and polish their skis into two identical masterpieces. It is an early part of the ritual, the psyching-up process, that culminates in the race itself.

Conversely, some people dread the chore, which they see as a time-consuming proposition, usually in a dreary basement. They think of ski tuning as just one of the many tasks they must perform before departure. Why not drop off your skis at the shop, pay $30, and spare yourself from the metal splinters and wax fumes? The simple answer is that many ski shops are not set up to put a true race tune on your skis. For certain snow conditions, the wax alone is almost three times the cost of a typical "full tune and wax." It is unlikely that you will enjoy shelling out over $100 for a ski tune every race. When you reach a level of ski racing where the difference between victory and defeat is less than a second, the precision with which your skis are tuned makes a big difference. Good ski shops do a perfectly good job tuning dozens of skis per night, but most of the work is done by machine, not by hand.

Hand tuning is not efficient for the bulk of their business. Less than a dozen ski shops in the country offer the personalized service, equipment, and know-how for a real race tune.

However, if you are completely "allergic" to ski tuning or if the margin between your time and the competition is 3 seconds or more, having your skis tuned at a reliable ski shop is fine and far better than not doing it at all. In addition, there are some ski tuning functions, in particular base patches and structuring (creating a three-dimensional pattern in the ski base to reduce friction) that can be done by hand but are better done with the equipment in a shop.

When to Prep Your Skis

Skiers who always demand the highest performance from their equipment prep their skis every time they go skiing. Although it is not necessary to tune your skis that much, every other time is a good idea. The more you ski, the more sensitive you become to the condition of your equipment. Similarly, if your skis are not in decent shape when you practice—free skiing or in gates—your progress will be hindered by your frustration, and your skis will not respond the same way in a race after they have been tuned.

Each ski tuning session is not necessarily a two-hour commitment. It might take ten minutes to deburr the edges and wax the bases. It depends on how many rocks you hit and the hardness and abrasiveness of the snow.

For frozen granular (hardpack) or icy conditions, your first concern should be the sharpness of your edges. The sharper the edge, the better it grips on ice. Icy conditions also tend to be abrasive to your bases, which strips them of wax, leaving them with the ski version of "cotton mouth." They even look white and a little fuzzy. Give them a generous coat of wax. If only the area of the base next to the edge turns dull gray or white, your ski has *edge burn.*

Edge burn indicates places where your base has worn. Black graphite bases are especially susceptible because they are more delicate. The graphite at the surface literally falls out of the base in the burned area. Ski technicians often call it "oxidation." It can happen after only one run, if you aggressively carve the ski on hard snow. When you see edge burn, it is definitely time to tune your skis. Edge burn slows you down and should be removed. It is also an indication that your bases desperately need wax.

When new snow falls, the powder may feel soft, but at the microscopic level the snowflakes are highly abrasive. New machine-made snow has even sharper crystals. Even though you haven't hit a rock, your bases will be thirsty for at least a brush and a wax after you have skied on fresh snow.

After the snow has been groomed and hundreds of skiers have manipulated it with their edges, the harsh new flakes turn into rounded old ones. Old packed powder is the gentlest on your ski bases. In these conditions, you may be able to fudge an extra day or two away from the wax room.

When conditions turn soft in the spring, the snow has a high water content. These are also easy conditions on your skis in terms of wear and tear, but it is not a good time to abandon your tuning regimen. Like the shrunken snow banks by the side of the road, corn snow is dirty because all of the impurities of the winter are condensed into it. Oil from the grooming machines and snowmobiles, crud from the trees, and soil that the grooming machines pull up from below all contribute to the "pollution." The area around the base lodge, the lift corrals, and the "cat tracks" (the roads that the grooming machines and skiers use to traverse the mountain) tend to be the dirtiest. The snow may appear white, but it can still be dirty. The grime sticks to your bases. Nothing could be slower.

As long as you ski regularly, there really isn't a break from ski tuning if you want to ski faster. The trick is to never let your skis go so long that they need the "works." You know your skis need a tune whenever the bases look dry, an edge gets a burr, or there are sizable nicks in the base. Of course, the night before a race is also a time to tune. Hopefully, you can get a decent weather report for the mountain, so that you can properly prepare your skis before you leave home. If a weather report is not available, use your best guess on the wax. You can always change it when you get there, but doing a decent tip-to-tail tune may be more of a challenge at the mountain because of lack of time and no place to do it.

Ski Racer's Tool Box

Race tuning may be labor-intensive, but the right tools make the job go more efficiently. Here is a list of what you need to tune and wax your skis for any type of skiing surface. A more detailed explanation on the use of each item comes later in this chapter.

1. **Workbench.** You can buy a portable bench made specifically for tuning and waxing skis, but any sturdy workbench will do as long as the height is approximately 35 inches, or about the height of an ironing board. If the bench is too low, your back will ache. If the bench is too high, you won't have the right leverage over the ski.

2. **Vises.** Trying to use regular vises from the hardware store is likely to be an exercise in frustration. The sidewalls of today's skis are rarely vertical. Sometimes they are wider at the base, or rounded on top. With a shaped ski, the pronounced sidecut of the ski also makes it difficult for a standard vise to grip it. Add the various protrusions and dampening devices on the top of the ski, and you are lucky to just rest the ski on the vise. Two blocks of wood would

Workbench set up for ski tuning with vises and an iron.

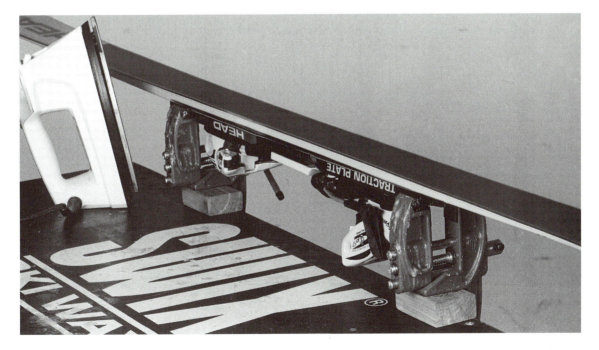

work as well. Investing in a good set of ski vises, about $60.00, is worth every penny. They adapt to the shape of the ski, holding it securely, and they are portable.

3. **An old iron.** There are several wax machines available that melt wax to a controlled temperature, then disperse it along the ski, however, an unwanted clothes iron, preferably one without steam holes and without a Teflon coating, is fine as long as it still works at the cooler temperature settings. If the ironing surface is rough, sand it smooth. Once you use an iron for waxing, keep it away from the ironing board so that it is not mistakenly used on clothes. Also keep in mind that with a household iron, you never know how hot it really is. Most ski bases have a melting point of 284°F. Your iron should be just hot enough to melt the wax, not the base.

4. **Stones.** Three types of stones—a diamond (DMT) whetstone, a pocket whetstone, and a Gummi stone—are the work horses of ski tuning. When you hit a rock, it casehardens the metal on your ski's edge. The diamond whetstone is the first line of attack on the burr. They come in three grits, coarse, medium and fine, and can be used wet or dry (although wet helps keep it cleaner). As the name implies, a pocket whetstone is a handy item to keep in your parka pocket for a quick deburring or to dull overly sharp edges. It is also a good tool for smoothing your edges after you remove the big burrs with the diamond whetstone.

A Gummi stone (A), pocket whetstone (B), and diamond whetstone (C).

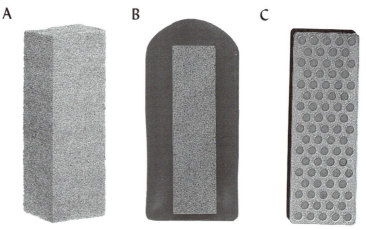

A   B   C

When a pocket whetstone becomes rutted, it should be replaced. A gummi stone is used primarily to detune (dull) a ski if it is too sharp, particularly the tips and tails of a new ski. It is too soft for working out burrs.

5. **Files.** A 6-inch mill bastard file is a good choice for side-filing. An 8-inch mill bastard file is the standard for base filing. The regular hardware store varieties work well but tend to wear out after only one or two tunes. Hard chromed files designed specifically for ski tuning cost a few dollars more, but they resist rust and last longer.

Mill bastard file.

6. **File brush.** After you make several strokes with a file, the file needs to be cleaned. A file brush quickly removes filings from the file teeth. Most professional ski tuners prefer a file brush over a file card because the file card can also dull your file.

File card.

7. **Edge tuner.** If you want to control the amount of bevel you put on your edges, an edge tuner holds the file at the desired angle. It also lessens the chance of the file slipping off the ski, causing a self-inflicted burr.

Edge tuner.

P-Tex candles.

Brass brush.

8. **P-Tex candles.** A P-Tex candle is used to repair minor holes and scratches in your ski base. They come in several colors. Black and clear are the most common. The color has no impact on performance. Whether you repair a clear base with black P-Tex or clear P-Tex is purely a cosmetic decision.

9. **Wooden kitchen matches or cigarette lighter.** P-Tex candles take much longer to light than a wax candle. Long wooden kitchen matches generate more heat for a longer time. A cigarette lighter is even better. Whatever your source of flame, the object is to reduce the chance of burning your fingertips when trying to ignite the P-Tex candle.

    Note: Some ski technicians use a propane torch to light P-Tex candles quickly with less carbon buildup, but this method is only advisable in a ventilated area by someone who is familiar with the characteristics of both propane torches and P-Tex candles. *Never* pack a propane torch in your bags for air travel. It can explode in the event of a drastic pressure change and thus is illegal on airplanes.

10. **Metal scraper.** After the P-Tex repair cools on your base, you need a smooth, sharp metal scraper to take off the excess P-Tex.

11. **Base sanding paper.** Sandpaper, with grits ranging from a coarse 100 to a fine 320, is used to put a structure on your ski base by hand. The colder the day, the finer the grit. As with files, ski technicians favor a specific type of sandpaper for ski tuning, a stearated (white) or a silicon carbon sheet (pale gray), over the hardware-store variety (light brown).

12. **Brass or bronze brush.** After structuring your bases, a metal brush is used to clean out the base (this is called *opening the structure*), and to help align the P-Tex fibers in one direction. The brushing action also raises microfibers, which can then be cut away by scrubbing the base with Fibertex.

13. **Fibertex.** At a glance, Fibertex (nylon abrasive hand pads) looks a lot like the scouring pad (Scotch-Brite) that you use to scour dirty pots. However, Fibertex for skis comes in three different levels of abrasiveness: hard, soft, and nonabrasive. The hardest is used after sanding to remove

small, unwanted particles and fibers that have adhered to the base material. It should be used alternately with a brass brush. The soft abrasive Fibertex is used to remove dirt from the base just before waxing. The nonabrasive Fibertex polishes the base, which is the final step after waxing, scraping, and brushing.

14. **Fiberlene.** Fiberlene is a durable, lint-free tissue that is handy for a number of things: wiping the base just before waxing; cleaning up excess wax; and as a separator to keep skis from rubbing at the tip and tail during transportation.

15. **Base cleaner.** Apply sparingly! Base cleaner takes off all dirt and wax. Use it only when your skis are really dirty. It dries out your bases.

16. **Wax.** Wax may be the smallest word on the list, but it takes up the most space in your wax kit. There are waxes for every temperature, plus mix waxes to enhance the primary wax if the snow is dirty, extremely cold, very dry, or wet. You need to stock them all if you want to ski fast on any type of snow.

17. **Acrylic plastic scraper.** A plastic scraper about 3/16ths inch thick is used to remove excess wax from your skis. It also comes in handy in springtime for removing the top layer of grime if there is a lot of dirt on your bases.

18. **Horsehair brush.** A few hard strokes with this brush are usually considered the final step after hot waxing and scraping, particularly if you are using softer fluorocarbon waxes. It opens the base structure. It is also the brush to use at the starting gate to open up your base structure just before your run, on all but the coldest days. (On cold days, the wax is

Examples of fluorinated waxes for ski racing.

Right
Horsehair brush.

Far Right
Synthetic cork.

so hard that this soft-bristle brush won't affect it.)

19. **Synthetic cork.** A synthetic cork is used at the start to apply rub-on wax to your ski bases. After applying the wax, rubbing it with the cork distributes the wax more evenly and creates heat, which helps it adhere to the base.

20. **True-bar.** Treat this little bar with tender loving care to keep it straight, smooth, and clean. By laying a True-bar across the base of your skis, you can determine whether your bases are flat, edge high, or base high.

These are just the basics. There are many more items that you can add to your skier's tool box. As you become more experienced with ski tuning and waxing, you will surely find your own tricks of the trade.

Using a True-bar to check how flat a ski base is. You have to put your face very close to the base to see under the bar. Be sure to check along the entire length of the ski; it's common for some areas, such as the shovel and under the binding, to be more concave than the rest of the ski. **(A)** Flat: no light appears under the True-bar. **(B)** Edge high: base is concave relative to the edges; light appears below the middle of the True-bar. **(C)** Base high: the base is convex; light appears below the sides of the True-bar, above the edges.

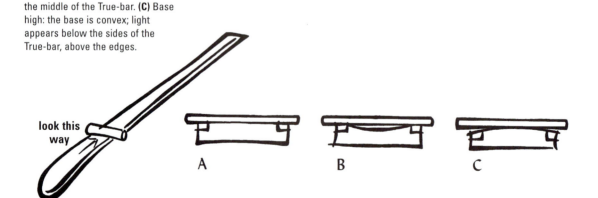

look this way

A   B   C

Base Repair

Serious racers have at least two pairs of skis for each discipline in which they compete, one pair for training and the other for racing. These skis feel similar on the snow. That way, a racer always has a pair of skis in perfect shape for racing. However, most people don't race frequently enough to justify or cannot afford a quiver of skis. Having a separate pair of race skis is still not a guarantee that your race skis will remain pristine. Sometimes you have to ski on them outside of a course, even if it is just skiing from the top of the lift to the starting gate, which puts you at risk of nicking the base or an edge. A course may have a rock hidden in it, too.

The first step in prepping your skis for a race is repairing the bases. If a gouge is bigger than a dime or goes through the base material into the core of the ski, bring the ski into a reliable ski shop to have it patched. If a gouge is moderate, clean out the hole, then score it to give the P-Tex something to grab.

Light the P-Tex candle by holding it over a flame (kitchen match or cigarette lighter). P-Tex candles don't have wicks, and

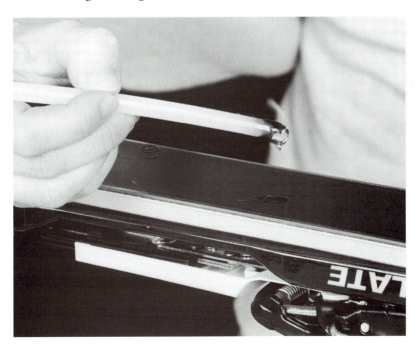

Hold the lighted P-Tex candle over the hole to be filled.

they ignite at a higher temperature than table candles. It may take several moments and several matches. After it lights, a bulb of liquid P-Tex will form at the tip of the candle. At first, a lot of black carbon will appear on the bulb. At this point it is important to hold the candle away from your skis, but over an inflammable surface, such as a concrete floor. Allow the candle to drip a few times until it begins to drip clear. Then, holding the candle like a pencil, a couple of inches above the ski base, fill the hole. Extinguish the P-Tex candle immediately after the hole is filled.

A hot P-Tex candle can inflict serious burns. Treat it with respect. If the candle begins to flow rather than drip, quickly extinguish it, then carefully hold it upright until the P-Tex starts to cool. Otherwise the hot P-Tex may stretch toward the ground. After a minute, place it on the end of a shelf or the workbench where it can't be knocked off, with the hot bulb hanging off the edge. Put a weight on the other end of the candle and leave it there until it has completely cooled.

When the new P-Tex on your ski base has cooled, use a sharp metal scraper to remove the excess. Always scrape toward the tail of the ski. Don't worry if the hole is not completely filled. You may have to repeat the process, filling and scraping, two or three times. When you scrape your skis, hold the scraper with two hands, thumbs toward the middle, with the scraper angled away from you. That way, any small ridges you create, will run with the ski rather than against it. In other words, push the scraper away from you and toward the tail of the ski.

Unlike your ski base, P-Tex candles contain trace amounts of wax to help them burn, which sometimes interferes with adherence. If the hole is a little rough on the inside, the P-Tex fills the roughness, forming fingers into it as it hardens. Sometimes, despite your painstaking efforts, your repair job doesn't hold after a day on the hill. An alternative to P-Tex is a special base repair powder, which irons on. If base powder doesn't hold, you should bring the ski into a respected ski shop to have the gouge professionally patched.

Don't worry about small scratches on your base. If you can't decide whether a scratch is deep enough to fill, do not fill it, espe-

cially if it travels tip to tail. P-Tex is not as receptive to wax as normal base material. If you go nuts with a P-Tex candle, your skis won't soak up wax as efficiently, which will prevent you from skiing faster.

The proper way to hold a scraper.

Base Structuring

As your skis travel down the hill, the surface tension between the skis and the snow creates friction, which in turn causes the snow surface to melt and a small film of water to form between the two. If the bottom of your skis were shiny smooth, friction would be greatest, and glide would be slowest. The skis would feel as if they were suctioned to the snow. A ski also glides poorly if the base is worn and dry from excessive exposure to the snow without wax.

Creating a three-dimensional pattern in the base material, called *structuring* the base, helps dissipate friction and removes general oxidation and edge burn, allowing the ski to glide more quickly and smoothly. There are a number of patterns that can be produced, but they all fall into three basic categories: fine, medium, and coarse. Fine base structures are used when the snow is dry and cold (10°F or colder), or if the snow is fresh or falling when temperatures are cold. Medium structures are the most common. They are used when temperatures range between 10° and 32°F and when the snow crystals are old and rounded, such as those on the race hill, which are subjected to grooming machines daily. Coarse structures work best when there is free water in the snow at temperatures warmer than 32°F. When the temperature is above freezing, the water layer between the ski and the snow is thicker, requiring a more pronounced structure to break the suction.

Base structure is more important in speed events, which isn't to say that a skier should change base structure as often as wax. Top downhill and Super G skiers have a selection of skis that have been prepped for specific snow conditions. For slalom and giant slalom, you should pick one structure that matches the predominant weather patterns in your area.

Stone Grinding

The two most common ways to structure the base of a ski are with a machine called a *stone grinder* or by hand using sandpaper wrapped around a block. Some ski technicians would never let a machine touch a race ski. However, when your bases are so damaged that it is too much to do by hand, it is time to have them stone ground. If they aren't damaged, some experts recommend one stone grinding mid-season to rejuvenate your ski bases. If you are using last year's skis, it is a good idea to do it at the beginning of the season, too, but that is it! Monthly stone grindings are too much. It removes a lot of base material as well as most of the wax that has become impregnated into your skis.

When you opt for a professional stone grinding, be sure that is what you are getting. A good stone grinding machine is very, very expensive, over $20,000. Although rarer now, shops that cannot afford a stone grinder may use a belt sander. Belt sanders stop just short of wrecking a good pair of skis. They remove a lot of base material and not much edge, leaving your skis concave (edge high). They also rough up the base terribly rather than creating a pattern in it. It will be almost impossible to turn on the snow, and you will feel like you are dragging a hundred small tacks under each ski. You create hours more work for yourself after your skis are belt-sanded.

Assuming the shop has a stone grinder, be sure the person running it knows how to use it. It takes a subtle, smooth touch to do stone grinding well. Shaped skis with plates, dampening devices, and three-dimensional top-skins make stone grinding even trickier. The ski should move with constant speed and downward pressure over the stone with absolutely no pauses.

Once your skis are stone ground, you should treat them like new skis. In other words, you still have a bit of hand tuning to do, as described later in this chapter.

Hand Structuring

A skilled ski tuner may spend more time structuring a ski base by hand, but the end result is less risk of trauma to the base and equal or better performance. Select a grit of sandpaper based on the type of structure you want to create. The coarser the sandpaper, the coarser the structure. You should use 100-grit sandpaper sparingly, only if conditions are very warm and wet, or if you need to remove a lot of base material (when your bases are convex relative your edges). A grit of 150 works well when temperatures are in the high 20s or higher. A grit of 180 is the workhorse of ski sandpapers, good for most temperatures and conditions, particularly from 10° to 32°F. When temperatures dip below 15°F, a finer grit, 220 or 320 (if the snow is very dry), works best. Overlap among the grits and temperatures exists primarily because of humidity. When humidity exceeds 75 percent, you can go slightly coarser with your base structure with fast results.

To create a base structure using sandpaper, always wrap the paper around a sanding block or a file. Work from tip to tail, applying even, moderate pressure and making long, smooth strokes. The number of passes varies depending on the condition and the structure of your bases when you start, but you know you are done when the base has a consistent look from tip to tail.

Magnified views (x100) of **(A)** an uneven base, **(B)** a sanded ski base, and **(C)** ski base after several rounds of Fibertex-ing and brushing.

Sanding creates a lot of microscopic polyethylene fibers, which should be removed. After sanding, you should brush your ski base vigorously with a brass brush, working from tip to tail, then scrub it with coarse Fibertex. The technique for "Fibertex-ing" is the same as sanding. Wrap the Fibertex around a file or a sanding block and, using moderate pressure, work from tip to tail in long, smooth strokes. You should alternate brushing and Fibertex-ing several times before moving on to the next step, sharpening your edges.

Edge Sharpening

Before you can actually sharpen your skis, you have to deburr them. When the steel edge of your ski hits a rock, the brief burst of heat tempers, or *case hardens*, the outer layer of steel, making it harder than the rest of the edge. Trying to file a case-hardened burr will only dull your file. To remove the burr, use a coarse diamond whetstone or a pocket whetstone. If you can't get the area totally smooth with a stone, try rubbing some 320-grit sandpaper in the localized area on both sides of the edge. If the burr is really deep, you may never be able to remove it, but the area should at least be smooth. If the burr is not too deep after you have smoothed it out, you may be able to remove it completely by filing.

Don't forget to check the tip area and back edge of your ski for burrs. If the tail is made of metal, it can become rough from standing your skis on it. As with a burr on the side edge, burrs in the tail can damage your file when you try to remove them and they can feel like a rudder gone awry while skiing.

Filing the base of the ski is called *flat filing* because in theory, you are filing the flat base. However, sometimes the base material is lower than the edge. When the edges are high, the skis are *railed* (resembling railroad tracks), making them very difficult to turn. If you have a pair of skis that appear to be in good shape but they only want to go straight, most likely they are railed. The only way to make your edges the same level as your bases is to flat file them.

To flat file your skis, secure them in the vises. Hold an 8- or 10-inch file with two hands, one on each side of the ski, with your thumbs pressing over the edges. The file should be at an angle so that the teeth bite when you pull the file toward yourself. Work your way down your ski, filing in only one direction, toward the

Proper way to hold a file for flat filing. Here the technician uses a file guide to create a bevel on the base side of the edge. The guide bevels only one edge at a time, the one without the sleeve on it.

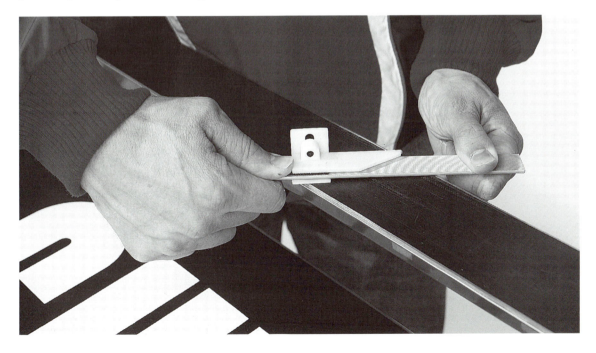

tail, not up and down. After one pass down the ski, wipe the ski with Fiberlene and clean the file to remove the metal filings. If you don't keep the ski and file clean, the filings can score the base or the edge.

Rather than flat filing, which affects both edges simultaneously, many ski tuners now prefer to file one edge at a time with a file guide, a tool that holds the file precisely next to the edge. File guides prevent the file from bending as you press downward through your file stroke. If you do not use a file guide, be careful not to contort your body as you pull the file down your ski. Try to apply consistent pressure.

After flat filing, you should turn your ski on its side so that the base is away from you and secure it again in the vices. Side file each edge, using a small 6-inch file in a file guide. The side edge is where most of the bevel work is done. Beveling refers to the angle of the edge compared to 90 degrees. If the ski edge forms a 90-degree angle, the base bevel and the edge bevel are both 0 degrees. Base bevels are usually 0 to 1 degree, whereas side bevels vary between 0 and 4 degrees. Extreme 4-degree bevels, where the edge forms an acute 86-degree angle, are reserved for very aggressive skiers on icy conditions, such as a World Cup slalom. Edge bevel is a personal thing. The amount of bevel greatly influences a ski's performance. Accuracy is paramount, hence the file guide. If you don't have an opinion, you should stick with the manufacturer's recommended bevel, particularly with shaped skis, which is usually not 0 degrees. "An edge that forms a 90-degree angle won't work with shaped skis if you use a high edge angle when you turn," says Mike DeSantis, Product Development Manager for Volkl USA and a former World Cup technician.

Comparing degrees of base and side bevel. **(A)** No bevel: the side edge and base edge are flat, forming a 90-degree angle. **(B)** One-degree side bevel: the base edge is flat, but the side edge has a 1-degree bevel, forming an 89-degree angle. **(C)** Four-degree edge bevel: the base edge has a 1-degree bevel, and the side edge has a 3-degree bevel, forming an 86-degree angle.

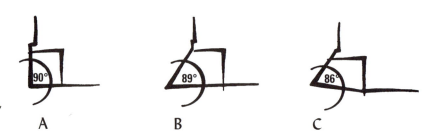

A   B   C

"With a 90-degree edge [no bevel], as a shaped ski bends in an arc, the top part of the edge, nearest the sidewall, releases the back part of the edge in a high-speed turn. You need some side bevel to carve cleanly. Side beveling cuts away the top part of the edge. This is also why [the cross section of] some skis have a trapezoidal shape."

After sharpening and beveling the edges, use a fine diamond whetstone to polish them. Polishing removes the slight burr that filing leaves behind on the base side of the edge. Polished edges are the frosting that sweetens the turn. Your skis glide smoothly, with enhanced edge grip. A smooth, polished, sharp edge feels good even when snow conditions are soft, but a sharp edge with a burr feels grabby.

The tendency is to always make your edges razor sharp, so you could literally shave with them. The degree of sharpness should be determined by snow conditions. If conditions are spring-like, warm and soft, your edges should not be so sharp or you risk catching an edge. The same is true on certain types of machine-made snow. It is trickier to judge machine-made snow. It can

---

PRO TIP: MIKE DeSANTIS

Mike DeSantis is one of the country's foremost experts on ski tuning. A graduate of the Stratton Mountain School, he raced for the University of Vermont and worked as a coach at Stratton Mountain. From 1991 to 1996, he held the joint positions of Director of International Racing and World Cup Technician for Volkl Skis. During that time he was responsible for the skis of numerous World Cup stars, including Hilary Lindh, Kate Pace (Canada), Heidi Voelker, Kim and Krista Schmidinger, Chris Puckett, and Jason Rosener. He is now Product Development Manager for Volkl USA. After a lifetime around ski equipment, he has gained some valuable insights into how to prepare a ski for racing. "Base bevel is the most important thing, even more than how sharp the edge is," says DeSantis. "The base bevel not only determines how easy you can initiate a turn, but also provides the necessary resistance for you to roll the ski up on edge. It is the single biggest influence on the overall characteristics of the ski."

It follows that reproducing the same base bevel time after time is equally important. "To prevent the ski from performing differently every time, keep it simple," advises DeSantis. "Small, finite tweaks, such as varying the tip and tail bevel a half-degree from the rest of the ski, don't matter. On the World Cup, I lived by a 1-degree bevel from tip to tail."

DeSantis swears by a specific base edge beveler made by Sun Valley Ski Tools (about $23), which is the only beveler he has found that has a full cradle on both sides of the file, creating a stable enough platform for it. "You should file only the edge, not the base material," explains DeSantis. "If you bring the ski base into the bevel, it effectively thickens the edge, making it harder to turn the ski. The ski feels like it is railed. You can start the turn, but not finish it." DeSantis warns that a precision tool like this requires dexterity and a subtle feel. He does not recommend it for novice ski tuners.

appear to be hard-packed, yet when you turn on it, it feels grippy. The best strategy is to sharpen your skis the night before the race but bring a piece of very fine sandpaper with you on the hill. If your skis grab in your turns during your warm-up, dull them slightly.

There are two sections of edge that should never be sharp, the extreme tips and tails. Many racers go even further, dulling 2 to 3 inches down the running surface on the inside edge, and 3 to 5 inches on the outside edge. Dulling does not mean rounding. "Don't round off the tip and tail," says Mike DeSantis. "You must still maintain the shape of the edge. Think of your edges like fine cutlery. Knives go dull, not round." If your tips are too sharp, it is more difficult to initiate a turn. If your tails are too sharp, it can be difficult to release a turn. Dulling the tips and tails of the ski is commonly called *detuning*. The best tool for the job is a Gummi stone or a piece of fine grit sandpaper.

Waxing

Ski wax for racing is dominated by two brands, Swix and Toko. A third brand, Dominator, is a relative newcomer, but it is developing a loyal following, too. It is a good idea to pick one line of wax and learn it. Although all three manufacturers have their marquee products, such as Cera F in the case of Swix, and Wet Jet in the case of Toko, which outperform the others under specific conditions, day after day, race after race, you will be more successful hitting the right wax if you stick to one brand.

The more you wax your skis, the better your intuition becomes regarding what wax to use. Every manufacturer publishes temperature charts based on color-coded wax. You can make waxing exceedingly complicated, taking snow temperatures and humidity readings and measuring the reflective trend of the snow (How much of the sun's radiation is being absorbed? Is the snow cooling or warming?), or you can keep it simple. Simple is much easier, less time-consuming, and less nerve-wracking. Pick the wax based on what you think the air temperature will be when you race. As previously mentioned in this chapter, make your best guess. Remember, the race may start at 10:00 A.M., but you may not go until 11:30 A.M. Then feel confident in your choice.

Cleaning Your Bases

Before you wax your skis, you should clean them, preferably by a method called *hot scraping*. Select a soft (warm-weather) hydrocarbon wax, which melts easily. As your iron heats up, wipe the old wax off it with some Fiberlene. With your ski secured in vises, hold the bar of wax against the warm iron, dripping the wax down the length of the ski base. As a rule of thumb, the iron should be just hot enough to melt the wax, but not smoking.

Next, iron the wax into the base of the ski until the wax along the entire length of the ski stays liquid at the same time, and the top skin of the ski (now upside down) feels warm. It takes a few minutes. Keep the iron moving smoothly, working your way down your ski to avoid hot spots. If you stop the iron, it could cause irreparable heat damage to your ski bases. "Use a little upward pull for a buttery finish," advises Mike DeSantis. "If you press down on the iron or just let the weight of the iron rest on the ski, the wax comes more out the side than into the base."

While the wax is liquid, scrape it off with a plastic scraper. The hot wax pulls dirt away from the base material, suspending it. When you scrape off the wax, the dirt comes too. You should continue to apply wax and scrape it until the wax comes off clean.

If possible, avoid using chemical base cleaners, which oxidize and dry out the base. There are two exceptions. You should use a chemical base cleaner when the base is so brown that you can see dirt but can't scrape it off and would not want to hot wax over it, and when the temperature has changed drastically, requiring an equally drastic wax change, particularly when going from warm to cold, and the last wax you applied was a high fluorocarbon wax (an explanation of fluorocarbon waxes is in the next section.) If you do use a chemical base cleaner, put it on a rag, not directly on your ski base, then rub it on. Wait only a short moment, then wipe it off. After using a base cleaner, it is a good idea to hot scrape your skis before applying your race wax to remove any residue of the cleaner.

Types of Wax

You do not need a degree in chemistry to select the right wax, just a wax chart, a reliable weather report, and a few insights, beginning with the difference between hydrocarbon and fluorocarbon waxes. Hydrocarbon waxes are simply "regular" ski waxes, economical paraffins that remain acceptable for training, traveling, storage, and recreational races, such as NASTAR races. However, hydrocarbon waxes as serious race waxes have been displaced by fluorocarbon waxes for all but the coldest and driest days.

About a decade ago, the first fluorinated waxes made their debut on the World Cup circuit. The results were outstanding, particularly on wet snow on warm days. Fluorinated waxes last longer, repel dirt better, and, most importantly, run faster. They hate water. Compare how water reacts to no wax, hydrocarbon wax, and fluorocarbon wax: if you put water on an unwaxed ski base, it runs off in a sheet, which is a high-friction situation. If you put water on a ski base treated with a hydrocarbon wax, the water beads up, then runs off. If you put water on a ski base treated with a fluorinated wax, the water barely has time to bead up before it sprints off. In terms of your time on a course, the difference can be significant, a second or two quicker. If you are serious about skiing faster, you need to take fluorocarbon waxes seriously.

When fluorinated waxes were first introduced, they were reserved for temperatures above 25°F. Today, as with regular waxes, fluorinated waxes have been developed for different temperatures. You can also buy waxes with *low*, *high*, and *pure* amounts of fluoridation. Pure wax is not 100 percent fluorocarbon, but it contains a higher percentage compared with low and high fluorinated waxes. Many racers put only fluorinated waxes on their race skis, trying to get as much of the stuff impregnated into their bases as possible.

If fluorocarbons are so fast, why don't racers just use the purest variety all the time? For starters, the cost is prohibitive. For example, a 30-gram vial of powdered Cera F, a pure fluorinated wax made by Swix, will set you back close to $100. Thirty grams is enough wax for about five pairs of skis. The higher the percentage of fluorocarbons in the wax, the more expensive it is. Second, the purest fluorinated waxes tend to be most effective when temperatures are above 25°F and the snow has a high moisture content. If you can easily make a snowball, you are in the pure fluorocarbon wax range. Finally, pure fluorocarbon wax is not recommended as a melted wax. When heated, it chemically bonds to your base, clogging the structure and permanently creating a temperature-specific ski. To avoid this problem, most racers apply it to their skis cold, at the start, just before they go. Because of the cost and the limited use of pure fluorocarbon waxes, many racers save it for big events when conditions warrant it.

High fluorinated waxes, although still costly, are about 40 percent less expensive than pure fluoros. They make excellent race waxes, which can be applied by hand at the start, or ironed onto the ski. If you opt for ironing, a high fluoro wax is not the only wax you should use. It is strictly the top layer, applied last, after a base wax. To conserve wax, instead of dripping it in clumps on your skis, touch the bar of wax briefly to the iron, then rub the iron on the ski. When the base is covered with wax, iron it as usual to even it out and to make the base absorb it.

If you are making the investment in high fluoro waxes, you should add low fluoro waxes to your shopping list, too. Low fluoros are the bulk wax in this category. They are used for hot scraping and as the base wax for racing. In the latter case, after you iron it on, allow it to cool completely, then scrape your skis thoroughly. If you are the type who only lets fluorocarbon waxes touch your race skis, low fluoro wax is also your wax of choice for travel and storage.

Special Waxing Conditions

There are certain snow conditions that make waxing more challenging: extremely cold temperatures, low humidity levels, dirty snow, and new machine-made snow.

When temperatures plummet, skis stick. "Getting rid of excess wax from the ski's structure is extremely important to the overall glide of the ski," says Geoff Hamilton, Alpine Service Technician for Swix Sports USA. "Brush thoroughly with a stiff brush, such as a bronze brush. The base may look fine, but it is not ready to be skied on again until you cannot produce any wax dust."

FIVE STEPS TO APPLYING A FLUORINATED WAX AT THE START

Pure fluorinated waxes, such as Cera F by Swix and Wet Jet by Toko, are the fastest waxes on the hill in spring conditions. High fluorinated waxes are fast at a variety of temperature ranges as long as humidity is above 70 percent. The application is a five-step process.

1. Scrape your skis thoroughly until the base wax seems entirely gone. Don't worry, there is still wax on your skis.
2. Brush your bases aggressively to clear excess wax out of the base structure.
3. Rub the pure or high fluorinated wax onto your ski bases, working from tip to tail. In the case of powdered Cera F, sprinkle on the wax, then use a horsehair brush to distribute the wax evenly along the ski.
4. Using a synthetic cork, rub the wax vigorously until it blends into the base.
5. Brush the base with a horsehair brush to open the base structure.

If you miss the wax, this is also the same method for rewaxing your skis on the hill right before the start. The correct wax might or might not be a pure fluorocarbon wax, depending on the weather and snow conditions, but the application process is the same.

When it comes to waxing for subzero days, Hamilton recommends adding graphite (black) wax to your base wax. "Don't go fluoro crazy," warns Hamilton. "If the humidity is above 40 percent, a low-fluoro wax will be fast. High fluoros need at least 65 percent humidity to differentiate from low flouros. If the humidity is below 40 percent, a hydrocarbon wax, combined with a graphite additive, works best." Hamilton also recommends scraping as soon as the wax is cool, not the next morning. Cold weather wax is very hard. The longer it sits on your skis, the more likely it will chip off rather than scrape off smoothly.

Graphite additives have more uses than just on cold days. Graphite is a dry lubricant. It helps you ski faster whenever the humidity is below 40 percent, even when the temperature is 32°F, a situation more likely to occur in the Rockies than in the Green Mountains. Graphite is also a great base wax when the snow is old and dirty, particularly if you have black bases. It literally cuts down the static cling between the ski and the snow. However, it is possible to overuse graphite. You should keep the ratio of graphite to base wax at one to one or less. To ensure a one-to-one ratio, hold both bars of wax together and evenly against the base of your iron, letting them drip simultaneously onto your ski base. If you rub a layer of wax on your skis first, it helps the graphite disburse more evenly.

As already mentioned, high or pure fluorocarbon waxes are also a good choice when the snow is dirty, because they don't allow particles to penetrate. It also helps to have a coarse base structure, which cuts down on the suction between the ski base and the snow. Brush your skis thoroughly just before your race run to open the structure as much as possible.

New machine-made snow tends to have sharper crystals, which remove wax quickly from the ski base, making it more susceptible to edge burn and general dryness. "Adjust your wax mixture three to four degrees colder than the wax chart suggests for increased durability," says Geoff Hamilton. "If that doesn't drop the wax down a color, then add a little of the next colder wax to the recommended one to harden it."

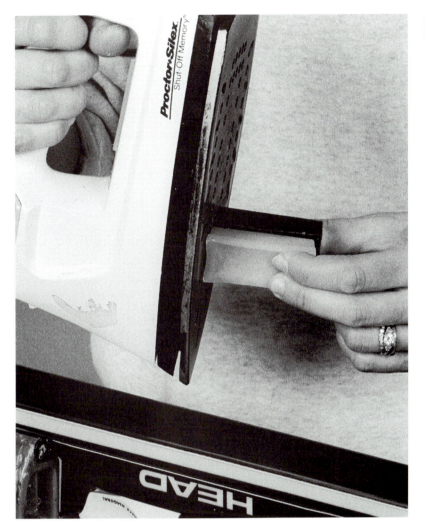

Using two bars of wax simultaneously.

Travel Wax

For traveling, whether by airplane or by automobile, having a coat of wax on your skis is a must. It protects the bases from dirt and your edges from dings and rust. If you are racing the next morning, your travel wax is effectively your base wax for the race. If the race is not the next morning and you have a place and the time to wax at the ski area, use a soft wax (rated for warmer temperatures) for travel. It penetrates the base easily and scrapes off with minimal effort, even after it has been sitting on your bases for awhile. When you put your skis away for the summer, it is a good idea to travel wax them, too.

FIRST PERSON: WHAT I PUT IN MY FANNY PACK

The night before a race, I always tune and wax my skis. Regardless of my prerace diligence, I inevitably want to do something to my skis at the start. Usually, I scrape my skis, rub on a high fluoro wax, cork it in, then brush it out. However, sometimes I notice a burr on my edge that was incurred during warm-up or inspection, and sometimes, I completely miss the wax. I've come to expect the unexpected, preparing for it with the contents of my trusted fanny pack.

I have left my fanny pack at the starting gate of every race for the last 15 years. It is a treasure trove of useful items for quick fixes. Some of these you would expect. Others are my own secrets. I share them with you now:

- Two ski-brake bands. These handy loops hold my ski brakes in the "up" position so that I can work on the area of my skis near my bindings with ease. Because I have a strap for each ski, I don't have to move one back and forth.
- A large screwdriver. I always carry a large screwdriver in case I need to make a quick binding adjustment. I only need it about once a winter, but interestingly, at least one other racer borrows it at every race.
- A pocket whetstone and a two-sided stone that is Gummi on one side and a diamond whetstone on the other. With these two stones, I'm ready to tackle any burr or to dull my skis if they are too sharp.
- A 6-inch file. Some days, my skis are not sharp enough. A quick side-file at the start puts a little more hum on them. Once in a while, I hit a major rock, so I have to file the edge after stoning it.
- An extra ski pole basket. Baskets come off. I always carry a spare. Pushing out of the start is impossible without baskets on both poles. Many ski areas require pole baskets for safety reasons.
- An extra ski boot buckle. Buckles break. However, carrying an extra buckle only helps if your buckles are screwed on rather than riveted in place. If your buckles are fixed, bring an extra bail (the thin wire part of the buckle).

Paste Wax

Paste waxes, such as Swix F-4, are meant for high-performance recreational use. They are based on fluorocarbon technology. Although they have a wide temperature range and can be applied quickly, they also come off quickly, lasting about 100 yards if conditions are hardpacked or icy.

Universal waxes of any sort, liquid, paste, or bar form, are not meant for racing. Racing takes precision, not only with technique and equipment, but also with wax. Precise waxing produces infinitely faster skis than universal waxes, which are better than nothing, but generally slower.

New Skis

New skis are a thrill. It is so exciting to get a pair that it is hard to imagine that they are not perfect out of the box. Often they are

- Two plastic scrapers. As an Alpine Masters racer, I rarely scrape my race skis at home. I wait until just before the start, then take off any wax that I haven't skied off. I always bring an extra scraper, because other racers inevitably want to borrow one, and I want to be sure one is always available and sharp.
- Two horsehair brushes. One brush is for general brushing (and lending to others), the other is in a plastic sandwich bag, reserved for pure and high fluorocarbon waxes only. The more fluoros in the brush, the more they will penetrate into my ski.
- A brass brush. If I miss the wax, or if my wax is really hard (on colder days), the brass brush opens the structure of my bases.
- A square of Fibertex. I never know when my bases may need a scrub or a polish.
- One or two packets of liquid universal wax. In the spring, when the snow is dirty, I use it to clean my bases while adding a little wax to them.
- Three bars of high fluorocarbon waxes to cover the range of winter temperatures. At this point in my life, I mainly race in New England, where the humidity is usually greater than 60 percent. I almost always rub a high fluoro wax on my skis before the start of a race, except when the temperature nears freezing and the snow starts to change to slush. Then, I up the ante with a pure fluoro if the competition is high and I really want to win.
- A vial of Swix Cera F wax and a bar of Toko Wet Jet wax. Although both of these pure fluoros are lightning fast in warm, wet snow, I find Cera F to be a little faster at the point where the snow is changing over from dry to wet, whereas Wet Jet seems to have the edge when the snow is downright slushy.
- A synthetic cork. It doesn't do much good to put a fluorocarbon wax on my bases at the start if I don't rub it in.
- A rag. I never know when I might need to wipe something off, like my edges, my bases, my hands, or my nose.

not. When you get a new pair of skis, plan to spend some time getting them ready for the slopes.

The first step is to use a True-bar to see if the bases are concave or convex compared to the edges. Manufacturers are getting much better at delivering skis with the correct tune and bevel, but not always. If the bases aren't flat, then you've either got some scraping or some filing to do, probably the latter. You may have to change the bevel to fit your preference, too. The next step is to detune the tips and tails, as described earlier in this chapter.

It is not worth changing the structure of the bases unless the snow is really wet, but it is important to alternate scrubbing your bases with Fibertex and brushing them with a stiff bronze brush. "Scrub the base for at least 100 passes," recommends Geoff Hamilton of Swix. "This rips out the microscopic polyethylene hairs which create drag, especially on cold days. These hairs also melt into the base when you hot wax, sealing the base from wax."

Finally, hot scrape to clean your ski bases, then saturate them with wax. The softer the wax, the deeper the penetration. "Temperature range is not an issue," explains Hamilton. "Waxing is a layering process. Start with a soft warm-weather wax, which allows other layers to adhere better to the base. The more wax you can put on new skis, the better."

Safety Considerations

Over the last few years, there has been a fair amount of publicity about the harmful effects of fluorocarbon wax fumes in the skiing trade press. In fact, it is the base cleaner fumes that are the most dangerous, depending on the type of cleaner you use. If you use high-quality waxes, they are inert as long as they are not exposed to open flame or a heat source greater than 570°F. However, it is a good idea to work in a well-ventilated wax room.

In addition to fresh air, be sure you have good lighting above your work bench. Ski tuning is a precise task, which often involves melting P-Tex and always involves sharp edges. Good lighting lowers the risk of burning or cutting yourself. If you tend to cut yourself a lot while tuning your skis, wrap athletic tape around those spots on your fingers while you work. (Adhesive bandages don't stay on, and gloves don't give you a fine enough feel for your work.)

Race Day

No two race courses are ever the same. There are always unknown variables, which are the source of excitement, the true test, the magnet that draws you back to the starting gate, time after time.

Wake-Up Call

When the alarm goes off on the morning of a race, especially an important race, it is tough to contain your excitement. Your nerves buzz with anticipation. You can almost feel yourself skiing faster as you go about your morning routine. *Routine* is the operative word. Race day is not the day to turn over the proverbial new leaf and change your habits. The optimal morning routine is one that can be followed without much effort. It is not stressful, and it should allow you to start the process of focusing your physical and mental abilities on your skiing. That means 90 percent of what you do should have a positive, skiing-minded approach. The other 10 percent should cover mundane personal maintenance, such as brushing your teeth and combing your hair.

Some aspects of personal maintenance can influence your performance on the slopes. For example, do not skip a shower. The water is soothing yet stimulating. If you are prone to neck and shoulder pain, stretch those areas in the shower. It will help relieve stress and prevent muscle tweaks later in the day.

It is also a good idea to limber up for a few minutes after your shower. Work your joints in circles, particularly your hips, knees, and ankles, and stretch a little. This stretching is not meant to be flexibility training, as described in chapter 2. It is merely to help you wake up, loosen up, and feel athletic by pushing a little more

Shower exercises for the neck and shoulders.

A. Press head forward.

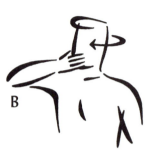

Turn head to one side, then the other, trying to look over each shoulder.

Circle shoulders to the front, then to the back.

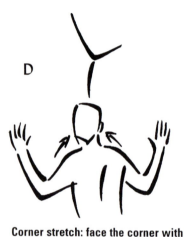

Corner stretch: face the corner with your hands on the walls, elbows bent 90 degrees; press your chest toward the corner.

Pull one arm across your body, then reverse arms and direction.

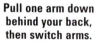

Pull one arm down behind your back, then switch arms.

Bend your arm behind your head. Press down on your elbow with your other hand to stretch your triceps. Switch arms.

blood into your major muscle groups. Imagine yourself as a cat waking from a nap, stretching to lengthen your body, not to contort it. As with any stretching, only press into the position, don't bounce. Stretch easily, don't push your muscles, even if you are nowhere near the position that you usually reach. Your muscles are just waking up. Also remember to *breathe*! Exhale as you extend in each position.

Some people are so nervous the morning of a race that they avoid eating. It is important to have a good breakfast on race day for several reasons. First, your body needs the fuel. Skiing is a cold-weather sport that requires about 500 calories per hour in body heat alone. Second, it is difficult to concentrate on the course when your stomach is empty and begging for food.

Breakfast does not have to be a five-course meal, nor does it have to involve a half bottle of Tabasco sauce. Racing with heartburn or indigestion is not pleasant. Stick to light, nutritious fare, such as a bowl of cereal. Mild food may not tickle your taste buds, but it is much easier on a nervous stomach.

Go easy on simple sugars. A double dose of Danish pastries may satisfy your taste buds and fill your stomach, but the inevitable "sugar low" is not a favorable condition for faster skiing. Breakfast meats, such as bacon and sausage, also are not good choices because they take a long time to digest. Complex carbohydrates, such as cereal and whole-wheat toast, fruit, yogurt, and other light foods, are the safest bets. Many athletes are superstitious about breakfast on race days, preferring to eat the same thing they did on the morning of their most successful race. What you eat does have an impact on your performance, but if you become too single-minded about it and you can't find that particular food on race morning, you may suffer a subconscious defeat before you even leave your house or hotel. Keep an open mind. If you must eat a particular food for breakfast and you are not staying at home, bring it with you.

The rules for coffee are the same as for food. Stick with your normal routine. Whether you typically have one cup or six cups in the morning, drink the same on race day. Understimulation makes you feel sluggish; overstimulation only serves to increase your pre-race jitters, and both conditions make it difficult to concentrate.

Ski Area Ritual

When you see the mountain on race day, your heart beats a little faster. Like a first date, feelings of excitement and anticipation are juxtaposed with anxiety, nervousness, and hope. Here's what to expect and how to ensure the rest of the day goes smoothly:

SEVEN RACE-DAY STRESS BUSTERS

Race day is stressful, not in the same way as work or school, but in an exciting, adrenaline-pumping way. Ski racing involves physical and mental output. Too much extraneous stress saps your energy. To perform at your peak, you must be able turn stress into a state of relaxed concentration. You may still feel energy surge through your body, but it is focused. Here are seven ways to avoid negative stress and to encourage relaxed concentration.

1. Prepare your skis the night before the race. As discussed in chapter 9, prepping your skis in advance can save you an hour or more on race day. Use the time to do more stretching, free skiing, or sleeping (if you arrive sleep deprived).

2. The night before the race, pack everything you need in one bag, and lay out your clothes down to your underwear. Getting out of the house or hotel on race day can be a panic, especially if you are nervous and excited about the day. The less you have to find, the lower the stress level and the less time it takes to get ready. Densmore's Corollary states that the more you have to pack on race day, the more things you are likely to forget.

3. Give yourself plenty of time on race day. Rushing is stressful. If you get up early, arriving at the slopes on time, you will be more relaxed throughout the day. You will have plenty of time before your first run to register, inspect the course, tweak your wax, limber up, and socialize.

4. Don't skip breakfast. If you don't feed your competitive fire, it won't burn. Nothing deflates enthusiasm more than hypoglycemia.

5. Take several free-skiing runs. Free skiing before your start not only reinforces your technique and helps you find your balance over your skis, but also helps calm your nerves. Don't worry about leaving the race hill for a run or two. You may have fun, which is the object of the day.

6. Wherever anxiety strikes—in your hotel, in the base lodge, or on the chairlift—exhale, sit back, and close your eyes. Many racers put on headphones and listen to music, which helps keep them focused and calm. If you are inside, try to find a quiet section of the day lodge. Stretch your major muscle groups, then lie on the floor for a second to relax while visualizing yourself skiing well. When your mind believes you can perform, your body will follow.

7. Check your neck and shoulders. Are they tight? Many skiers carry stress in their neck and shoulders without realizing it. If you feel stress, it is difficult to relax this area of your body. A simple technique is to consciously tense the muscles more, then exhale and release the contraction. If you do it three times, you will notice a significant decrease in your overall body tension.

Arrival

On race day, you should arrive at least 1½ hours before the scheduled start, earlier if parking is in a remote area. That leaves you 30 minutes in the base lodge to register, put on your gear, and say your hellos and an hour on the hill to warm up and inspect the course.

Although the entry fees for many races must be paid a week or more in advance, for 99 percent of all ski race events you are required to stop at a registration area to pick up your bib. In some cases, your bib must be visible at all times. It would be a shame to be disqualified for this small technicality. If you will be stripping off a layer or two for your race run, be sure to check whether this rule is in effect. If so, wear your bib over your parka until just before your run, then switch it over your racing clothes.

Lycra bibs that fit over your race clothes like a sleeveless shirt are issued for most USSA-sanctioned races. They are very stretchy and form-fitting. However, stiff cloth or coated paper bibs are typically used at other events. A cloth bib is secured with fabric ribbons, which are really extensions of the trim fabric at the bottom corners of the bib. How you tie them will depend on the diameter of your waist versus the length of the ribbons. If the ribbons reach, many racers prefer to tie the two back ones together in front, and the two front ones together in back, rather than at the sides. The bows should be doubled to prevent the ribbons from untying in the middle of the race, then tucked under the bib. This tends to be slightly more aerodynamic than tying the bows at the sides, because the bib hugs your body more. In addition, no bows or strings interfere with your angulation and pole plant zones.

Paper bibs are held in place by thin, stretchy bands with metal tabs on each end that you punch through the corners of the bib. They are standard issue for NASTAR-type races and many charitable events because they are cheap to produce, disposable, and easy to customize with sponsor logos. With paper bibs, use one elastic band on each side to connect the front and back panels. If you push the metal tab through the bib panel from the front surface to the back (so the tabs end up under the bib), the bands will

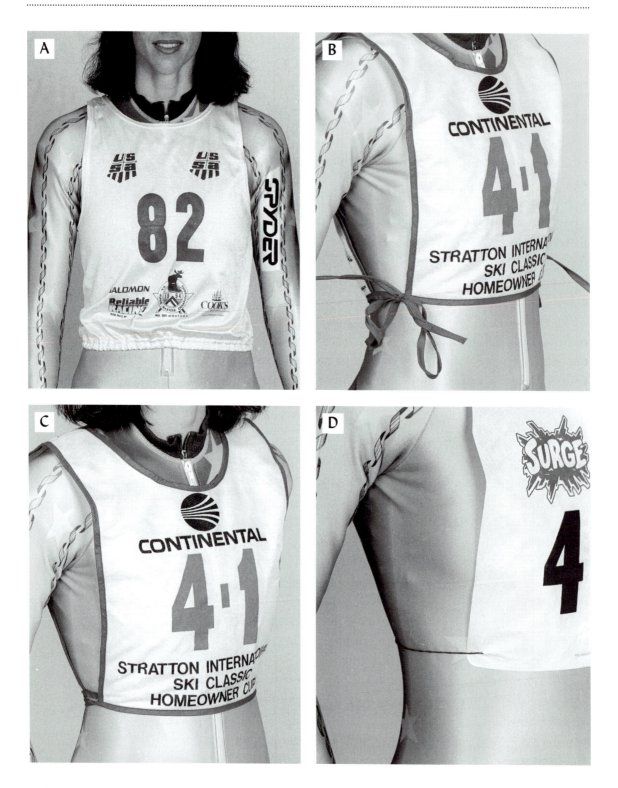

hold the edges of the bib closer to your body. Always be sure to put several extra elastic bands in your pocket at registration. They have a tendency to break or disappear.

Sometimes paper bibs have only a front panel. In this case, the bands are long enough for one to go around your neck, and the other around your back, like a halter top. As with two-panel bibs, insert the metal tabs from the front surface of the bib to the back so that they hold down the edges. The aerodynamic advantage is slight, but in many cases, every little bit helps.

Do not wear paper bibs around your thigh or lower leg. Many people do it, but not the fastest racers. First, the bib can rotate into a distracting position or a position that interferes with your leg work. Second, the start and finish officials have a more difficult time seeing the number.

In addition to picking up your bib and whatever other handouts come with the event, it is also a good idea to confirm the start time for each run, the running order (which may not coincide with your bib number), the race trail's name and location, and the closest warming hut with bathrooms. If you are not familiar with the ski area, ask specifically which lift to take and how to find the trail.

Opposite Page
Four most common styles of race bibs. **(A)** Lycra bib. **(B)** Cloth bib tied on the sides. **(C)** Cloth bib tied front and back with bows tucked under the bib. **(D)** Paper bib with tabs to the inside.

WHAT TO DO WHEN YOU FORGET YOUR SKIS (OR SOME OTHER CRITICAL PIECE OF EQUIPMENT)

Unless you are a sponsored athlete and it is early in the season, before all inventory is sold, if you forget your skis, you have only two options. You can either rent skis or borrow a pair from a friend. Hopefully your friend uses the same size skis and boots as you do. Many ski shops offer high quality demo skis. You may be able to find the exact model that you normally use. Whether borrowed or rented, always check the tune and how the bindings are adjusted. You may have a few hours of work ahead of yourself.

The worst thing you can forget is your ski boots. Most people own only one pair of ski boots. Even if you could find someone with an extra pair, the odds of them fitting you and being comfortable are very low. Ski shops don't offer high-end demo boots as a rule. Your options are limited to entry-level rental boots or buying a new pair and, time permitting, having them fit. The bottom line is do not forget your boots!

All other pieces of equipment or articles of clothing may be borrowed or purchased quickly at most ski areas, except for possibly a speed suit or protective gear for slalom racing. If you can't borrow loaners from your co-racers, try one of the local ski club coaches. A pair of running tights and a turtleneck over your long underwear will work in a pinch for a speed suit, although such an outfit will not be quite as aerodynamic or wind resistant. It is more difficult to find substitutes for pads and a slalom helmet .

Forgetting anything is a hassle, but several items present more of a hassle than others. Before you start your car to drive to the race site, run through a mental checklist of critical items: skis, boots, poles, helmet, gloves, goggles, socks, money!

Getting lost before you have seen the course can easily send your blood pressure soaring. Also, Densmore's Race Rules state that no matter how many times you go to the bathroom on the morning of a race, you will still have to go just before your run. You might as well find the most convenient place, preferably indoors.

Warm-Up

As in any other form of athletic competition, to ski your best, you must get your blood flowing before the start. It is particularly critical in alpine skiing because of its stop-and-go nature, because it takes place in a cold environment, and because you have to put your body in unnatural, angulated positions. Warming up is not simply stretching. It includes free skiing and possibly some time in the base lodge. Eventually, all racers develop a warm-up routine of their own, but here are a few of the basics.

At most ski areas, you have time to take four runs during the hour before the race, two to inspect the course and two to warm up. Assuming a 10:00 A.M. start time, you should be on the hill by 9:00 A.M. Your muscles will be cold and stiff after traveling from your hotel to the mountain and your first chairlift ride. Avoid a quick limbering up routine at the top of the lift. An athletic trainer would suggest you get your muscles moving first. Make a run down the hill. Take it easy the first run, especially at the top. Concentrate on finding the center of your skis in each turn, and look ahead, way down the hill, to reinforce that habit. About halfway down the run, pull over to the side of the trail and take a moment to limber up. At this point, your muscles have started to warm up, and the location is less conspicuous.

This exercise sequence need not be performed all at once. You can mix it up while free skiing. It is also an excellent way to stay loose in the start area while waiting for your race run.

By your second free-skiing run, you should begin to feel like a ski racer. Find an empty trail (not the race hill) and test your accelerator while obeying the speed limits for the ski area. If the race is a technical event, work up to race speed while being courteous to other skiers. Concentrate on looking ahead and making perfect carved turns of the appropriate radius.

Sometimes a coach will set up a short practice course near the race course. Some racers avoid practice courses on race day, believing that if they haven't learned how to run gates by then, it is too late. They also don't want to risk the blow to their ego in the event they don't ski the practice course well. Skiing a practice course should be avoided if a poor run could kill your confidence or if the course has deteriorated past the surface conditions that you will see during your race run. On the other hand, practice courses can be helpful. If you typically need a couple of runs in a course in training to have your best run of the session, then the same will be true on race day. A practice course may also reveal the true snow conditions of the race course and how the course will wear. In the final analysis, skiing a practice course is a judgment call based on your mood and the snow conditions. If you decide to run it, do so after your regular warm-up and course inspection.

If you have time for only one run free skiing, forget the practice course, save the exercises for the start area, and just focus on your skiing. You must condense two runs into one. Still start slowly, finding your balance and a feel for the snow, but plan your run so that you can do some fast skiing before you reach the bottom.

Trailside Stretches

Arm circles. Take your pole straps off, then swing one arm at a time. Start slowly, then increase speed until blood centrifuges into your fingertips. Reverse direction.

Course Inspection

You should give course inspection equal priority to a good warm-up unless you arrive so late that you only have time for one run. In that case, you should inspect the course. Course inspection is not an exact science. As with your warm-up, over time you will find what works best for you.

The biggest issue with many racers is whether to memorize the course. In technical events, most top racers do not memorize

Trailside Stretches *continued*

Crawl/backstroke. "Swim" your arms forward. Start with a relaxed, controlled motion. As your muscles loosen up, increase the speed, but never to the point that your neck muscles become tense. Then reverse direction, swimming your arms backward.

Side stretch. Raise one arm above your head, then bend to the opposite side. Be sure your knees are bent slightly to prevent undue stress on the lower back.

every gate. They check out the terrain, the rhythm of the course, and any tricky combinations. "I used to memorize courses when I was younger," says Felix McGrath, former top slalom skier in the United States who now coaches the University of Vermont ski team. "That's okay. It never hurts to go through the course in your mind, but it's more important to memorize the terrain, the fall-aways, knolls, and turns in the trail, especially if you have never skied there."

McGrath points to another U.S. Ski Team member, Matt Grojean. Grojean had a reputation for skiing well in training but underperforming in competition. At races, he diligently studied the course. In training, Grojean's first run was always his best, even though his course inspection was cursory. A coach recommended that he use less mental preparation on race day, too. It worked. "It is better to be fast with a few mistakes, than to calculate your run and be slow," says McGrath. "Some racers think too much."

Trailside Stretches *continued*

Side-to-side arm swings. Start with your arms at shoulder height. Swing them both to the left, then both to the right. Be sure your knees are slightly bent. Swing them higher above your head, then lower around your waist.

To avoid over-thinking the course, plan on only two inspection runs. Get the big picture the first run, while also noticing the tricky sections. Take more time the second run to look at each combination of gates. Try to detect places where you may be able to put a few tenths between you and the competition. It may be helpful to run sections of the course in your mind as you look at it. You do not need to know the exact number of open gates between two flushes, but you should sense the rhythm and know that the exit gate in the first flush is a bit of a fall-away (see page 78 on how to ski fall-away gates.)

It is also important to notice the texture of the snow. Will the course rut up because of soft snow? Will it become chattery as a result of icy conditions and tight turns? Will it stay relatively smooth and firm?

If there is a section of the course that remains cloudy in your mind, take a third inspection run (time permitting), concentrat-

Trailside Stretches *continued*

Hip circles. With your hands on your hips and your knees slightly bent, rotate your hips several times in one direction, then the other direction.

Knee circles. With your hands on your knees, circle your knees several times in one direction, then the other direction.

ing primarily on that section where you are unsure of yourself. It may be helpful to watch one or two racers run that section before you make your run, but beware of forerunners unless their ability is equal to or better than yours. You may see a less expert skier make a mistake and, when it is your turn, ski that section with caution only to find the section in question was easy. Good skiers leave good images in your mind. Bad skiers leave bad images.

Two places you should make a point to study are the start and the finish. If the start referee allows you to stand in the starting gate, do it at least once to determine the steepness of the ramp and to better understand the line through the first few gates. How you ski those first few gates sets the tone for your entire run. If you are not allowed to stand in the starting gate, hike up to it from below. You want to avoid any surprises, such as looking down the start ramp moments before you push off and becoming

Trailside Stretches *continued*

Fore-aft leg swings. Click your downhill ski boot out of its binding if you haven't done so already. Using your poles for balance, swing your leg front and back, starting with low, slow kicks. Work up to higher kicks, but never so high that it becomes uncomfortable.

intimidated by how steep (or flat) it is. If you are a newcomer to ski racing, plan a strategy for the first few gates that allows you to establish your composure and rhythm, especially if the start ramp is steep. If you crush the first three gates, you may jam your edges roughly in the next dozen.

Always examine the last three or four gates thoroughly, too. They are often quite straight, but maybe not. In particular, note the location of the last gate in relation to the finish line. Is it off-set or a straight shot? Look for the path of least resistance, which is often not through the center of the finish line. Check out the finish area, too. How much room do you have to stop? How rough is it? The finish area is typically the least maintained section of the course. As a result, many injuries occur there because people are tired. They let up to stop, just as the snow becomes much rougher. Remember, the run is not over until you've come to a complete stop and have gotten out of the way.

Trailside Stretches *continued*

Side-to-side leg swings. Using your ski poles for balance, swing your leg to the side, then across your body like a pendulum.

Course inspection is an individual activity. Don't rush or try to keep up with others. Go at your own pace, but try to keep moving. It is fine to stop momentarily to study a certain section, but don't buy property there. If you want to chat with a long lost friend, move away from the course, so that you don't distract or block the view of another racer.

In general, course inspection is done by slowly side-slipping or snowplowing, which also smoothes out the snow. However, many of the organizations that sanction races have rules that forbid you from going through the gates. In such instances, you must side-slip next to the course to inspect it. You may traverse into the course to examine the line from a particular vantage point, but then you must slide back out again to descend farther down the trail.

In any case, turning through a gate is completely against proper course inspection etiquette and may lead to immediate

Trailside Stretches *continued*

Hamstring stretch. Using your poles for balance, put the tail of one ski in the snow in front of you. For most, this is enough stretch. For more stretch, press your chest toward your knee.

Quad stretch. Using a pole for balance, put one ski tip in the snow behind you.

disqualification, depending on who sees you do it. This rule ensures that everyone has an equal opportunity to win because no one has had practice on the course. It also prevents the premature development of ruts in the course. Even hitting a gate while sideslipping is frowned on. You may hug as close to a gate as you wish, but not bend it. Like a branch snapping back after you brush against it in the woods, the pole could hit the racer right behind you. Sometimes the course opens for inspection before the gates are securely screwed into the snow, particularly for the second run. Hitting one could knock it out of the snow and send it barreling down the hill.

If the biggest no-no during course inspection is making a turn through a gate, shadowing the course—skiing alongside it, copying the turns—is a close second. It is against the rules, and it can be dangerous. If you are skiing fast down the side of the course, someone may unknowingly push backward out of the

Trailside Stretches *continued*

Side lunge. Using your poles for balance, lunge to the side, angling one ski away from your body. Be sure your bent knee is pointing in the same direction as your foot.

Calf stretch. Slide one ski back while keeping it in contact with the snow.

course into your path. Any fast skiing on the race hill except during your race run is inappropriate and potential grounds for disqualification. There are too many people on the hill, most of whom are concentrating on the gates and not on someone skiing toward them.

If the temperature is above freezing, the course may be "salted" with a nitrogen-based fertilizer to help firm up the snow. It takes approximately 20 minutes for the salt to set up, during which time you may not go into the course. The salt is typically applied about 30 minutes before the scheduled start time. If you think the course may be salted, plan your inspection and warm-up accordingly, perhaps taking both inspection runs first, then free skiing.

Last-Minute Preparation

If you are the kind of person who needs to be at the airport a full hour before flight time, you should plan to arrive at the starting area at least 15 minutes before you race. If you are the type who walks up to the gate as your flight is boarding, you should still give yourself at least 10 minutes at the start. You may have a lot to do.

First, check your skis. Scrape off any visible wax that you haven't already scraped or skied off. Don't forget the sidewalls. If needed, rub on the appropriate wax for that race run and cork it thoroughly. Regardless of whether or not you rub on wax, you should brush out the structure of your base. You also need time to limber up, take off your warm-up clothes, buckle your boots snugly, and collect your thoughts.

Focusing

One of the most difficult aspects of ski racing is focusing. Some athletes listen to music that either has a beat or words that pump them up. Some hike away from the crowd to stretch and prepare their skis. Some socialize with others around the start and even cheer loudly for everyone. Some cannot watch. Because skiing is an individual sport, each racer has a unique ritual that ends in tunnel vision down the course. Here are some of the ways members of the 1999 U.S. Alpine Masters Ski Team make themselves race ready:

❅

"I put aside all other factors in life until the race is over. This is relatively easy once I get out on the mountain, on a chairlift, and take a free run down the hill."
—Charlene Braga (Women's Class 5, Ages 45–49)

❅

"I don't call home until after the race."
—John Woodward (Men's Class 12, Age 80 +,
Member of the U.S. National Ski Hall of Fame)

❅

"I try to concentrate on the race and not let other factors bother me. I try to keep a positive mental outlook by telling myself that I am going to ski well." —Margaret Vaughn (Women's Class 4, Ages 40–44)

"I have discussions with my husband [who is also a racer]. He's definitely more focused than I am."

—Nancy Godsil (Women's Class 6, Ages 50–54)

❋

"I picture myself running gates in my mind."

—Joan Skiff (Women's Class 9, Ages 65–69)

❋

"I use the mental imagery of racing through a course."

—Gary Konza (Men's Class 5, Ages 45–49)

❋

"The race must be the most important study when I am on the hill. I try to be unconscious to external distractions."

—Greg Sarkis (Men's Class 3, Ages 35–39)

❋

"I try to stay in the moment."

—Nick Maracich (Men's Class 4, Ages 40–44)

❋

"I enjoy the moment."   —Coralue Anderson (Women's Class 8, Ages 60–64)

❋

"For me, all races leading up to big races are, at some level, training runs. I don't want to give too much. I may only have a set number of winning runs inside me, so I save that sort of energy and focus for the big races."

—Christian Woll (Men's Class 2, Ages 30–34)

❋

"All races are big races. The preparation, physically and mentally, for every race is the same for me. I have a relaxation ritual that I do in combination with stretching when I line up at the start. A joke or two with my confreres doesn't hurt. When I get in the starting gate, the only thing that matters is

my skiing and the course. I cleanse my mind of all the negative vicissitudes of my daily life."

—Bob Broadbent (Men's Class 11, Ages 75–79)

❋

I always try to relax before a race. In my career, I've made about all the dumb mistakes one can in ski racing. I try not to forget them." —Norma Lausmann (Women's Class 11, Ages 75–79)

The Race

When the moment of truth finally arrives and you enter the starting gate, if you are not perfectly clear on how the count down works, ask right away. Normally, you have 30 to 60 seconds in the starting gate before it is really your turn. After the course is proclaimed "clear," the starter asks if you are ready. If you are not, say "no," as long as the excuse is physical, such as an open buckle or a last minute adjustment to a pole strap. At this point, a delay should not last more than a moment or two. If you miss your start in a local or regional race, most, but not all, start officials, allow you to go either at the end of your seed or at the end of your gender group. At a national or international race, you forfeit your start.

Start Cadences

At all but short, coin-operated recreational race courses, a starter prompts you when to go, but the prompt could be one of several formats.

In USSA-style slaloms, in which one racer goes at a time, the starter simply gives you a 10-second warning, then tells you to "Go when ready." However, the starter doesn't really mean it. He or she is really saying, "Go within the next few seconds, or I will disqualify you."

In giant slaloms, the starter gives you a 10-second warning, then a count down, "Five, four, three, two, one, GO!" You don't have to wait for "GO!" to go. You may leave the gate any time within 3 seconds before or after "GO!"

The cadence for dual races varies slightly from event to event. In pro racing, the starter asks, "Red course ready?" The racer must clearly say, "Yes." Then the starter asks, "Blue course ready?" That racer must also say, "Yes." Then the starter says, "Courses clear. Racers ready. Three, two, one . . .," but instead of saying "GO!," a loud buzzer sounds. In some cases, the starter doesn't say the count down. Racers watch red lights blink sequentially down a pillar to a green light, similar to the light "tree" used in drag racing. On the buzzer and the green light, gates similar to those used in horse racing open, allowing the racers to go at exactly the same time.

In some charity-oriented races, especially when people of differing levels of ability, such as a top racer and a recreational skier, go against each other, a handicap system may be used. In such cases, one starting gate opens earlier than the other. In both pro-style and handicap starts, you never see your time from top to bottom. You only see the difference between yourself and the person on the other course. In other words, the first person to cross the finish line starts the clock. The second person stops it.

In most other dual races, even though two racers are going side by side, each receives a time. In this case, it is still important to know the start cadence, because there is an advantage to having the faster start. You are less likely to be distracted by the other person if that person is behind you.

Start Technique

A strong start is not just a prelude to a fast run, you can literally win or lose the race because of it. Racers can gain or lose 2 seconds or more in the start. Muscular strength and technique are equally important.

A typical starting gate has a timing wand across it, about shin high. When you go through the gate and push the wand open, the clock starts. The wand is sensitive. *Don't touch it prematurely!* If you accidentally hit the wand before you are supposed to go, tell the starter. The starter can confer with the timer at the bottom via radio and have it reset if necessary.

Your entire starting motion should create momentum down the hill before you push open (through) the wand. When you enter the starting gate, place your poles on the other (downhill) side of the wand. Pole holes probably exist in the starting ramp. Use them if they are in a comfortable place and if there is no risk of your poles getting stuck in them. If the holes are deep in ice or wet, easy-to-pack snow, the odds of losing a pole at the start are greater. If you can't widen the hole by circling your poles in them, plant your poles in a different spot.

A common mistake is planting your poles too far ahead of your feet. They should be about halfway between the toe pieces of your bindings and your ski tips, so that you have leverage over

---

FIRST PERSON: EXHALING MY WAY TO VICTORY

When I was 14 years old, I qualified for the North American Trophy Series (now called the VISA Super Series) for the first time. By midwinter, I had posted a number of top ten results and had moved into the first seed (top 15 racers), but I had not won a race at that level. One weekend, two giant slalom races were held at Stratton Mountain, Vermont. I was excited about the races and knew the race hill well, since I was attending the Stratton Mountain School, an academy for ski racers, at the time.

I expected a long, fast course, and that was what I found. By the time I reached the bottom on my first run, my legs were so tired that I was barely able to turn. I just tried to maintain my speed without crashing. I was in fourth place after the first run, itching to move up into the medals, but not sure I could ace the course on the second run because of the overwhelming fatigue I had felt. My legs were still tired an hour after I had finished the first run.

Feeling a bit rejuvenated after lunch, I headed up the chairlift to check out the second course. Rather than setting a straighter, faster line, as was usually the case, the course setters had made the second course turnier and more demanding. I knew that was part of the game, but the thought of it made my legs ache.

I can't say I wanted to win that day more than anything else in the world. In truth, I felt winning would be nice, but unlikely. I went through my prerace routine—prepping my skis, stripping off my warm-ups, limbering up, buckling my boots. . . . Just before I got into the starting gate, my coach, an Austrian named Fritz Vallant, whispered one word in my ear, "Breathe." This was the mid-1970s, a decade before performance-enhancing breathing techniques had become mainstream.

At first this word of advice surprised me. Then I thought about my first run and wondered if I had taken one breath the whole way down. Then my mind jumped to weight training and the rule to exhale when you lift a weight.

I got into the starting gate. On "GO!," I exhaled as I gave a strong push. I exhaled in every turn. When I reached the last few gates, my legs still felt strong and my head was clear. I was winded in the finish area, but nowhere near collapse. When I heard my time, I nearly fainted. I had beaten the rest of the field by 2.5 seconds, enough to win the race. It was the first significant victory of my ski-racing career.

The moral of the story is exhale consistently all the way down the course. You will fatigue less quickly and have more power at the end of the run. Don't worry about inhaling. It happens automatically.

Fritz Vallant is now the Head Technical Coach of the Austrian Ski Team.

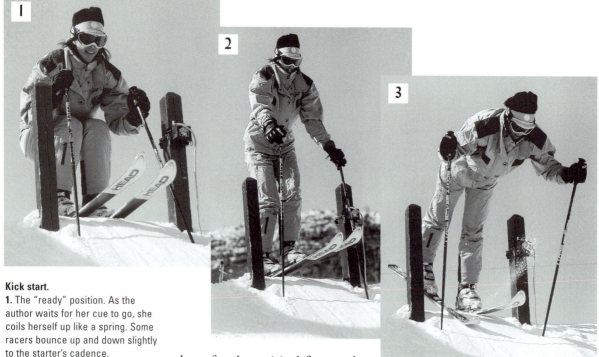

Kick start.
1. The "ready" position. As the author waits for her cue to go, she coils herself up like a spring. Some racers bounce up and down slightly to the starter's cadence.
2. Initial step. On "go," she uncoils her legs, making a powerful step with her left foot, but she doesn't open the wand yet.
3. The kick. As she stomps the ground with her left foot, her right leg extends behind her and her body straightens. She uses her poles for support.

them for that critical first push.

Once your poles are set in the snow, pull your shins toward the wand so that they are close but not touching it. Some racers lower and raise their hips to the starter's cadence, using the rhythm and upward movement to aid their first push. Other racers prefer to stand still, hips low, with their entire bodies coiled like springs. The start is a full-body explosion, not just a push with the arms and shoulders. In the first moment, one foot makes a singular, powerful step, initiating the forward push as your arms pull your torso over your ski poles. In the next moment, your stomach muscles contract powerfully, like doing a stomach crunch.

To a casual observer, it looks as if you are kicking both feet into the air behind you, which is why this technique is sometimes called a "kick start," but really all effort is forward. After that first step, your feet simply follow. You want your entire body to be heading toward the first gate before your lower legs or feet push the wand open. They are the last part of your body to leave the starting gate.

Focus

When you post a scorching fast time, you rarely remember much of your run. That doesn't mean your brain turned off, it just went on automatic pilot. With enough practice, anyone is capable of finding this *racer's high*. Reaching this state of ultimate performance requires practice to acquire the muscle memory, familiarity with gates, and feel for the terrain. It also requires focus.

Focus implies concentration on something specific. To ski faster, you must develop a single-minded mantra, such as "look ahead," "breathe," or "let 'em run." Begin using it before you enter the starting gate. Remember to just pick one! Too often, skiers try to micromanage their runs, sometimes talking to themselves all the way down the course. A race run is no time to correct prob-

4. Within a moment, her left leg follows, also extending behind her. She has not touched the wand yet.
5. Foward push. Her legs come forward with as much momentum as she can muster, opening the wand.
6. The stomach crunch. As she pushes out of the start using her arms, shoulders, and stomach muscles, she makes a powerful skating step foward.

lems with technique. If you coach yourself down the entire course, you will be slow, and there will be little flow to your skis.

Trouble-Shooting

In ski racing, as in any of life's more interesting pursuits, unanticipated variables appear. Some of these are merely challenging, others highly problematic. The weather changes. You misjudge the line. You fall. How you react to adversity plays a big role in your success as a ski racer. Here are some of the common things that can go wrong and how to overcome them:

Incorrect Wax

Picking the wax before race day is an educated guess. If you miss the wax, scrape your skis thoroughly, then brush them aggressively. It helps to ski on them as much as possible to wear off the old wax. Just before your start, rub on the correct wax of the day, cork it in, and then brush it out (see chapter 9). Odds are, you will glide with pride.

Low Line

If you misjudge a turn and suddenly find yourself on a line that is too low, don't try to correct the mistake all at once. As long as you can stay in the course, recover gradually over the next two or three gates. Your time will be faster if you let your skis run as much as possible, rather than jamming a turn to recover immediately.

Edges Too Dull, Too Sharp, or Burred

Hopefully, you will figure out these little nuisances with your ski edges before you get on the course. That's why you bring a fanny pack to the start. If your edges are too dull, a quick side-filing followed by a few passes with a stone usually does the trick. Burrs can also be smoothed out with a stone and removed completely if they aren't too deep (see chapter 9).

Edges that are too sharp can be dulled quickly with a gentle pass of ultrafine grit sandpaper. If you have to dull your edges, do so cautiously, just a tiny bit at a time. After your first effort, ski on your skis, then dull them slightly again, if necessary, repeating the process until they feel right. It is a lot easier to dull skis than to sharpen them at the start.

Falling on the Course

The rules about falling vary depending on the sanctioning body for the race. In USSA races, if you fall you may finish unless your ski comes off. Finishing, even though you are miles behind the leader, is frequently a prerequisite for taking a second run. In collegiate racing or other team racing, finishing after a fall may be critical to the team's overall results. In general, if you fall and both skis stay on, plan to finish, as long as you can get back in the course quickly. The next racer is only 30 to 60 seconds behind you. If you cannot resume your run without interfering with the next person, be courteous and don't continue. At that point, your time will be so slow, it won't matter anyway. If you can get back in action quickly, most likely you will have to hike a few steps to a gate that you missed. If the course is set USSA-style, in which two poles or panels make one gate, be sure both boots cross the imaginary line between the two poles, otherwise your effort will be for naught. If you are unsure whether you crossed the line, the only person who is authorized to tell you is the gatekeeper. You have to ask. The gatekeeper is allowed to answer only "yes" or "no."

Imaginary line through a gate. In order for you to pass "legally" through a gate on a USSA-style course, both of your feet must cross the imaginary line between the two poles or panels that designate the gate.

Deep Ruts

After a snow storm—even if the snow has been rolled—or when springtime conditions exist, ruts form around each gate.

The later your start number, the deeper the ruts. The trick to skiing ruts well is not fighting them. Use them, even if they might not be in the exact place that you had hoped to turn. Enter the rut where everyone else did, but try not to ride it to the very end. An early exit will keep you on a more comfortable line. In slalom, don't worry how far you are away from the poles. If you are too far away to cross-block, which is usually the case, keep your body oriented down the hill and concentrate on what your feet are doing. If you have to lean into the hill for the sake of blocking the pole, your skis will skid and you will be slow. Forget about cross-blocking until you are able to ski a tighter line.

Path of the skis through a rut. Enter the rut where previous racers did, but try to exit the rut earlier (higher). Don't ride it to the end or you may be late or too low to make the next turn a good one.

Losing Your Grip on a Ski Pole

Losing your grip on your ski pole is annoying to say the least. It usually happens as you leave the starting gate or if your hand hits a gate. The common reaction is to frantically grab for it with the hand that lost its grip. Instead, make a decisive grab for the upper third of the pole with the other hand and place the grip back in the correct hand. A decisive movement takes much less time than trying to stab at or swing the pole over and over again.

If your grip (the rubber or plastic piece you hold) comes off your pole, if your pole breaks in a race, or if you drop it completely, keep skiing and hold that hand forward in its normal position for balance. It may help your timing to fake the pole plant.

Leg Burn

If your legs are dying with a third of the course to go, remind yourself to breathe! In giant slalom, the rhythm of the course usually matches the rhythm of your breathing. Exhale as you make your turns. Inhale during the transitions between turns. In the other racing disciplines, your respiratory effort may not coincide with your turns, but your muscles still need oxygen. If you concentrate on breathing from the start, you will delay the buildup of lactic acid in your leg muscles.

Visibility Problems

Races are not supposed to take place if visibility is less than two or three gates, but it is a discretionary call. Often a storm or fog will worsen, then let up, over and over again. The conditions during your run are sheer luck, good or bad. When you enter the start, be sure your goggles are clear. On wet days, keep your goggles tucked inside your coat or under your bib until the last second. Tuck a lens cloth up your sleeve for a final swipe across your lens just before you start. Don't use your glove, sleeve, or a tissue on your goggle lens, particularly on the inside where the anti-fog coating has been applied, because you will scratch it. If it is raining, a coating of Rain-X on the outside of the lens helps improve your vision. As on the windshield of a car, Rain-X causes water to bead up and scurry away.

On stormy or foggy days, take extra care to learn the course. Looking ahead may seem fruitless as you race through the gates, but keep trying. Ski smoothly and safely. Try to stay loose. If you stay within the limits of your ability and visibility, you will finish well. Remember, everyone else is fighting the same battle. In technical events, if it becomes impossible to see through your goggles, take them off over your head with a sweep of your hand, assuming your helmet allows it. You may be uncomfortable squinting through the snow or rain, but at least you'll be able to see something.

If conditions seem unreasonable, stop! There is no sense getting hurt. You may protest to the race officials if the race is important enough.

An Uphill (Head) Wind

You need a bit of luck to avoid the worst wind on gusty days. Your only defense is to ski with a more compact, lower body position, as long as it doesn't inhibit your technique. Don't try to tuck more than the course would normally warrant. Otherwise, the tails of your skis will probably skid, which is certainly slower than a carved turn.

Extreme Weather

Extreme weather can mean very cold or very hot. If the temperatures are subzero, dress warmly and stay that way until the last possible moment. Cold muscles are not conducive to fast skiing. If you normally stretch out at the start, do it inside a lodge. Go free skiing with discretion; do it enough to get your muscles working, but not so much that your warm-up is really a freeze up. It may help to wear an extra pair of long underwear under your speed suit and a thin balaclava under your helmet.

If the weather is hot, stay out of the sun, stay hydrated, wear strong sunscreen, and use eyewear that protects 100 percent against ultraviolet and infrared rays. Snow is highly reflective, worse than a lake or the ocean. The sun saps energy and can cause serious sunburn, especially at high altitudes. When you inspect the course, wear a hat to shield your face. If you wear sunglasses during warm-up, don't forget to switch to goggles for your race run; your eyes will water behind sunglasses at faster speeds. Even shatterproof glasses can cause serious facial and eye wounds if you accidentally hit a gate with your face.

Forgotten Bib

If you forget or lose your bib, go to the registration desk for a replacement. If you are about to take your run, tell the starter that you forgot your bib and give your number to the starter. He or she will radio the timer that you will be next on course. Although it is frowned on, in most cases, you will be allowed to race without a bib.

Finish Technique

Like the start, a strong finish can mean the difference between first and fifth. During course inspection, you should have noticed the fastest line through the last few gates to the finish. Besides noticing where to cross the finish, how you do it is important.

In slalom racing, you will likely push through the finish, but in giant slalom, you could be going too fast to push. In that case, you should drop into a tuck. In speed events, you will already be in your tuck, so just stay there. Do not sit back! Many knee injuries occur in the finish area because racers rock back onto the tails of their skis. From that position, all it takes is a simple jolt to the knee as you turn to stop or to recover from a potential fall to tear your anterior cruciate ligament.

Some racers try to reach a hand forward to break the light beam across the finish line to stop the clock. If you are accurate in your attempt, the technique can help, particularly in dual races. At the very least, driving forward with a hand pulls the rest of your body forward. Don't worry about reaching for the finish line if there is any chance that the action will throw you off balance. It is never a good idea to kick a foot forward, which increases the odds of sitting back and falling.

Be sure you have crossed the finish line before you begin to slow down. Once again, after you cross the finish line, don't stop concentrating until you have stopped. Remember, the run is not over until you have come to a complete stop.

Congratulations! You have just skied faster!

Resources

Books and Other Publications

Ski Racing

Ski Racing International
P.O. Box 1125
6971 Main St., Suite 1
Waitsfield VT 05673
802-496-7700
http://www.skiracing.com

In addition to news, event coverage, profiles of athletes, instructional features
and race results, this newspaper also publishes annual lists of ski racing
academies and training camps. Twenty issues each year.

USSA Competition Guide, published annually by the U.S. Ski and Snowboard
Association (USSA; see address under Associations) and distributed to all
USSA members. Includes rules, race schedules, regional contacts, training
programs, and clubs throughout the United States.

USSA Masters Competition Guide, published annually by USSA (see address
under Associations) and distributed to all current members who hold masters racing licenses. Includes rules, race schedules, regional contacts, training programs, and clubs throughout the United States.

General Skiing

The following books are not specific to ski racing, but they do provide
more information on such topics as technique on shaped skis and the mental
aspects of the sport.

Foster, Ellen Post, and Alan Schonberger. *Skiing and the Art of Carving*.
Edwards CO: Turning Point Ski Foundation, 1996. A video based on the
book is also available.

Harb, Harald. *Anyone Can Be an Expert Skier: The Definitive Shaped Ski Owner's Guide.* 1998.

Hobart, Al. *Carving Turns Made Easy.* Alpine Racing R&D, Waitsfield VT, 1998. This is actually a colorful booklet, which doubles as flash-cards for the chairlift. A video based on the booklet is also available.

LeMaster, Ron. *The Skier's Edge.* Champaign IL: Human Kinetics, 1999. This book includes some excellent sequential photography of top ski racers.

Selder, Dennis, J. *Smart Skiing: Mental Training for All Ages and Levels of Skill.* San Francisco: Jossey-Bass, 1998.

Witherell, Warren, and David Evrard. *The Athletic Skier.* Boulder CO: Johnson Publishing, 1993. This book includes helpful tips on leg alignment and how it affects your skiing.

Yacenda, John, and Tim Ross. *High-Performance Skiing.* Champaign IL: Human Kinetics, 1998.

Good Reads

Durrance, Dick. *The Man on the Medal: The Life and Times of America's First Great Ski Racer.* Aspen CO: Durrance Enterprise, 1995.

Wilson, Mike. *Right on the Edge of Crazy: On Tour with the U.S. Downhill Ski Team.* New York: Time Books, 1993.

Videos

America's World Championships Medal Moments, by Jalbert Productions (1998). This video is more of an historical documentary than an instructional video, but inspiring nonetheless. Available through the Colorado Ski Museum, P.O. Box 1976, Vail CO 81658, 800-950-7410.

Fast Thinking (1998), featuring A. J. Kitt and Hilary Lindh. Available from *Ski Racing International* (see under Books and Other Publications).

Fast Tuning (1998), featuring World Cup technicians Willi Wiltz (Dynastar) and Bill Farwig (Salomon). Available from *Ski Racing International* (see under Books and Other Publications).

Norwegian Alpine Ski Team Advanced Coordination Training for Alpine Skiers. Available from USSCA (see under Associations).

Norwegian Alpine Ski Team Dryland Training and Skiing Fundamentals. Available from USSCA (see under Associations).

U.S. Ski Team Free Skiing & Advanced Elements of Alpine Ski Technique. Available from USSCA (see under Associations).

U.S. Ski Team Speed Elements Training. Available from USSCA (see under Associations).

Winning Runs: SL, GS, SG & DH

A collection of winning runs in all four ski racing disciplines, men and women, for a given year or big event (World Championships, Olympics). Pick your year of interest, from 1989 to present. Available from USSCA (see under Associations).

Clubs

The USSA Alpine Competition Guide and the USSA Alpine Masters Competition Guide include listings by state of ski clubs and other ski racing programs throughout the United States.

Ski Racing Academies

The following college preparatory schools (high schools) specialize in combining ski racing (and other winter sports) and academics. They are geared toward the dedicated student-athlete whose primary goal is to reach his or her potential as a ski racer. They offer intensive training and racing opportunities, without sacrificing academic requirements for college. Most members of the U.S. Ski Team are either currently attending or have previously attended a ski racing academy.

Burke Mountain Academy
East Burke VT
802-626-5607

Carrabassett Valley Academy
Carrabasett ME (Sugarloaf)
207-237-2250

Crested Butte Academy
Crested Butte CO
970-349-1805

Green Mountain Valley School
Waitsfield VT (Sugarbush)
802-496-6819

Killington Mountain School
(late fall–winter only)
Killington VT
802-773-3233

The Lowell Whiteman School
Steamboat Springs CO
970-879-1350

National Sports Academy
Lake Placid NY (Whiteface Mountain)
518-523-3460

Rowmark Academy
Salt Lake City UT (Park City, UT)
435-355-7494

Stratton Mountain School
Stratton Mountain VT
802-297-1886

Vail Valley Academy
(late fall–winter, only)
Vail CO
970-476-5119

Waterville Valley Academy
(late fall–winter, only)
Waterville Valley NH
603-236-4246

The Winter Sports School
Park City UT
435-649-8760

In addition to the ski racing academies listed above, a number of private college prep schools, such as the Holderness School (Plymouth NH) and Gould Academy (Bethel ME), have outstanding ski racing programs, while offering a full range of high school classes and extracurricular activities. These schools do not specialize in the athletic development of ski racers, but are an excellent choice if ski racing is your passion but making the U.S. Ski Team is not your all-consuming goal.

Associations

American Ski Racing Association (ASRA)
P.O. Box 467
Chinchilla PA 18410
717-344-2772
http://www.asra.org

NASTAR
P.O. Box 5447
Snowmass Village CO 81615
970-923-6278
http://www.nastar.com

Professional Ski Instructors of America (PSIA)
133 South Van Gordon Street, Suite 101
Lakewood CO 80228
303-988-1111
http://www.psia.org

United States Ski and Snowboard Association (USSA)
P.O. Box 100
Park City UT 84060
435-649-9090
http://www.ussa.org

U.S. National Ski Hall of Fame
P.O. Box 191
Ishpeming MI 49849
906-485-6323
http://www.portup.com/skihall

U.S. Ski Coaches Association (USSCA)
USSA Coaches Educational Publications
P.O. Box 100
Park City UT 84060
435-649-9090
http://www.ussa.org

Mail Order

Most of the equipment, clothing, and accessories mentioned through this book are available through specialty ski shops. In addition, most ski equipment manufacturers have websites that are easy to find with a web search engine. If you are interested in a particular brand, consult its website, which usually includes a list of retailers nearest you. Here are a few of the better-known mail-order catalogs for ski racing products.

ARTECH
Enfield NH
603-632-9152
E-mail: ARTECH@endor.com

Finish Line Sports
Boise ID
800-741-3985
http://www.finishlinesport.com

Michel Pratte Alpine Ski Co.
1141 E. Cochand
Ste.-Adele PQ
Canada J8B 2X8
800-641-3327
http://www.mprattesport.com

Race Place
Bend OR
800-814-RACE (7223)

Reliable Racing Supply
Glens Falls NY
518-793-5677; 800-274-6815
http://www.reliableracing.com

World Cup Supply
Fairlee VT
802-555-0593

Index

About the Author

Lisa Feinberg Densmore began ski racing at the age of eight. Although she trained and competed all over the world as a junior racer, then spent four years as a member of Dartmouth College's NCAA ski team (1980–83), she is best known for her success on the Women's Pro Ski Racing Tour. She was a member of the pro tour for six years (1985–90), achieving a ranking of 10th in the world.

Since retiring from the pro tour, Ms. Densmore has been one of the most decorated alpine masters skiers in the United States. She has won countless races, including fifteen national titles since 1991. *Ski Racing International* named her Alpine Masters Skier of the Year in 1992 and 1994 and presented her with the Masters Recognition Award in 1999. She received the prestigious Al Sise Outstanding Alpine Masters Racer award in 1992 and 1994 from the United States Ski and Snowboarding Association (USSA), the sport's national governing body. In addition, she has been named to the U.S. Alpine Masters Ski Team, an honorary team that recognizes the number-one ranked man and woman in each masters age group, in five of the seven years that she was eligible.

Ms. Densmore's recognition is not limited to her ski racing. She is also the two-time winner of the Harold S. Hirsch Award for Excellence in Broadcast, the highest award given annually by the North American SnowSports Journalists Association (NASJA). A versatile, accomplished journalist, she appears frequently as a commentator and reporter during sports coverage on CBS, ESPN, ESPN2, FoxSportsNet, and the Outdoor Life Network, not only for skiing, but also for snowboarding, in-line skating, roller hockey, running, and a number of other sports. She has also hosted two series, *Ski New England* and *New England Outdoors*, on the Travel Channel, as well as *Skiing Magazine's Private Lessons* on the Weather Channel. She is currently an anchor on the morning show and host of a series of skiing and in-line skating tips on Resort Sports Network and a field producer for the nationally syndicated show *More Than a Game*.

Ms. Densmore is also a prolific writer. She has published hundreds of articles for magazines and periodicals as varied as *Men's Journal*, *Women's Sports & Fitness*, *Outdoor*, and *Inline*. She is a regular contributor to *Ski Racing International* and was formerly the Instruction Editor for *Mountain Sports & Living* (*Snow Country*), which included acting as Director of the Mountain Sports & Living Training Centers, a series of instructional clinics at major ski resorts around the United States. She is the featured instructor at the Head/Subaru Women's Ski Clinics, a national program that raises money for the National Breast Cancer Coalition. She is also a popular speaker and coach at sports-related trade and consumer shows, fund-raising events, sales meetings, and youth camps.

Ms. Densmore currently serves as a member of the Dartmouth College Athletic Council and the USSA Eastern Alpine Masters Committee, as a Trustee of the Stratton Mountain School, and on the boards of the New England Ski Museum and New England Masters Skiing, Inc. She is on the nominating committee for the New England Women's Sports Hall of Fame and for NASJA's Outstanding Competitor Award.